WHERE ARE WE ?

Earth

according to the Bible

To Christa,
   It was great chatting
with you. I look forward to
hearing the fruit that comes
from your willingness to share
The Truth!

—

WHERE ARE WE ?

Earth

according to the Bible

By Chad Taylor

Published by Rustic Trail Productions LLC

    Mailing address:
Rustic Trail Productions LLC
14241 NE Woodinville Duvall Road
Suite 190
Woodinville, WA 98072

For information please e-mail info@rustictrailproductions.com

First Edition: December 2017

ISBN-13: 978-0-9993221-0-9 (pbk.)

ISBN-10: 0-9993221-0-9 (pbk.)

For additional copies of this book:

Both paperback and ebook copies are available at:

www.wherearewethebook.com

Paperback copies are available in bulk at a discount, please visit the website above for more details.

You can also simply scan the code below:

This book is dedicated to my Dad. With the heart of a humble country boy he took the road less traveled, time and time again. His example stays with me always; come what may, hang right at the fork and push on.

It's not goodbye, it's see you later.
We love you Dad.

CONTENTS

©2017 Chad Taylor

INTRODUCTION

Do you happen to remember what you were doing on the evening of June 10th, 2009? I do. I was standing on a mountain top, gazing up at the stars in the sky after watching the sun disappear behind snowcapped mountains.

It was late spring in Northwest Montana. I was in my mid twentys at the time and about two years into my second business. It seemed like I was at one of those frustrated points in life where I just needed a short break for reflection and re-focus. It was a last minute decision, but I felt a need to just get away from it all and head out into the woods.

There are countless places to go in Montana and have peace and quiet. Most of my outings were hikes to the top of a mountain somewhere. I guess it came with a sense of accomplishment. I would usually pick the places that had great views and hopefully some fishing along the way.

This hike was going to be different though. I felt a drawing, like I just needed to get away for a couple of days and hit a reset button. A reset on what? I didn't know at the time but it was just one of those gut feelings like it was something I needed to do.

It was a last minute decision to take off that Wednesday afternoon. I frantically flipped through the pages of my hiking book until I found a mountain I hadn't been to before. *"There it is,"* I exclaimed. A few minutes later I was off, heading into the wild, into the Great Bear Wilderness.

It was around 3:00 pm when I finally pulled into the trail head and parked the truck. With a backpack on my back and a dog by my side, I was off. Heading into some of the most beautiful and hostile country most people will ever go.

Southward view from Mount Furlong
Great Bear Wilderness, Montana.
June 11th, 2009.

About half way up the mountain I realized I should have planned this trip better. Wearing running shoes in snow is less than ideal. *"Oh well, nothing a campfire can't dry out,"* I said to my four legged companion.

I spent the hike admiring the scenery while scanning for animals, especially dangerous ones. While I walked, my dog would run ahead, then past me and behind, then past me and ahead again. He always loved the outdoors, I'll bet for every mile I walked, he ran two or three.

We would have reached the peak much sooner had I not missed the trail we were supposed to turn onto. I didn't really mind the added time to the hike, *"we will get there when we get there, even if it's in the dark."*

We reached the peak just in time to watch a beautiful sunset. While admiring the few remaining minutes of daylight, I quickly set up the tent before it got too dark to slow the process. Within a few minutes my feet were warming by a campfire as I gazed up at countless stars that were now visible. Montana is called Big Sky Country and that night the Big Sky was full of bright stars.

Now, for those of you that have never done it, sleeping on the ground in an area with a very high Grizzly Bear population is known to keep a person awake. A thin layer of nylon separating you from a 600 pound meat eater is less than comforting. I was not concerned about big toothed critters this night though. I hadn't seen any sign of life near the top of the mountain.....this night I slept like a baby.

It was going on 10:30 a.m. by the time I finally unzipped the tent to see just how beautiful the day was. My dog had been up for hours strolling around the area. I could always tell when he returned from exploring. He had his own vestibule to sleep in and upon his return would greet me with a nudge through the screen. After getting out and moving around, I made my way to the snacks I picked up on the drive. While standing there eating 'breakfast,' I gazed out over endless miles of Montana mountains, straining my eyes to pick out the ones I had already been to. A person could probably spend a lifetime out there and not set foot on each one.

I brought my Bible with me on this trip. One of the main reasons I felt I needed to go into the wilderness was to open it up and read it in a quiet, remote place. I looked forward to reading it that morning, even though I hadn't opened it in the last......who knows how long, probably years. I really felt like this day was going to be a big turning point.

I was at a point in life where I wanted to get closer to God. It felt like today things would open up for me like never before, it just seemed so right. This was the same Bible I was given at nine years old. It even had my name stamped on the front of it. With being fairly old it still looked almost new, chalk it up to years of procrastination I guess.

After enjoying the views, I realized the moment had finally arrived. It was time to open God's Word and get closer to Him. I sat, resting my back against a log that looked like it'd been there for years. Even though there was still snow nearby, the sun was warm and bright. Sitting down with the black book in my hands it dawned on me..... *"Where do I start?"*

After a pause I said to myself, *"Why not the beginning? Duh."* I turned a few pages until I got to Genesis, Chapter One, Verse One. I began reading the story of creation, how everything came to be. *"What?"*.............. *"Huh?"*................ *"Hmm,"*................*"I don't get it."*

Over......and over.......and over I read Chapter One. Each time growing more and more confused. *"A dome in the waters, what the heck is that?!"* At some point my frustration got the better of me. I decided to cut my much anticipated Bible reading short.

I stood up and stretched after reading for not nearly as long as I planned on. Standing in front of the log, gazing out at the scenery, I was dumbfounded at what I had just attempted to read. I looked over at my dog, that by now was probably on his third nap. I felt the warmth of the sun shining bright above me. I smelled the fresh mountain breeze as it blew over the mountain. I took all of it in and I thought to myself; *"There has to be something I am missing."*

I believed what I read, but I absolutely did not understand it. *"How did all of this come to be? Where are we? I don't understand."* What I read about creation is nothing like we are told in school, or even at church for that matter.

©2017 Chad Taylor

Westward view from Mount Furlong
Great Bear Wilderness, Montana.
June 11th, 2009.

"What is going on? What are we missing? Is this why it seems like everyone I have heard talk about creation speedily skips through Genesis Chapter One? Is it because they don't have a clue what it means either?"

Feeling totally frustrated and confused I took the tent down and packed it away into my pack. I placed it right by the book, still warm from the tense hands that were just holding it. After snapping a couple more pictures of the views I whistled to my dog that it was time to go.

I had walked uphill with such hope of finding answers and getting closer to God. Now I was walking downhill through snow, in running shoes, feeling totally defeated. My hope and anticipation only turned into deeper questions. *"A dome in the waters?.......a dome in the waters...?"* Just some of the frustrated mumbles I said to myself on my way back down the trail.

Upon reaching the truck, I dropped the tailgate and sat down. Resting there for a few moments, I peered up at the mountain I was just on top of. I thought to myself, *I really want to get closer to God. I thought this was going to be a big step forward, but it feels like I just tripped.*

Little did I know it then, but six years, two businesses, four moves, a wedding, a funeral, and a baby later, the questions I had on that mountain would be answered. Yes, there was a big turning point for me that day. It was the day I started to ask, *"Where are we?"*

I wasn't ready for the answers on that mountaintop in 2009, are you ready now?

DISCLAIMER

Sanctify them in the truth; your word is truth.
- John 17:17 - (ESV)

Imagine standing outside on a cool summer night. You gaze up at the moon and countless stars lighting up the sky. There in the dark, with your head tilted back, your issues and distractions seem to go away. Even though it is brief, you feel a sense of awe. A certain stillness as you try to comprehend the seemingly infinite depth you are witnissing.

What is out there? Where are we? Where is heaven and where is God?

I didn't know it at the time, but the seed for this book was planted that day in the wilderness. It was a seed planted out of frustration and apparent failure. Out of that frustration sprang a strong desire to find answers, to find The Truth.

After returning from the wild, I was much more attentive to what people had to say regarding creation in the Bible. I was never satisfied with the explanations I heard. My questions only seemed to bring dismissive responses from those I assumed had the answers. I wanted details, but all I heard was fluff. I never doubted the Bible as The Truth, I just didn't want someone to tell me fluff and expect me to be satisfied. Over the years I realized nobody I'd ever met had the insight I was looking for.

Has this been your experience too? Has anyone given you a good explanation of the creation account? Have you asked a pastor to explain Genesis chapter one? Did they squirm when you asked, "what is a firmament?" Is it obvious they have no clue what they are talking about on the subject? Please don't feel bad towards them, they don't know what they don't know. They are simply repeating what they were told...fluff.

This entire book started out of a deep frustration for not being able to understand the first chapter of the most important book ever assembled. Over the years my longing to understand creation grew into a strong desire to understand *where we are, where heaven is and where God is.*

You may be saying to yourself; *Don't we already know where we are?* or *I've always wondered what the Bible said about earth and where we are!* Or maybe you are the kind of person that likes to avoid uncomfortable subjects and are saying to yourself; *This isn't a salvation issue, why are we discussing this?*

However you have approached this book, relax. You and I are about to take a wonderful journey through the pages of the Bible. Imagine discovering insights written down for thousands of years that we missed. Insights that were right in front of us but we were blind to them. What if all of these seemingly small insights together paint a clear picture of the location of earth, heaven *and* God! Together, you and I will turn the pages of God's Word and find out, once and for all.

Only a day or two into assembling this book, I realized it needed to be simple and easy to understand. This subject affects us all, therefore we should all be able to understand it. I needed to take what could be considered a complicated subject and simplify it, so that's what I did.

This Book is by no means a comprehensive list of every verse in the Bible that describes earth and *where we are.* It is intended to be an introduction to *where we are* according to God's Word. I believe a book that contained every example on this subject in the Bible would take more than a lifetime to assemble. It would also be many times the size of this book.

For every one example in this book there are many more that could have been used that describe the same thing. One of the hardest parts of making this book was not trying to find verses that describe *where we are,* but rather trying to decide how many examples to stop at.

In summary, there are countless more examples about *where we are* remaining in the Bible, than are found in this book. Every one of them only reinforces what we are going to see on our journey through these pages.

How the Bible is used in this book:

Every example in Parts 1-3 use at least four Bible versions. They are the **King James Version** (KJV), **New International Version** (NIV), **English Standard Version** (ESV) and the **New Revised Standard Version** (NRSV). I chose the first three because from my research, they are the most popular versions today with millions of copies sold every year. I added the (NRSV) as the fourth version because this is the version I grew up with and is the version I brought with me on the mountaintop in the introduction.

In addition to the four versions listed above, there are also some examples from the **New Living Translation** (NLT). The (NLT) is also one of the most popular versions of the Bible today. On our journey, we will see how all of these versions work together. If you normally read from a different translation than one of these, I suggest you bring your Bible along on our Journey. The examples we will see are in the same order they are found in the Bible. Will all of them paint a clear and consistent picture about the location of earth, heaven and God?

Will a single book, comprised of 66 smaller books, written over a 1500 year period, by 40 different authors, all inspired by God, paint a consistent picture of God's creation? We are going to find out.

All scripture is given by inspiration of God, and is profitable for doctrine, for reproof, for correction, for instruction in righteousness: That the man of God may be perfect, thoroughly furnished unto all good works.

- 2 Timothy 3:16-17   (KJV)

How definitions and highlights are used in this book:

Along with every example in this book are dictionary definitions of key words used in the example verse(s). The words with definitions are <u>underlined</u> in each example. The purpose of having words defined is to help in forming a picture of what is being described in the examples. See pages 288-291 for more information.

There are also **phrases highlighted** in most of the examples. The purpose for highlighting is to bring extra attention to phrases that we may naturally read right over and possibly miss important details.

> <u>Special note:</u> (In case you wonder when we get there on our journey), I was not permitted to underline words or highlight phrases in one of the Bible versions used in this book. With that said, I am grateful I was permitted to use their version as well as all of the other Bible versions in this book.

How images are used in this book:

The images that apply to each Biblical example are meant to be a very simplified rendering of what is being described. Every effort was made to duplicate what is being said into an image to better understand each example. Keep in mind the images are not to scale, nor would it be possible to do so. They are just a nice way to visually see what is being described in each example. Will the images remain consistent from beginning to end? Will puzzle pieces spanning 1500 years fit with each other? What is the picture going to be?

<u>Final thoughts before we start our journey:</u>

We all live our lives looking through lenses we have developed since birth. Whether we know it or not. They are filtering lenses of opinions and biases that determine how we interact and perceive the world around us. I mention this, because we bring those exact same perceptions and biases to the Bible when we read it.

There are tens of thousands of Christian denominations in the world today. Can they all be 100% right? Can they all be 100% wrong? Or could they all be somewhere inbetween with a mixture of truth and lies? One liberating question I believe we can all ask ourselves is this; *"Is my understanding about _____ wrong?"* Fill in the blank with any subject you like.

The first few times I didn't agree with something and stopped to ask myself that question, it was very uncomfortable. It is hard for any of us to admit we are wrong in something we believe. But I have learned that is when real growth can happen. The more we allow ourselves to be corrected by The Truth, the easier and better life gets.

You may be brand new to the Bible or you may have read it many times over. This book is assembled in a way that regardless of your experience, you will come to a much better understanding of *where we are,* according to the Bible. There is no need to feel inferior if you have little or no experience with the Bible. We all start out that way and in some ways, to be new may actually benefit you on our journey.

Regardless of your experience with the Bible, I want to give you a great quote from my friend Victor;

"Don't go to the Bible to prove what you have already chosen to believe, go to the Bible to find out what to believe."

It may seem like the same thing. However, allowing God's Word to tell you what to believe is vastly different than searching out verses that can be twisted to reinforce what you have already chosen to believe. Do we naturally keep things in context? Do we naturally leave out things we don't agree with or understand?

I know it is not easy, but could you allow the Bible to correct you if something you have chosen to believe is incorrect? Can you remain humble and allow God to guide your understanding? Do you really want to know *where you are?* Do you really want to know what the Bible says about creation? Do you really want to know *where heaven is?* Do you really want to know *where God is?*

If you are like me and have a longing to truly understand where earth, heaven and God are, this is going to be very special. Let's begin our journey.......

PARTS SUMMARY

PART ONE

The Seven Days of Creation

In part one, we will journey through the creation account in the first book of the Bible; Genesis. We will go through each day and see what discoveries can be made when we examine the words used. Does the first chapter of Genesis lay the foundation for what will be uncovered in the following parts? We are going to find out.

PART TWO

Descriptions of Earth and its surroundings

In part two, we will journey through more accounts of creation as well as stories describing earth and it's surroundings. Will all of them work together and fit into what we discover in part one? We are going to find out. The examples we will see are in the same order they are found in the Bible.

PART THREE

Clues about Earth in Biblical Stories

In part three, we will journey through stories that build on what we discover in parts one and two. Will the stories line up with the descriptions from the first two parts? We are going to find out. The examples we will see are in the same order they are found in the Bible.

PART FOUR

Common Themes and Review

In part four, we will review any common themes we discover on our journey through parts one, two and three. Will there be consistency through all three parts? Can a book whose writing spanned 1500 years remain consistent? We are going to find out.

PART FIVE

Questions and Conclusions

In part five, we will bring any discoveries from our journey through the Bible to the present day. What questions do any new understandings present us with? When comparing the Bible to what we see in our daily lives, what can we conclude about *where we are?* *Where is heaven and where is God?*

PART ONE

The Seven Days of Creation

May the glory of the LORD continue forever!
The LORD takes pleasure in all he has made!

- Psalm 104:31 (NLT)

DAY ONE

Genesis 1:1-5

¹ **In the beginning God created the heaven and the earth.** ² And the earth was without form, and void; and darkness was **upon the <u>face</u> of the <u>deep</u>.** And the Spirit of God moved **upon the <u>face</u> of the waters.** ³ And God said, **Let there be light:** and there was light. ⁴ And God saw the light, that it was good: and God divided the light from the darkness. ⁵ And God called the light Day, and the darkness he called Night. And the evening and the morning were **the first day.**   Genesis 1:1-5 (KJV)

¹ In the beginning God created the heavens and the earth. ² Now the earth was formless and empty, darkness was over the surface of the deep, and the Spirit of God was hovering over the waters. ³ And God said, "Let there be light," and there was light. ⁴ God saw that the light was good, and he separated the light from the darkness. ⁵ God called the light "day," and the darkness he called "night." And there was evening, and there was morning—the first day.   Genesis 1:1-5 (NIV)

¹ **In the beginning, God created the heavens and the earth.** ² The earth was without form and void, and darkness was over the **<u>face</u> of the <u>deep</u>.** And the Spirit of God was hovering over the **<u>face</u> of the waters.** ³ And God said, "Let there be light," and there was light. ⁴ And God saw that the light was good. And God separated the light from the darkness. ⁵ God called the light Day, and the darkness he called Night. And there was evening and there was morning, **the first day.**   Genesis 1:1-5 (ESV)

¹ **In the beginning when God created the heavens and the earth,** ² the earth was a formless void and darkness covered the **<u>face</u> of the <u>deep</u>,** while a wind from God swept over **the <u>face</u> of the waters.** ³ Then God said, "Let there be light"; and there was light. ⁴ And God saw that the light was good; and God separated the light from the darkness. ⁵ God called the light Day, and the darkness he called Night. And there was evening and there was morning, **the first day.**   Genesis 1:1-5 (NRSV)

Face: any of the plane surfaces that bound a geometric solid / an inscribed, printed, or marked side (p. 289)

Deep: extending far downward (p. 289)

DAY ONE

Light
(Day)

Dark
(Night)

©2017 Chad Taylor

Spirit of God

Face of
the deep

Genesis 1:1-5

DAY TWO

Genesis 1:6-8

⁶ And God said, Let there be a <u>**firmament**</u> <u>**in**</u> the <u>**midst**</u> of the waters, and let it <u>**divide**</u> the waters from the waters. ⁷ And God made the <u>**firmament,**</u> and <u>**divided**</u> the waters which were <u>**under**</u> the <u>**firmament**</u> from the waters which were <u>**above**</u> the <u>**firmament**</u>: and it was so. ⁸ And **God called the <u>firmament</u>** Heaven. And the evening and the morning were **the second day.**   Genesis 1:6-8 (KJV)

⁶ And God said, "Let there be a vault between the waters to separate water from water." ⁷ So God made the vault and separated the water under the vault from the water above it. And it was so. ⁸ God called the vault "sky." And there was evening, and there was morning—the second day.   Genesis 1:6-8 (NIV)

⁶ And God said, "Let there be an <u>**expanse**</u> in the <u>**midst**</u> of the waters, and let it <u>**separate**</u> the waters from the waters." ⁷ **And God made the <u>expanse</u> and <u>separated</u>** the waters that were <u>**under**</u> the <u>**expanse**</u> from the waters that were <u>**above**</u> the <u>**expanse.**</u> And it was so. ⁸ **And God called the <u>expanse</u>** Heaven. And there was evening and there was morning, **the second day.**   Genesis 1:6-8 (ESV)

⁶ And God said, "Let there be a <u>**dome**</u> in the <u>**midst**</u> of the waters, and let it <u>**separate**</u> the waters from the waters." ⁷ So God made the <u>**dome**</u> and <u>**separated**</u> the waters that were <u>**under**</u> the <u>**dome**</u> from the waters that were <u>**above**</u> the <u>**dome.**</u> And it was so. ⁸ God called the <u>**dome**</u> Sky. And there was evening and there was morning, **the second day.** Genesis 1:6-8 (NRSV)

- ⌐ **Firmament:** the vault or arch of the sky (p. 289)
- ⌐ **Vault:** an arched structure of masonry usually forming a ceiling or roof (p. 291)
- ⌐ **Dome:** a large rounded roof or ceiling that is shaped like half of a ball / a large hemispherical roof or ceiling (p. 289)
- ⌐ **Expanse:** Firmament / great extent of something spread out (p. 289)
- ⌐ **In:** used to indicate location or position within something (p. 290)
- ⌐ **Midst:** the middle or central part (p. 290)
- ⌐ **Between:** in the space that separates (two things or people) (p. 288)
- ⌐ **Divide:** to separate (something) into two or more parts or pieces (p. 289)
- ⌐ **Divided:** separated into parts or pieces (p. 288)
- ⌐ **Separate(d):** to stop being together, joined, or connected / to become separate (p. 291)
- ⌐ **Under:** in or into a position below or beneath something (p. 291)
- ⌐ **Above:** in or to a higher place than / over (p. 288)

DAY TWO

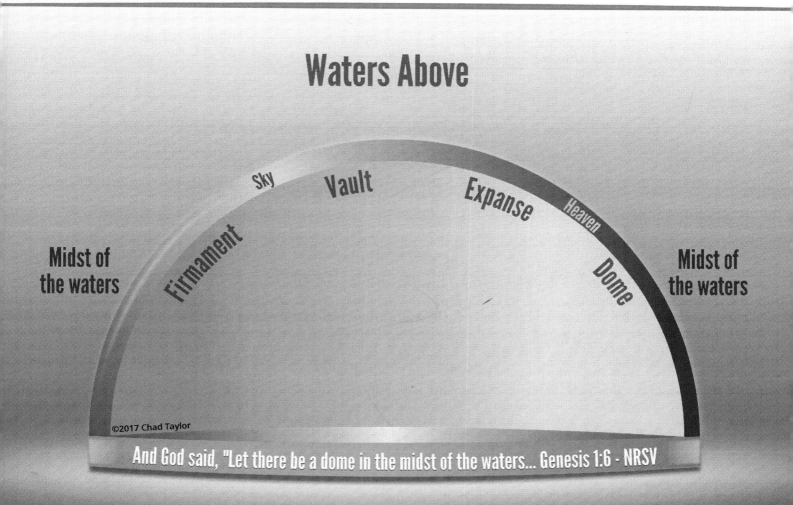

Waters Above

Midst of the waters

Firmament · Sky · Vault · Expanse · Heaven · Dome

Midst of the waters

©2017 Chad Taylor

And God said, "Let there be a dome in the midst of the waters... Genesis 1:6 - NRSV

Waters Below

Genesis 1:6-8

DAY THREE

Genesis 1:9-13

⁹And God said, **Let the waters <u>under</u> the heaven be gathered together unto <u>one</u> <u>place</u>, and let the dry land <u>appear</u>:** and it was so. ¹⁰And **God called the dry land Earth;** and the gathering together of the waters called he **Seas:** and God saw that it was good. ¹¹And God said, **Let the earth bring forth grass,** the herb yielding **seed,** and the **fruit tree** yielding **fruit** after his kind, whose seed is in itself, upon the earth: and it was so. ¹²And the earth brought forth grass, and herb yielding seed after his kind, and the tree yielding fruit, whose seed was in itself, after his kind: and God saw that it was good. ¹³And the evening and the morning were **the third day.** Genesis 1:9-13 (KJV)

⁹And God said, "Let the water under the sky be gathered to one place, and let dry ground appear." And it was so. ¹⁰God called the dry ground "land," and the gathered waters he called "seas." And God saw that it was good. ¹¹Then God said, "Let the land produce vegetation: seed-bearing plants and trees on the land that bear fruit with seed in it, according to their various kinds." And it was so. ¹²The land produced vegetation: plants bearing seed according to their kinds and trees bearing fruit with seed in it according to their kinds. And God saw that it was good. ¹³And there was evening, and there was morning—the third day. Genesis 1:9-13 (NIV)

⁹And God said, **"Let the waters <u>under</u> the heavens be gathered together into <u>one</u> <u>place</u>, and let the dry land <u>appear</u>."** And it was so. ¹⁰God called the dry land **Earth,** and the waters that were gathered together he called **Seas.** And God saw that it was good. ¹¹And God said, **"Let the earth sprout vegetation,** plants yielding seed, and fruit trees bearing fruit in which is their seed, each according to its kind, on the earth." And it was so. ¹²The earth brought forth vegetation, plants yielding seed according to their own kinds, and trees bearing fruit in which is their seed, each according to its kind. And God saw that it was good. ¹³And there was evening and there was morning, **the third day.** Genesis 1:9-13 (ESV)

⁹And God said, "Let the waters <u>under</u> the sky be gathered together into <u>one</u> <u>place</u>, and let the dry land <u>appear</u>." And it was so. ¹⁰**God called the dry land Earth,** and the waters that were gathered together he called **Seas.** And God saw that it was good. ¹¹Then God said, **"Let the earth put forth vegetation:** plants yielding seed, and fruit trees of every kind on earth that bear fruit with the seed in it." And it was so. ¹²The earth brought forth vegetation: plants yielding seed of every kind, and trees of every kind bearing fruit with the seed in it. And God saw that it was good. ¹³And there was evening and there was morning, **the third day.** Genesis 1:9-13 (NRSV)

⌐   **Under:** in or into a position below or beneath something (p. 291)

⌐   **One:** being a single unit or thing (p. 290)

⌐   **Place:** a certain area or region of the world (p. 290)

⌐   **Appear:** to come into sight (p. 288)

DAY THREE

Downward view:

Waters gathered into one place

Sea

Sea

Sea

Sea

©2017 Chad Taylor

Dry land appears, called Earth

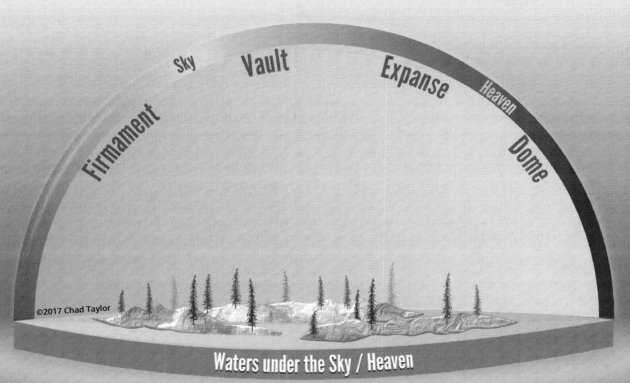

Sky   Vault   Expanse   Heaven

Firmament   Dome

©2017 Chad Taylor

Waters under the Sky / Heaven

Genesis 1:9-13

DAY FOUR

Genesis 1:14-19

¹⁴ And God said, **Let there be lights <u>in</u> the <u>firmament</u> of the heaven to divide the day from the night; and let them be for signs, and for seasons, and for days, and years:** ¹⁵ And let them be for lights **<u>in</u> the <u>firmament</u> of the heaven** to give light upon the earth: and it was so. ¹⁶ And God made **<u>two</u> great lights;** the **greater light** to rule the day, and the **lesser light** to rule the night: he made the **stars** also. ¹⁷ And **God <u>set</u> them <u>in</u> the <u>firmament</u> of the heaven to give light upon the earth,** ¹⁸ And to rule over the day and over the night, and to divide the light from the darkness: and God saw that it was good. ¹⁹ And the evening and the morning were **the fourth day.** Genesis 1:14-19 (KJV)

¹⁴ And God said, "Let there be lights in the vault of the sky to separate the day from the night, and let them serve as signs to mark sacred times, and days and years, ¹⁵ and let them be lights in the vault of the sky to give light on the earth." And it was so. ¹⁶ God made two great lights—the greater light to govern the day and the lesser light to govern the night. He also made the stars. ¹⁷ God set them in the vault of the sky to give light on the earth, ¹⁸ to govern the day and the night, and to separate light from darkness. And God saw that it was good. ¹⁹ And there was evening, and there was morning—the fourth day. Genesis 1:14-19 (NIV)

¹⁴ And God said, **"Let there be lights <u>in</u> the <u>expanse</u> of the heavens** to separate the day from the night. And let them be for signs and for seasons, and for days and years, ¹⁵ and let them be **lights <u>in</u> the <u>expanse</u> of the heavens to give light upon the earth."** And it was so. ¹⁶ And God made **the <u>two</u> great lights—the greater light** to rule the day and the **lesser light** to rule the night—and the **stars.** ¹⁷ **And God <u>set</u> them <u>in</u> the <u>expanse</u> of the heavens to give light on the earth,** ¹⁸ to rule over the day and over the night, and to separate the light from the darkness. And God saw that it was good. ¹⁹ And there was evening and there was morning, **the fourth day.** Genesis 1:14-19 (ESV)

¹⁴ And God said, **"Let there be lights <u>in</u> the <u>dome</u> of the sky** to separate the day from the night; and let them be for signs and for seasons and for days and years, ¹⁵ and let them be **lights <u>in</u> the <u>dome</u> of the sky to give light upon the earth."** And it was so. ¹⁶ **God made the <u>two</u> great lights—the greater light** to rule the day and the **lesser light** to rule the night—and the **stars.** ¹⁷ **God <u>set</u> them <u>in</u> the <u>dome</u> of the sky to give light upon the earth,** ¹⁸ to rule over the day and over the night, and to separate the light from the darkness. And God saw that it was good. ¹⁹ And there was evening and there was morning, **the fourth day.** Genesis 1:14-19 (NRSV)

☐   **In:** used to indicate location or position within something (p. 290)

☐   **Two:** being one more than one in number (p. 291)

☐   **Set:** to put or fix in a place or condition (p. 291)

☐   **Firmament:** the vault or arch of the sky (p. 289)

☐   **Vault:** an arched structure of masonry usually forming a ceiling or roof (p. 291)

☐   **Expanse:** Firmament / great extent of something spread out (p. 289)

☐   **Dome:** a large rounded roof or ceiling that is shaped like half of a ball / a large hemispherical roof or ceiling (p. 289)

DAY FOUR

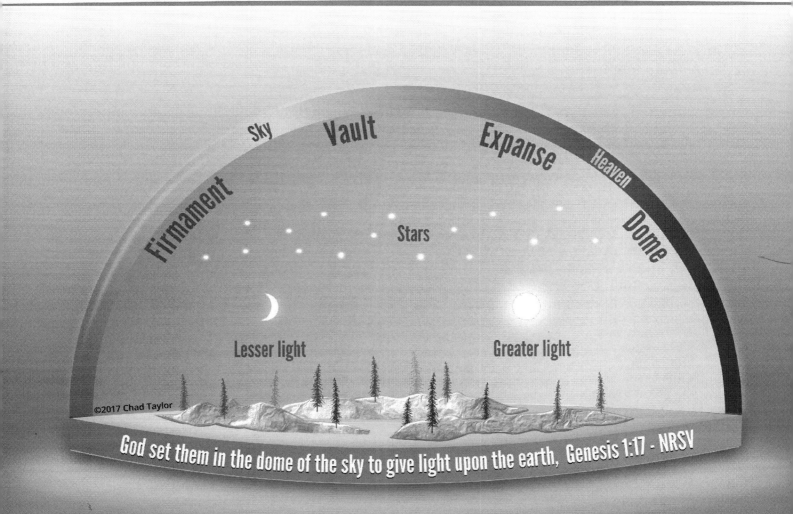

God set them in the dome of the sky to give light upon the earth, Genesis 1:17 - NRSV

Genesis 1:14-19

DAY FIVE

Genesis 1:20-23

²⁰ And God said, **Let the waters bring forth abundantly the moving creature that hath life, and fowl that may fly above the earth <u>in</u> the <u>open</u> <u>firmament</u> of heaven.** ²¹ And God created great **whales,** and every living **creature** that moveth, **which the waters brought** forth abundantly, after their kind, and **every winged fowl** after his kind: and God saw that it was good. ²² And God blessed them, saying, Be fruitful, and multiply, **and fill the waters in the seas, and let fowl multiply in the earth.** ²³ And the evening and the morning were **the fifth day.** Genesis 1:20-23 (KJV)

²⁰ And God said, "Let the water teem with living creatures, and let birds fly above the earth across the vault of the sky." ²¹ So God created the great creatures of the sea and every living thing with which the water teems and that moves about in it, according to their kinds, and every winged bird according to its kind. And God saw that it was good. ²² God blessed them and said, "Be fruitful and increase in number and fill the water in the seas, and let the birds increase on the earth." ²³ And there was evening, and there was morning—the fifth day. Genesis 1:20-23 (NIV)

²⁰ And God said, **"Let the waters swarm with swarms of living creatures, and let birds fly above the earth <u>across</u> the <u>expanse</u> of the heavens."** ²¹ So God created the **great sea creatures** and **every living creature that moves, with which the waters swarm,** according to their kinds, and **every winged bird** according to its kind. And God saw that it was good. ²² And God blessed them, saying, "Be fruitful and multiply and fill the waters in the seas, and let birds multiply on the earth." ²³ And there was evening and there was morning, **the fifth day.** Genesis 1:20-23 (ESV)

²⁰ And God said, **"Let the waters bring forth swarms of living creatures, and let birds fly above the earth <u>across</u> the <u>dome</u> of the sky."** ²¹ So God created the great **sea monsters** and every **living creature that moves, of every kind, with which the waters swarm, and every winged bird** of every kind. And God saw that it was good. ²² God blessed them, saying, "Be fruitful and multiply and fill the waters in the seas, and let birds multiply on the earth." ²³ And there was evening and there was morning, **the fifth day.** Genesis 1:20-23 (NRSV)

- ☐ **In:** used to indicate location or position within something (p. 290)

- ☐ **Open:** open air (p. 290)

- ☐ **Firmament:** the vault or arch of the sky (p. 289)

- ☐ **Across:** from one side to the other (p. 288)

- ☐ **Vault:** an arched structure of masonry usually forming a ceiling or roof (p. 291)

- ☐ **Expanse:** Firmament / great extent of something spread out (p. 289)

- ☐ **Dome:** a large rounded roof or ceiling that is shaped like half of a ball / a large hemispherical roof or ceiling (p. 289)

DAY FIVE

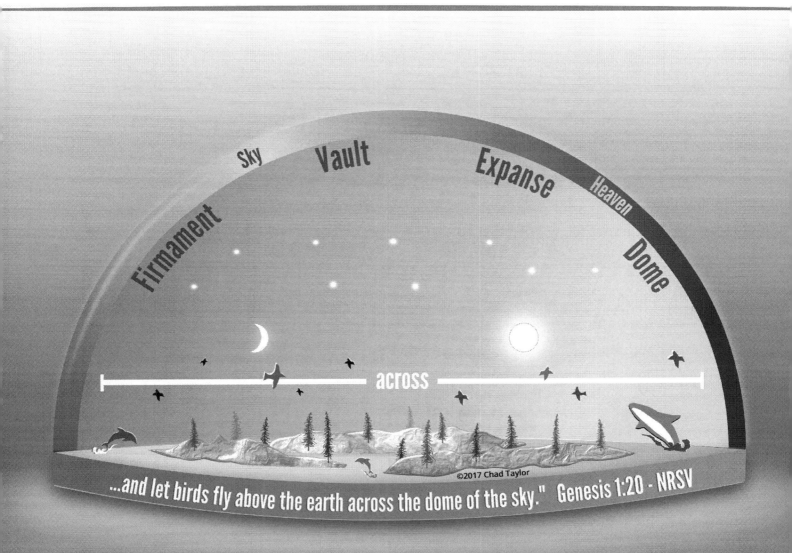

Genesis 1:20-23

DAY SIX

Genesis 1:24-31

²⁴ And God said, **Let the earth bring forth the living creature after his kind, cattle, and creeping thing, and beast of the earth after his kind:** and it was so. ²⁵ And God made the beast of the earth after his kind, and cattle after their kind, and every thing that creepeth upon the earth after his kind: and God saw that it was good. ²⁶ **And God said, Let <u>us</u> make man in <u>our</u> image, after <u>our</u> likeness: and let them have dominion over the fish of the sea, and over the fowl of the air, and over the cattle, and over all the earth, and over every creeping thing that creepeth upon the earth.** ²⁷ **So God created man in <u>his</u> own image, in the image of God created he him; male and female created he them.** ²⁸ **And God blessed them, and God said unto them, Be fruitful, and multiply, and replenish the earth, and subdue it: and have dominion over the fish of the sea, and over the fowl of the air, and over every living thing that moveth upon the earth.** ²⁹ And God said, Behold, I have given you every herb bearing seed, which is **upon the <u>face</u> of <u>all</u> the earth,** and every tree, in the which is the fruit of a tree yielding seed; to you it shall be for meat. ³⁰ And **to <u>every</u> beast** of the earth, and **to <u>every</u> fowl** of the air, and **to <u>every</u> thing that creepeth** upon the earth, wherein there is life, **I have given <u>every</u> green herb for meat:** and it was so. ³¹ And God saw every thing that he had made, and, behold, it was very good. And the evening and the morning were **the sixth day.** Genesis 1:24-31 (KJV)

²⁴ And God said, "Let the land produce living creatures according to their kinds: the livestock, the creatures that move along the ground, and the wild animals, each according to its kind." And it was so. ²⁵ God made the wild animals according to their kinds, the livestock according to their kinds, and all the creatures that move along the ground according to their kinds. And God saw that it was good. ²⁶ Then God said, "Let us make mankind in our image, in our likeness, so that they may rule over the fish in the sea and the birds in the sky, over the livestock and all the wild animals, and over all the creatures that move along the ground." ²⁷ So God created mankind in his own image, in the image of God he created them; male and female he created them. ²⁸ God blessed them and said to them, "Be fruitful and increase in number; fill the earth and subdue it. Rule over the fish in the sea and the birds in the sky and over every living creature that moves on the ground." ²⁹ Then God said, "I give you every seed-bearing plant on the face of the whole earth and every tree that has fruit with seed in it. They will be yours for food. ³⁰ And to all the beasts of the earth and all the birds in the sky and all the creatures that move along the ground—everything that has the breath of life in it—I give every green plant for food." And it was so. ³¹ God saw all that he had made, and it was very good. And there was evening, and there was morning—the sixth day. Genesis 1:24-31 (NIV)

²⁴ And God said, "Let the earth bring forth living creatures according to their kinds—livestock and creeping things and beasts of the earth according to their kinds." And it was so. ²⁵ And God made the beasts of the earth according to their kinds and the livestock according to their kinds, and everything that creeps on the ground according to its kind. And God saw that it was good. ²⁶ Then God said, "Let <u>us</u> make man in <u>our</u> image, after <u>our</u> likeness. And let them have dominion over the fish of the sea and over the birds of the heavens and over the livestock and over <u>all</u> the earth and over <u>every</u> creeping thing that creeps on the earth." ²⁷ So God created man in his own image, in the image of God he created him; male and female he created them. ²⁸ And God blessed them. And God said to them, "Be fruitful and multiply and fill the earth and subdue it, and have dominion over the fish of the sea and over the birds of the heavens and over <u>every</u> living thing that moves on the earth." ²⁹ And God said, "Behold, I have given you <u>every</u> plant yielding seed that is on the <u>face</u> of <u>all</u> the earth, and <u>every</u> tree with seed in its fruit. You shall have them for food. ³⁰ And to <u>every</u> beast of the earth and to <u>every</u> bird of the heavens and to <u>everything</u> that creeps on the earth, <u>everything</u> that has the breath of life, I have given <u>every</u> green plant for food." And it was so. ³¹ And God saw everything that he had made, and behold, it was very good. And there was evening and there was morning, **the sixth day.** Genesis 1:24-31 (ESV)

²⁴ And God said, "Let the earth bring forth living creatures of every kind: cattle and creeping things and wild animals of the earth of every kind." And it was so. ²⁵ God made the wild animals of the earth of every kind, and the cattle of every kind, and everything that creeps upon the ground of every kind. And God saw that it was good. ²⁶ Then God said, "Let <u>us</u> make humankind in <u>our</u> image, according to <u>our</u> likeness; and let them have dominion over the fish of the sea, and over the birds of the air, and over the cattle, and over <u>all</u> the wild animals of the earth, and over <u>every</u> creeping thing that creeps upon the earth." ²⁷ So God created humankind in his image, in the image of God he created them; male and female he created them. ²⁸ God blessed them, and God said to them, "Be fruitful and multiply, and fill the earth and subdue it; and have dominion over the fish of the sea and over the birds of the air and over <u>every</u> living thing that moves upon the earth." ²⁹ God said, "See, I have given you <u>every</u> plant yielding seed that is upon the <u>face</u> of <u>all</u> the earth, and every tree with seed in its fruit; you shall have them for food. ³⁰ And to <u>every</u> beast of the earth, and to <u>every</u> bird of the air, and to <u>everything</u> that creeps on the earth, <u>everything</u> that has the breath of life, I have given <u>every</u> green plant for food." And it was so. ³¹ God saw everything that he had made, and indeed, it was very good. And there was evening and there was morning, **the sixth day.** Genesis 1:24-31 (NRSV)

☐ **Face:** any of the plane surfaces that bound a geometric solid / an inscribed, printed, or marked side (p. 289)

☐ **Whole:** not lacking or leaving out any part (p. 291)

☐ **All:** the whole, entire, total amount, quantity, or extent of (p. 288)

☐ **Us:** I and at least one other (p. 291)

☐ **Our:** relating to or belonging to us / made or done by us (p. 291)

☐ **His:** that which belongs to him (p. 289)

☐ **Every:** including each of a group or series without leaving out any (p. 289)

☐ **Everything**: all that relates to the subject (p. 289)

DAY SIX

Vault

Sky

Firmament

©2017 Chad Taylor

And God said, Let us make man in

Genesis 1:24-31

DAY SEVEN

Genesis 2:1-3

¹Thus the heavens and the earth were finished, and **all the <u>host</u> of them.** ²And on the seventh day God ended his work which he had made; and he rested on the seventh day from all his work which he had made. ³And God blessed the seventh day, and sanctified it: because that in it he had rested from all his work which God created and made. Genesis 2:1-3 (KJV)

¹Thus the heavens and the earth were completed in all their vast array. ²By the seventh day God had finished the work he had been doing; so on the seventh day he rested from all his work. ³Then God blessed the seventh day and made it holy, because on it he rested from all the work of creating that he had done.
Genesis 2:1-3 (NIV)

¹Thus the heavens and the earth were finished, and **all the <u>host</u> of them.** ²And on the seventh day God finished his work that he had done, and he rested on the seventh day from all his work that he had done. ³So God blessed the seventh day and made it holy, because on it God rested from all his work that he had done in creation. Genesis 2:1-3 (ESV)

¹Thus the heavens and the earth were finished, and **all their <u>multitude</u>.** ²And on the seventh day God finished the work that he had done, and he rested on the seventh day from all the work that he had done. ³So God blessed the seventh day and hallowed it, because on it God rested from all the work that he had done in creation. Genesis 2:1-3 (NRSV)

⊏⊐   **Host:** Army / a great number / multitude (p. 289)

⊏⊐   **Multitude:** a great number / host (p. 290)

DAY SEVEN

And on the seventh day God finished his work that he had done... Genesis 2:2 - ESV

©2017 Chad Taylor

Genesis 2:1-3

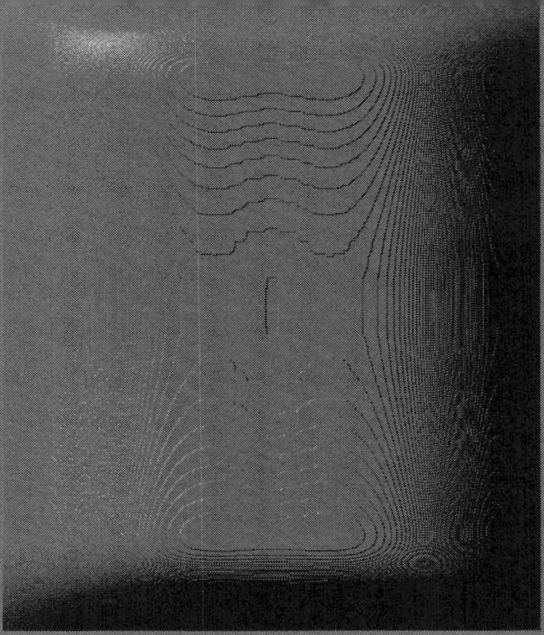

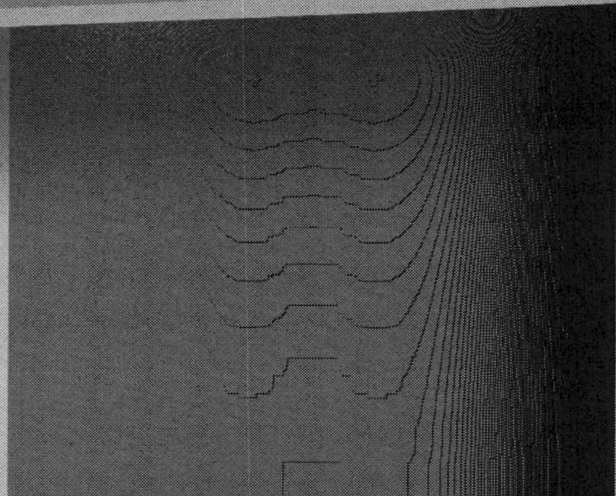

PART TWO

Descriptions of Earth and its surroundings

Look up into the heavens. Who created all the stars? He brings them out like an army, one after another, calling each by its name. Because of his great power and incomparable strength, not a single one is missing.

- Isaiah 40:26 (NLT)

1 Samuel 2:8

[8] He raiseth up the poor out of the dust, and lifteth up the beggar from the dunghill, to set them among princes, and to make them inherit the throne of glory: for **the pillars of the earth are the Lᴏʀᴅ's, and he hath set the world upon them.** 1 Samuel 2:8 (KJV)

[8] He raises the poor from the dust and lifts the needy from the ash heap; he seats them with princes and has them inherit a throne of honor. "For the foundations of the earth are the Lᴏʀᴅ's; on them he has set the world. 1 Samuel 2:8 (NIV)

[8] He raises up the poor from the dust; he lifts the needy from the ash heap to make them sit with princes and inherit a seat of honor. For **the pillars of the earth are the Lord's, and on them he has set the world.**   1 Samuel 2:8 (ESV)

[8] He raises up the poor from the dust; he lifts the needy from the ash heap, to make them sit with princes and inherit a seat of honor. **For the pillars of the earth are the Lᴏʀᴅ's, and on them he has set the world.** 1 Samuel 2:8 (NRSV)

Pillars: a firm upright support for a superstructure (p. 290)

Foundations: the natural or prepared ground or base on which some structure rests (p. 289)

Set: to place with care or deliberate purpose and with relative stability (p. 291)

On/upon: touching and being supported by the top surface of (something) (p. 290)

©2017 Chad Taylor

1 Samuel 2:8

Description:
The world is set on pillars / foundations.

©2017 Chad Taylor

1 Chronicles 16:30

30 Fear before him, all the earth: **the world also shall be <u>stable</u>, that it be <u>not</u> <u>moved</u>.**
1 Chronicles 16:30 (KJV)

30 Tremble before him, all the earth! The world is firmly established; it cannot be moved.
1 Chronicles 16:30 (NIV)

30 tremble before him, all the earth; **yes, the world is <u>established</u>; it shall <u>never</u> be <u>moved</u>.** 1 Chronicles 16:30 (ESV)

30 tremble before him, all the earth. **The world is <u>firmly</u> <u>established</u>; it shall <u>never</u> be <u>moved</u>.** 1 Chronicles 16:30 (NRSV)

    Stable: firmly established / fixed (p. 291)

    Firmly: securely or solidly fixed in place (p. 289)

    Established: to begin or create (something that is meant to last for a long time) / to bring into existence / to make firm or stable (p. 289)

    Cannot: can not (p. 288)

    Never: not ever (p. 290)

    Moved: to go from one place or position to another (p. 290)

Description:
Can not be moved.

Job 22:10-14

¹⁰ Therefore snares are round about thee, and sudden fear troubleth thee; ¹¹ Or **darkness, that thou canst not see; and** <u>abundance</u> **of waters** <u>cover</u> **thee.** ¹² **Is not God in the** <u>height</u> **of heaven?** and behold the **height of the stars, how** <u>high</u> **they are!** ¹³ And thou sayest, How doth God know? can he judge through the **dark cloud?** ¹⁴ Thick clouds are a covering to him, that he seeth not; and **he walketh in the** <u>circuit</u> **of heaven.**
Job 22:10-14 (KJV)

¹⁰ That is why snares are all around you, why sudden peril terrifies you, ¹¹ why it is so dark you cannot see, and why a flood of water covers you. ¹² "Is not God in the heights of heaven? And see how lofty are the highest stars! ¹³ Yet you say, 'What does God know? Does he judge through such darkness? ¹⁴ Thick clouds veil him, so he does not see us as he goes about in the vaulted heavens.' Job 22:10-14 (NIV)

¹⁰ Therefore snares are all around you, and sudden terror overwhelms you, ¹¹ or **darkness,** so that you cannot see, and **a** <u>flood</u> **of water** <u>covers</u> **you.** ¹² **"Is not God** <u>high</u> **in the heavens?** See the <u>highest</u> **stars, how** <u>lofty</u> **they are!** ¹³ But you say, 'What does God know? Can he judge through the **deep darkness?** ¹⁴ Thick clouds veil him, so that he does not see, and **he walks** <u>on</u> **the** <u>vault</u> **of heaven.'** Job 22:10-14 (ESV)

¹⁰ Therefore snares are around you, and sudden terror overwhelms you, ¹¹ or **darkness** so that you cannot see; **a** <u>flood</u> **of water** <u>covers</u> **you.** ¹² **"Is not God** <u>high</u> **in the heavens?** See the <u>highest</u> **stars, how** <u>lofty</u> **they are!** ¹³ Therefore you say, 'What does God know? Can he judge **through the deep darkness?** ¹⁴ Thick clouds enwrap him, so that he does not see, and **he walks** <u>on</u> **the** <u>dome</u> **of heaven.'** Job 22:10-14 (NRSV)

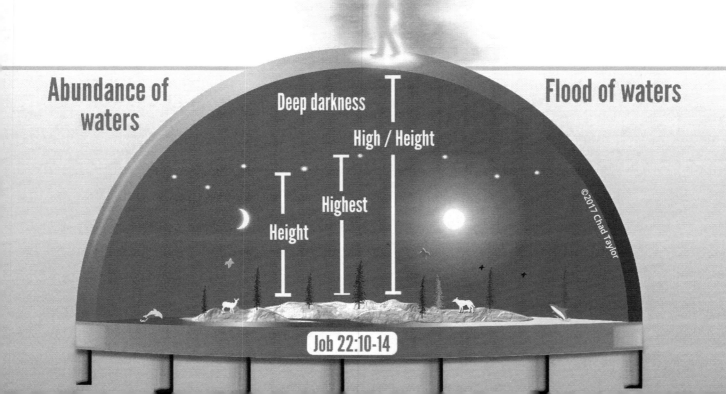

☐   **Abundance:** a large amount of something (p. 288)

☐   **Flood:** a large amount of water covering an area of land that is usually dry (p. 289)

☐   **Cover(s):** to be spread over or on top of (something) (p. 289)

☐   **High:** rising or extending upward a great distance (p. 289)

☐   **Height:** distance upward (p. 289)

☐   **Lofty:** rising to a great height (p. 290)

☐   **On:** touching and being supported by the top surface of (something) (p. 290)

☐   **Circuit:** a boundary line around an area / an enclosed space (p. 288)

☐   **Vaulted:** built in the form of an arch (p. 291)

☐   **Vault:** an arched structure of masonry usually forming a ceiling or roof (p. 291)

☐   **Dome:** a large rounded roof or ceiling that is shaped like half of a ball
            / a large hemispherical roof or ceiling (p. 289)

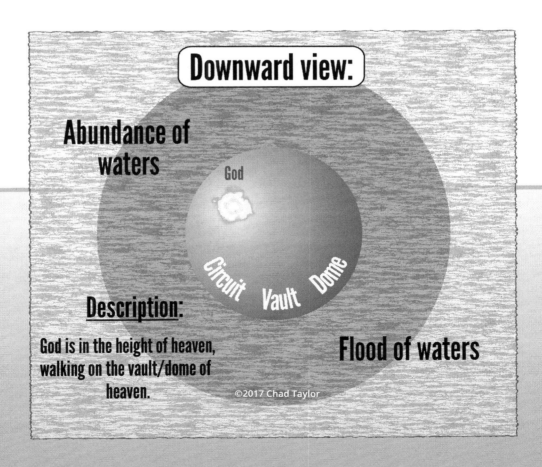

Downward view:

Abundance of waters

God

Circuit Vault Dome

Description:

God is in the height of heaven, walking on the vault/dome of heaven.

Flood of waters

©2017 Chad Taylor

Job 26:7-11

[7] He **stretcheth** out the north <u>over</u> the <u>empty</u> place, and <u>hangeth</u> the earth upon <u>nothing</u>. [8] He bindeth up the waters in his thick clouds; and the cloud is not rent under them. [9] He holdeth back the face of his throne, and spreadeth his cloud upon it. [10] He hath **compassed** the waters with **bounds,** until the day and night come to an end. [11] The **pillars** of heaven tremble and are astonished at his reproof.   Job 26:7-11 (KJV)

[7] He spreads out the northern skies over empty space; he suspends the earth over nothing. [8] He wraps up the waters in his clouds, yet the clouds do not burst under their weight. [9] He covers the face of the full moon, spreading his clouds over it. [10] He marks out the horizon on the face of the waters for a boundary between light and darkness. [11] The pillars of the heavens quake, aghast at his rebuke.   Job 26:7-11 (NIV)

[7] He **stretches** out the north <u>over</u> the <u>void</u> and <u>hangs</u> the earth on <u>nothing</u>. [8] He binds up the waters in his thick clouds, and the cloud is not split open under them. [9] He covers the face of the full moon and spreads over it his cloud. [10] He has inscribed a <u>circle</u> <u>on</u> the <u>face</u> of the **waters** at the boundary between light and darkness. [11] The **pillars** of heaven tremble and are astounded at his rebuke. Job 26:7-11 (ESV)

[7] He **stretches** out Zaphon <u>over</u> the <u>void,</u> and <u>hangs</u> the earth upon <u>nothing</u>. [8] He binds up the waters in his thick clouds, and the cloud is not torn open by them. [9] He covers the face of the full moon, and spreads over it his cloud. [10] He has described a <u>circle</u> <u>on</u> the <u>face</u> of the **waters,** at the boundary between light and darkness. [11] The **pillars** of heaven tremble, and are astounded at his rebuke. Job 26:7-11 (NRSV)

☐   **Stretches:** to extend in length (p. 291)

☐   **Spreads out:** to open, arrange, or place (something) over a large area (p. 291)

☐   **Over:** Above (p. 290)

☐   **Empty:** containing nothing (p. 289)

☐   **Void:** not containing anything (p. 291)

☐   **Hang(eth/s):** to attach or place something so that it is held up without support from below (p. 289)

☐   **Nothing:** not any thing (p. 290)

☐   **Compassed:** to make curved or circular (p. 288)

☐   **Bounds:** something that limits or restrains (p. 288)

☐   **On:** used to indicate the location of something (p. 290)

☐   **Face:** any of the plane surfaces that bound a geometric solid / an inscribed, printed, or marked side (p. 289)

☐   **Circle:** a closed plane curve every point of which is equidistant from a fixed point within the curve (p. 288)

☐   **Pillars:** a firm upright support for a superstructure (p. 290)

Descriptions:

1. The north is stretched over empty space.

2. Earth is not hanging from anything, it is set on pillars, (see previous and later examples for more details).

3. He inscribed a circle on the face of the waters and there is a boundary around the waters.

4. Heaven, (see p. 4), has pillars and they can shake at God's anger.

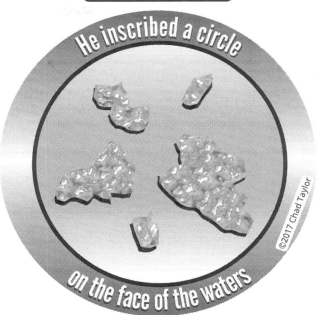

Downward View:

He inscribed a circle

on the face of the waters

©2017 Chad Taylor

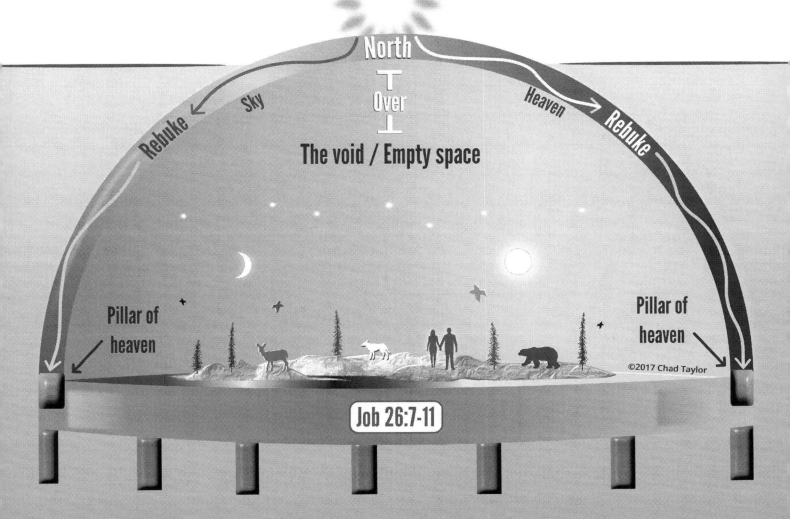

North

Over

The void / Empty space

Rebuke   Sky

Heaven   Rebuke

Pillar of heaven

Pillar of heaven

©2017 Chad Taylor

Job 26:7-11

Job 37:16-18 & 22

[16] Dost thou know the balancings of the clouds, the wondrous works of him which is perfect in knowledge? [17] How thy garments are warm, when he quieteth the earth by the south wind? [18] **Hast thou with him <u>spread out</u> the sky, which is <u>strong</u>, and as a molten looking glass?** [19..20..21..22] Fair weather cometh out of the north: with God is terrible majesty. Job 37:16-18 & 22 (KJV)

[16] Do you know how the clouds hang poised, those wonders of him who has perfect knowledge? [17] You who swelter in your clothes when the land lies hushed under the south wind, [18] can you join him in spreading out the skies, hard as a mirror of cast bronze? [19..20..21..22] Out of the north he comes in golden splendor; God comes in awesome majesty. Job 37:16-18 & 22 (NIV)

[16] Do you know the balancings of the clouds, the wondrous works of him who is perfect in knowledge, [17] you whose garments are hot when the earth is still because of the south wind? [18] Can you, like him, **<u>spread out</u> the skies, <u>hard</u> as a cast metal mirror?** [19..20..21..22] **Out of the north comes golden splendor; God is clothed with awesome majesty.** Job 37:16-18 & 22 (ESV)

[16] Do you know the balancings of the clouds, the wondrous works of the one whose knowledge is perfect, [17] you whose garments are hot when the earth is still because of the south wind? [18] **Can you, like him, <u>spread out</u> the skies, <u>hard</u> as a molten mirror?** [19..20..21..22] **Out of the north comes golden splendor; around God is awesome majesty.** Job 37:16-18 & 22 (NRSV)

⊏⊐   **Spread(ing) out:** to open, arrange, or place (something) over a large area (p. 291)

⊏⊐   **Strong:** not easy to break or damage (p. 291)

⊏⊐   **Hard:** very firm or solid (p. 289)

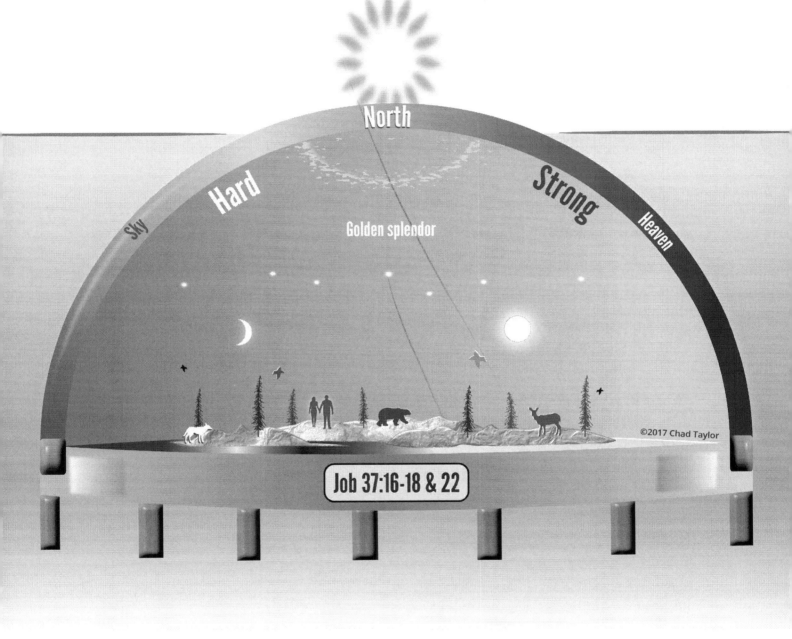

Job 37:16-18 & 22

©2017 Chad Taylor

Descriptions:

1. God spread out the sky, (see p. 4). It is described as being hard and strong. It is also described as being like a cast metal mirror.

2. God comes out of the north in golden splendor and awesome majesty. Read on for more verses regarding God and the north.

Job 38:4-7

⁴ Where wast thou when **I laid the <u>foundations</u> of the earth?** declare, if thou hast understanding. ⁵ **Who hath laid the measures thereof,** if thou knowest? or who hath <u>stretched</u> the line <u>upon</u> it? ⁶ Whereupon are the <u>foundations</u> thereof fastened? or who laid the <u>corner stone</u> thereof; ⁷ When the morning stars <u>sang</u> together, and all the sons of God shouted for joy?   Job 38:4-7 (KJV)

⁴ "Where were you when I laid the earth's foundation? Tell me, if you understand. ⁵ Who marked off its dimensions? Surely you know! Who stretched a measuring line across it? ⁶ On what were its footings set, or who laid its cornerstone— ⁷ while the morning stars sang together and all the angels shouted for joy?   Job 38:4-7 (NIV)

⁴ "Where were you when **I laid the <u>foundation</u> of the earth?** Tell me, if you have understanding. ⁵ **Who determined its measurements—surely you know!** Or who <u>stretched</u> the line <u>upon</u> it? ⁶ On what were its <u>bases</u> sunk, or who laid its <u>cornerstone</u>, ⁷ when the morning stars <u>sang</u> together and all the sons of God shouted for joy?   Job 38:4-7 (ESV)

⁴ "Where were you when **I laid the <u>foundation</u> of the earth?** Tell me, if you have understanding. ⁵ **Who determined its measurements—surely you know!** Or who <u>stretched</u> the line <u>upon</u> it? ⁶ On what were its <u>bases</u> sunk, or who laid its <u>cornerstone</u> ⁷ when the morning stars <u>sang</u> together and all the heavenly beings shouted for joy?   Job 38:4-7 (NRSV)

☐ **Foundation:** the natural or prepared ground or base on which some structure rests (p. 289)

☐ **Stretched:** to extend in length (p. 291)

☐ **Across:** from one side to the other (p. 288)

☐ **Upon:** on (p. 291)

☐ **Footings:** the base or foundation on which something is established (p. 289)

☐ **Bases:** the bottom or lowest part of something (p. 288)

☐ **Cornerstone:** a stone that forms part of a corner in the outside wall of a building and that often shows the date when the building was built (p. 288)

☐ **Sang:** to produce musical tones by means of the voice (p. 290)

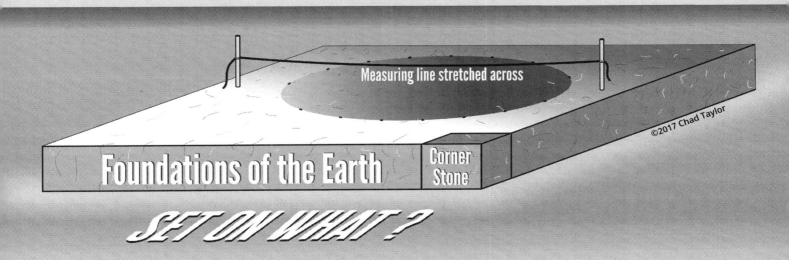

Morning Stars Sing

Measuring line stretched across

Foundations of the Earth

Corner Stone

SET ON WHAT ?

©2017 Chad Taylor

Psalm 19:1 & 4-6

[1] The heavens declare the glory of God; and **the firmament sheweth his handywork.** [2...3...4] Their line is gone out through all the earth, and their words **to the end of the world. In them hath he set a tabernacle for the sun,** [5] Which is as a bridegroom coming out of his chamber, and rejoiceth **as a strong man to run a race.** [6] His going forth is **from the end of the heaven, and his circuit unto the ends of it:** and there is nothing hid from the heat thereof. Psalm 19:1 & 4-6 (KJV)

[1] The heavens declare the glory of God; the skies proclaim the work of his hands. [2...3...4] Yet their voice goes out into all the earth, their words to the ends of the world. In the heavens God has pitched a tent for the sun. [5] It is like a bridegroom coming out of his chamber, like a champion rejoicing to run his course. [6] It rises at one end of the heavens and makes its circuit to the other; nothing is deprived of its warmth.   Psalm 19:1 & 4-6 (NIV)

[1] The heavens declare the glory of God, and **the sky above proclaims his handiwork.** [2...3...4] Their voice goes out through all the earth, and their words **to the end of the world. In them he has set a tent for the sun,** [5] which comes out like a bridegroom leaving his chamber, and, like a strong man, **runs its course with joy.** [6] Its rising is from **the end of the heavens, and its circuit to the end of them,** and there is nothing hidden from its heat. Psalm 19:1 & 4-6 (ESV)

[1] The heavens are telling the glory of God; and **the firmament proclaims his handiwork.** [2...3...4] yet their voice goes out through all the earth, and their words to the **end of the world. In the heavens he has set a tent for the sun,** [5] which comes out like a bridegroom from his wedding canopy, and like a strong man **runs its course with joy.** [6] Its rising is from **the end of the heavens, and its circuit to the end of them;** and nothing is hid from its heat. Psalm 19:1 & 4-6 (NRSV)

☐ **Firmament:** the vault or arch of the sky (p. 289)

☐ **Above:** in or to a higher place than / over (p. 288)

☐ **Tabernacle:** a dwelling place (p. 291)

☐ **In:** within a particular place (p. 290)

☐ **Tent:** something that resembles a tent or that serves as a shelter (p. 291)

☐ **End(s):** the part at the edge or limit of an area (p. 289)

☐ **Run(s):** to go without restraint (p. 290)

☐ **Circuit:** the route traveled (p. 288)

☐ **Course:** the path or direction that something or someone moves along (p. 289)

Downward View:

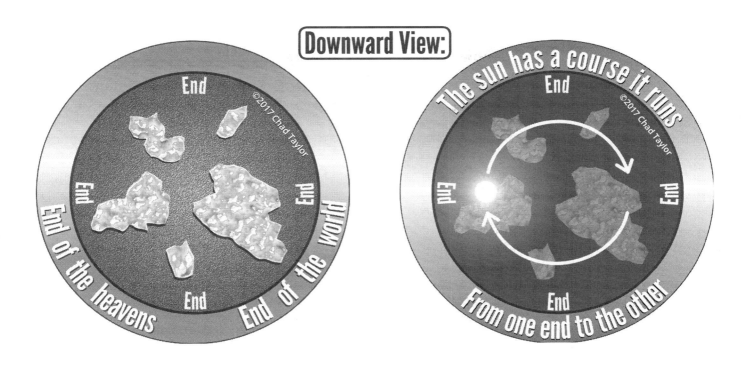

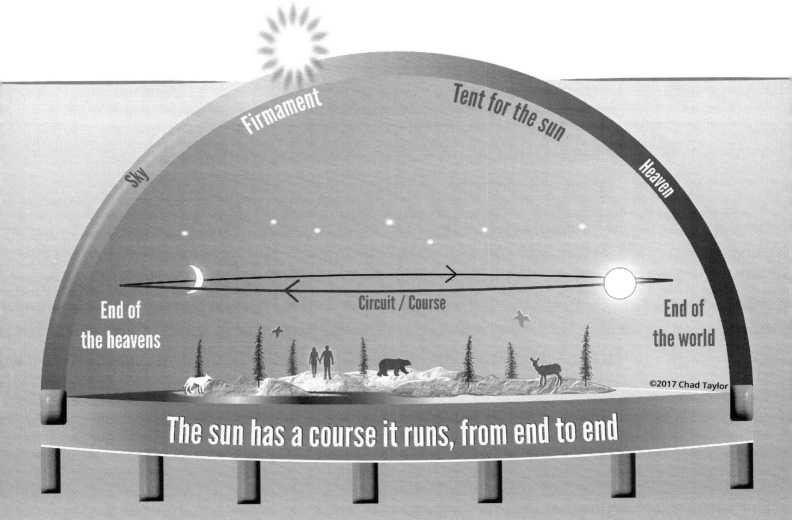

The sun has a course it runs, from end to end

Psalm 74:15-17

[15] Thou didst cleave the fountain and the flood: thou driedst up mighty rivers. [16] The day is thine, the night also is thine: thou hast prepared the light and the sun. [17] **Thou hast <u>set</u> all the <u>borders</u> of the earth: thou hast made summer and winter.** Psalm 74:15-17 (KJV)

[15] It was you who opened up springs and streams; you dried up the ever-flowing rivers. [16] The day is yours, and yours also the night; you established the sun and moon. [17] It was you who set all the boundaries of the earth; you made both summer and winter. Psalm 74:15-17 (NIV)

[15] You split open springs and brooks; you dried up ever-flowing streams. [16] Yours is the day, yours also the night; you have established the heavenly lights and the sun. [17] **You have <u>fixed</u> all the <u>boundaries</u> of the earth; you have made summer and winter.** Psalm 74:15-17 (ESV)

[15] You cut openings for springs and torrents; you dried up ever-flowing streams. [16] Yours is the day, yours also the night; you established the luminaries and the sun. [17] **You have <u>fixed</u> all the <u>bounds</u> of the earth; you made summer and winter.** Psalm 74:15-17 (NRSV)

⊏⊐   **Set:** to place with care or deliberate purpose and with relative stability (p. 291)

⊏⊐   **Fixed:** securely placed or fastened / stationary (p. 289)

⊏⊐   **Borders:** an outer part or edge (p. 288)

⊏⊐   **Boundaries:** something that indicates or fixes a limit or extent (p. 288)

⊏⊐   **Bounds:** something that limits or restrains (p. 288)

Downward View:

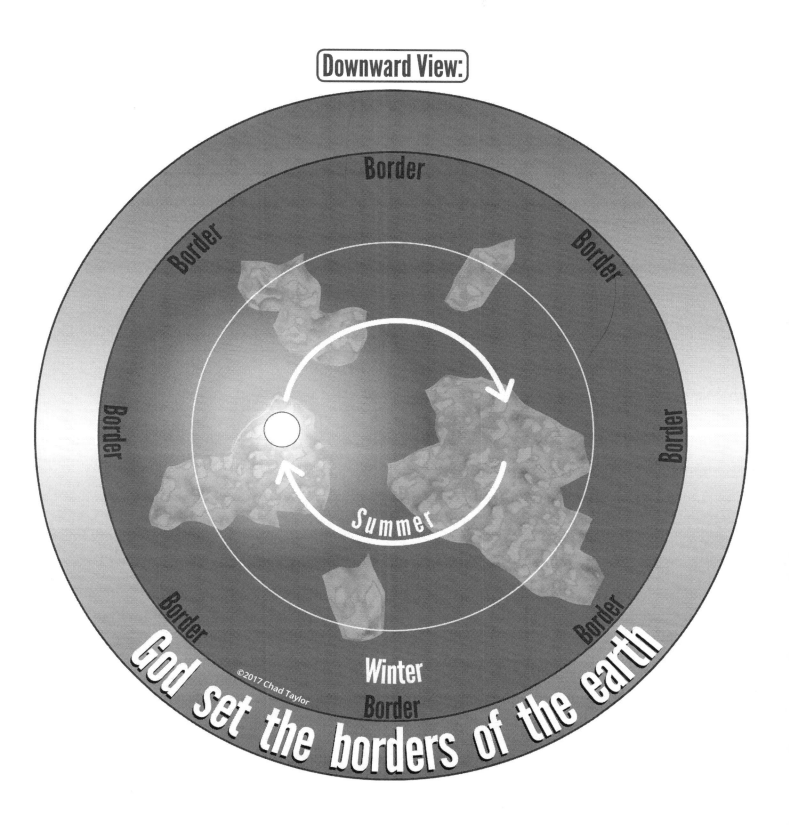

God set the borders of the earth

©2017 Chad Taylor

Psalm 75:3

³ The earth and all the inhabitants thereof are <u>dissolved</u>: I bear up the <u>pillars</u> of it. Selah. Psalm 75:3 (KJV)

³ When the earth and all its people quake, it is I who hold its pillars firm. Psalm 75:3 (NIV)

³ When the earth <u>totters</u>, and all its inhabitants, it is I who keep steady its <u>pillars</u>. Selah Psalm 75:3 (ESV)

³ When the earth <u>totters</u>, with all its inhabitants, it is I who keep its <u>pillars</u> steady. Selah Psalm 75:3 (NRSV)

- **Dissolved:** break up, disperse (p. 289)
- **Quake:** to shake violently (p. 290)
- **Totters:** Sway (p. 291)
- **Pillars:** a firm upright support for a superstructure (p. 290)
- **Firm:** securely or solidly fixed in place (p. 289)

God holds earth's pillars steady

©2017 Chad Taylor

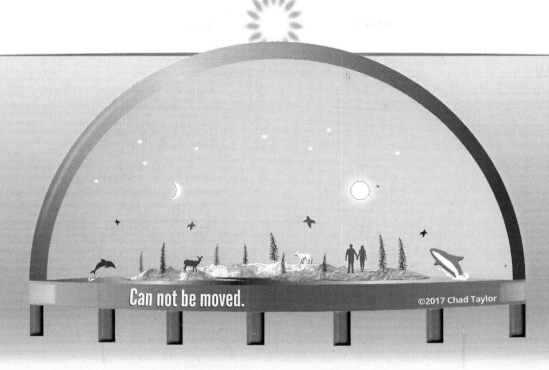

Can not be moved.

©2017 Chad Taylor

Psalm 93:1

¹ The LORD reigneth, he is clothed with majesty; the LORD is clothed with strength, wherewith he hath girded himself: **the world also is <u>stablished</u>, that it <u>cannot</u> be <u>moved</u>.** Psalm 93:1 (KJV)

---

¹ The LORD reigns, he is robed in majesty; the LORD is robed in majesty and armed with strength; indeed, the world is established, firm and secure. Psalm 93:1 (NIV)

---

¹ The Lord reigns; he is robed in majesty; the Lord is robed; he has put on strength as his belt. **Yes, the world is <u>established</u>; it shall <u>never</u> be <u>moved</u>.** Psalm 93:1 (ESV)

---

¹ The LORD is king, he is robed in majesty; the LORD is robed, he is girded with strength. **He has <u>established</u> the world; it shall <u>never</u> be <u>moved</u>;** Psalm 93:1 (NRSV)

- **Established:** to bring into existence / to make firm or stable (p. 289)

- **Firm:** securely or solidly fixed in place (p. 289)

- **Secure:** to put (something) in a place or position so that it will not move (p. 291)

- **Cannot:** can not (p. 288)

- **Never:** not ever (p. 290)

- **Moved:** to go from one place or position to another (p. 290)

Psalm 102:18-20 & 25

¹⁸ This shall be written for the generation to come: and the people which shall be created shall praise the LORD. ¹⁹ **For he hath looked <u>down</u> <u>from</u> the <u>height</u> of his sanctuary; <u>from</u> heaven did the LORD behold the earth;** ²⁰ To hear the groaning of the prisoner; to loose those that are appointed to death; ^{21..22..23..24..25} Of old hast **thou laid the <u>foundation</u> of the earth: and the heavens are the work of thy hands.** Psalm 102:18-20 & 25 (KJV)

¹⁸ Let this be written for a future generation, that a people not yet created may praise the LORD: ¹⁹ "The LORD looked down from his sanctuary on high, from heaven he viewed the earth, ²⁰ to hear the groans of the prisoners and release those condemned to death." ^{21..22..23..24..25} In the beginning you laid the foundations of the earth, and the heavens are the work of your hands. Psalm 102:18-20 & 25 (NIV)

¹⁸ Let this be recorded for a generation to come, so that a people yet to be created may praise the Lord: ¹⁹ that **he looked <u>down</u> <u>from</u> his holy <u>height</u>; <u>from</u> heaven the Lord looked at the earth,** ²⁰ to hear the groans of the prisoners, to set free those who were doomed to die, ^{21..22..23..24..25} Of old **you laid the <u>foundation</u> of the earth, and the heavens are the work of your hands.** Psalm 102:18-20 & 25 (ESV)

¹⁸ Let this be recorded for a generation to come, so that a people yet unborn may praise the LORD: ¹⁹ that **he looked <u>down</u> <u>from</u> his holy <u>height</u>, <u>from</u> heaven the LORD looked at the earth,** ²⁰ to hear the groans of the prisoners, to set free those who were doomed to die; ^{21..22..23..24..25} Long ago **you laid the <u>foundation</u> of the earth, and the heavens are the work of your hands.** Psalm 102:18-20 & 25 (NRSV)

⌐⌐   **Down:** from a higher to a lower place or position   (p. 289)

⌐⌐   **From:** used to indicate the starting point of a physical movement or action   (p. 289)

⌐⌐   **Height:** distance upward   (p. 289)

⌐⌐   **High:** rising or extending upward a great distance   (p. 289)

⌐⌐   **Foundation(s):** the natural or prepared ground or base on which some structure rests   (p. 289)

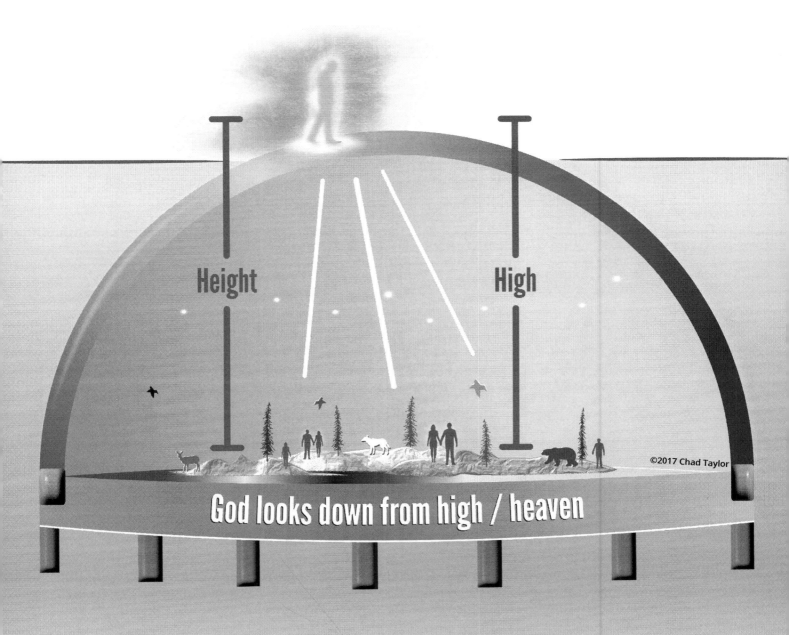

Height High

God looks down from high / heaven

©2017 Chad Taylor

Psalm 104:1-6

¹ Bless the LORD, O my soul. O LORD my God, thou art very great; thou art clothed with honour and majesty. ² Who coverest thyself with light as with a garment: **who stretchest out the heavens like a curtain:** ³ **Who layeth the beams of his chambers in the waters:** who maketh the clouds his chariot: who walketh upon the wings of the wind: ⁴ Who maketh his angels spirits; his ministers a flaming fire: ⁵ **Who laid the foundations of the earth, that it should not be removed for ever.** ⁶ **Thou coveredst it with the deep as with a garment: the waters stood above the mountains.** Psalm 104:1-6 (KJV)

¹ Praise the LORD, my soul. LORD my God, you are very great; you are clothed with splendor and majesty. ² The LORD wraps himself in light as with a garment; he stretches out the heavens like a tent ³ and lays the beams of his upper chambers on their waters. He makes the clouds his chariot and rides on the wings of the wind. ⁴ He makes winds his messengers, flames of fire his servants. ⁵ He set the earth on its foundations; it can never be moved. ⁶ You covered it with the watery depths as with a garment; the waters stood above the mountains. Psalm 104:1-6 (NIV)

¹ Bless the LORD, O my soul! O LORD my God, you are very great! You are clothed with splendor and majesty, ² covering yourself with light as with a garment, **stretching out the heavens like a tent.** ³ **He lays the beams of his chambers on the waters;** he makes the clouds his chariot; he rides on the wings of the wind; ⁴ he makes his messengers winds, his ministers a flaming fire. ⁵ **He set the earth on its foundations, so that it should never be moved.** ⁶ **You covered it with the deep as with a garment; the waters stood above the mountains.** Psalm 104:1-6 (ESV)

¹ Bless the LORD, O my soul. O LORD my God, you are very great. You are clothed with honor and majesty, ² wrapped in light as with a garment. **You stretch out the heavens like a tent,** ³ **you set the beams of your chambers on the waters,** you make the clouds your chariot, you ride on the wings of the wind, ⁴ you make the winds your messengers, fire and flame your ministers. ⁵ **You set the earth on its foundations, so that it shall never be shaken.** ⁶ **You cover it with the deep as with a garment; the waters stood above the mountains.** Psalm 104:1-6 (NRSV)

- **Stretch(es)(ing) out:** the act of stretching out / the state of being stretched out (p. 291)

- **Curtain:** a piece of cloth or other material that is hung to protect or hide something / a hanging screen usually capable of being drawn back or up (p. 289)

- **Tent:** something that resembles a tent or that serves as a shelter (p. 291)

- **Set:** to place with care or deliberate purpose and with relative stability (p. 291)

- **On:** to a position that is supported by (p. 290)

- **Foundations:** the natural or prepared ground or base on which some structure rests (p. 289)

- **Never:** not ever (p. 290)

- **Moved:** to go from one place or position to another (p. 290)

- **Covered:** to be spread over or on top of (something) (p. 289)

- **Garment:** a piece of clothing (p. 289)

- **Above:** in or to a higher place than / over (p. 288)

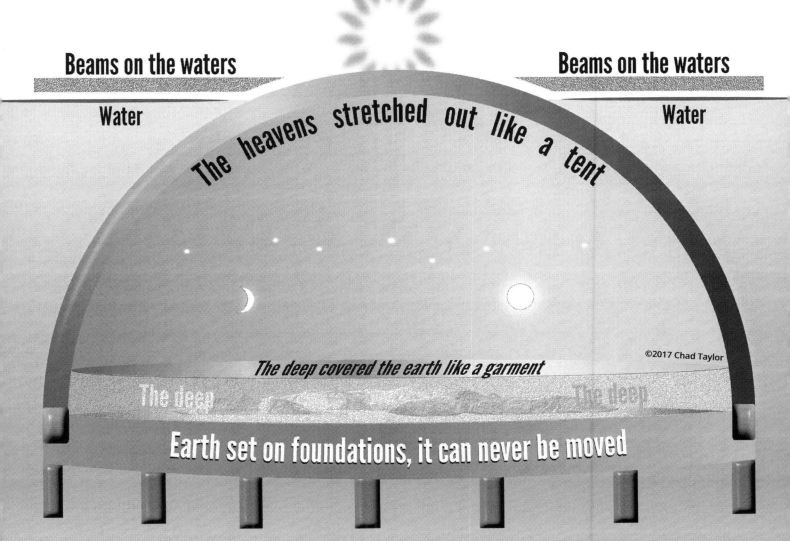

Psalm 108:4-5

[4] For thy mercy is great **above** the heavens: and thy truth reacheth unto the clouds. [5] Be thou exalted, O God, **above the heavens: and thy glory above all the earth;** Psalm 108:4-5 (KJV)

[4] For great is your love, higher than the heavens; your faithfulness reaches to the skies. [5] Be exalted, O God, above the heavens; let your glory be over all the earth. Psalm 108:4-5 (NIV)

[4] For your steadfast love is great **above** the heavens; your faithfulness reaches to the clouds. [5] Be exalted, O God, **above the heavens! Let your glory be over all** the earth! Psalm 108:4-5 (ESV)

[4] For your steadfast love is **higher** than the heavens, and your faithfulness reaches to the clouds. [5] Be exalted, O God, **above the heavens, and let your glory be over all** the earth. Psalm 108:4-5 (NRSV)

- **Above:** in or to a higher place than / over (p. 288)
- **Higher:** located far above the ground or another surface (p. 289)
- **Over:** Above (p. 290)
- **All:** the whole, entire, total amount, quantity, or extent of (p. 288)

God above the heavens

above/over all the earth

God's glory above all the earth

©2017 Chad Taylor

Psalm 148:1-5

¹Praise ye the LORD. Praise ye the LORD from the heavens: **praise him in the <u>heights</u>.** ² **Praise ye him, all his angels: praise ye him, all his <u>hosts</u>.** ³ **Praise ye him, sun and moon: praise him, all ye stars of light.** ⁴ **Praise him, ye heavens of heavens, and ye waters that <u>be</u> <u>above</u> the heavens.** ⁵ Let them praise the name of the LORD: for he commanded, and they were created. Psalm 148:1-5 (KJV)

¹ Praise the LORD. Praise the LORD from the heavens; praise him in the heights above. ² Praise him, all his angels; praise him, all his heavenly hosts. ³ Praise him, sun and moon; praise him, all you shining stars. ⁴ Praise him, you highest heavens and you waters above the skies. ⁵ Let them praise the name of the LORD, for at his command they were created, Psalm 148:1-5 (NIV)

¹ Praise the Lord! Praise the Lord from the heavens; **praise him in the <u>heights</u>!** ² **Praise him, all his angels; praise him, all his <u>hosts</u>!** ³ **Praise him, sun and moon, praise him, all you shining stars!** ⁴ **Praise him, you <u>highest</u> heavens, and you waters <u>above</u> the heavens!** ⁵ Let them praise the name of the Lord! For he commanded and they were created. Psalm 148:1-5 (ESV)

¹ Praise the LORD! Praise the LORD from the heavens; **praise him in the <u>heights</u>!** ² **Praise him, all his angels; praise him, all his <u>host</u>!** ³ **Praise him, sun and moon; praise him, all you shining stars!** ⁴ **Praise him, you <u>highest</u> heavens, and you waters <u>above</u> the heavens!** ⁵ Let them praise the name of the LORD, for he commanded and they were created. Psalm 148:1-5 (NRSV)

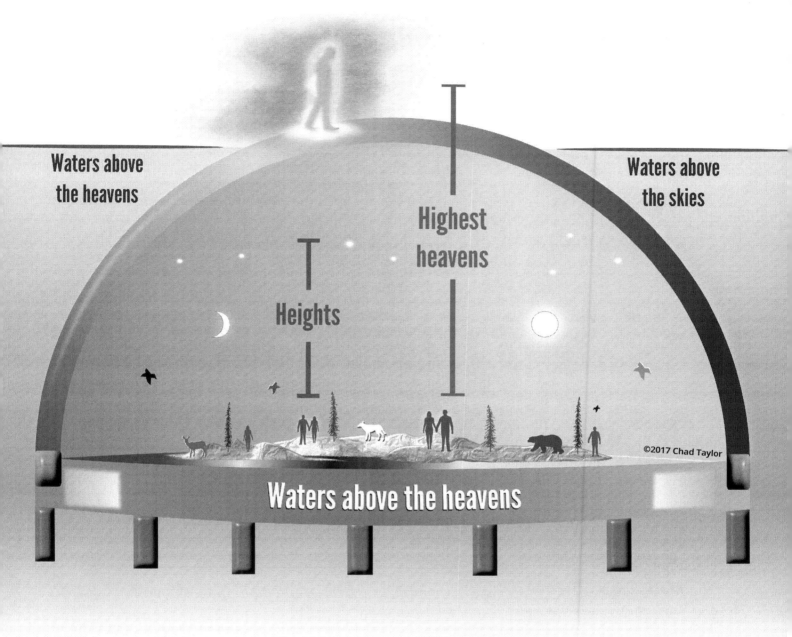

Waters above the heavens

Waters above the skies

Highest heavens

Heights

©2017 Chad Taylor

Waters above the heavens

⊏⊐ **Heights:** a high point or position (p. 289)

⊏⊐ **Highest:** a high or the highest point, place, or level; peak (p. 289)

⊏⊐ **Host(s):** Army / a great number / multitude (p. 289)

⊏⊐ **Be:** to occupy a place, situation, or position (p. 288)

⊏⊐ **Above:** in or to a higher place than / over (p. 288)

Proverbs 8:27-29

27 When he prepared the heavens, I was there: **when he set a <u>compass</u> upon the <u>face</u> of the depth:** 28 When he established the clouds above: when **he strengthened the <u>fountains</u> of the deep:** 29 When he gave to the sea his decree, that the waters should not pass his commandment: **when he appointed the <u>foundations</u> of the earth:** Proverbs 8:27-29 (KJV)

27 I was there when he set the heavens in place, when he marked out the horizon on the face of the deep, 28 when he established the clouds above and fixed securely the fountains of the deep, 29 when he gave the sea its boundary so the waters would not overstep his command, and when he marked out the foundations of the earth. Proverbs 8:27-29 (NIV)

27 When he <u>established</u> the heavens, I was there; when he <u>drew</u> a <u>circle</u> on the <u>face</u> of the deep, 28 when he made <u>firm</u> the skies <u>above</u>, when he <u>established</u> the <u>fountains</u> of the deep, 29 when he assigned to the sea its <u>limit</u>, so that the waters might not transgress his command, **when he <u>marked</u> out the <u>foundations</u> of the earth,** Proverbs 8:27-29 (ESV)

27 When he <u>established</u> the heavens, I was there, **when he <u>drew</u> a <u>circle</u> on the <u>face</u> of the deep,** 28 when he made <u>firm</u> the skies <u>above</u>, when he <u>established</u> the <u>fountains</u> of the deep, 29 when he assigned to the sea its <u>limit</u>, so that the waters might not transgress his command, when **he <u>marked</u> out the <u>foundations</u> of the earth,** Proverbs 8:27-29 (NRSV)

- **Set:** to put or fix in a place or condition (p. 291)
- **place:** a particular portion of a surface (p. 290)
- **Established:** to put (someone or something) in a position, role, etc., that will last for a long time (p. 289)
- **Marked:** to make or leave a visible mark on (something) (p. 290)
- **Drew:** to make (a picture, image, etc.) by making lines on a surface especially with a pencil, pen, marker, chalk, etc., but not usually with paint (p. 289)
- **Compass:** an instrument for drawing circles or marking measurements consisting of two pointed legs joined at the top by a pivot (p. 288)
- **Circle:** a closed plane curve every point of which is equidistant from a fixed point within the curve (p. 288)
- **Face:** any of the plane surfaces that bound a geometric solid / an inscribed, printed, or marked side (p. 289)
- **Firm:** securely or solidly fixed in place (p. 289)
- **Above:** in or to a higher place (p. 288)
- **Fountains:** the source from which something proceeds or is supplied (p. 289)
- **Boundary:** something that indicates or fixes a limit or extent (p. 288)
- **Limit:** something that bounds, restrains, or confines (p. 290)
- **Foundations:** the natural or prepared ground or base on which some structure rests (p. 289)

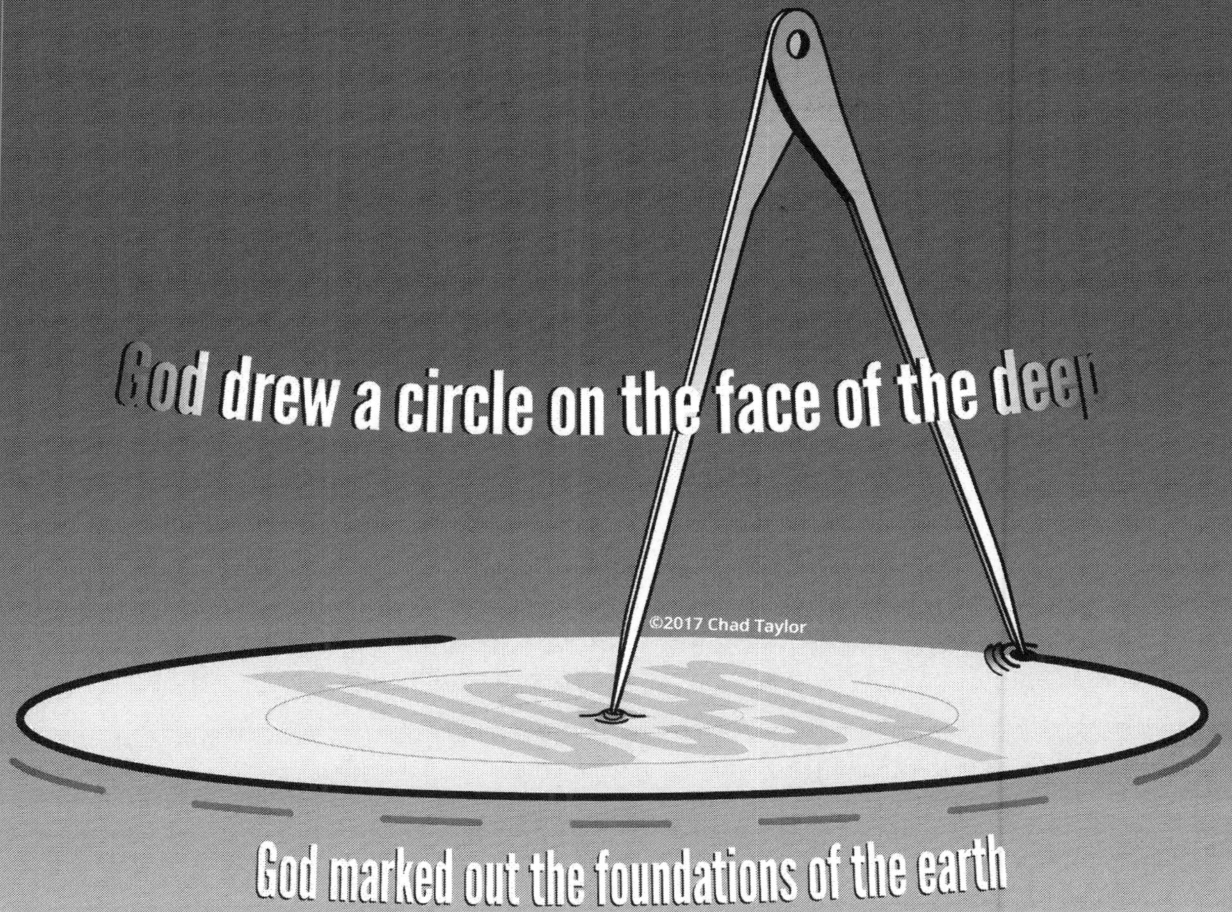

God drew a circle on the face of the deep

God marked out the foundations of the earth

©2017 Chad Taylor

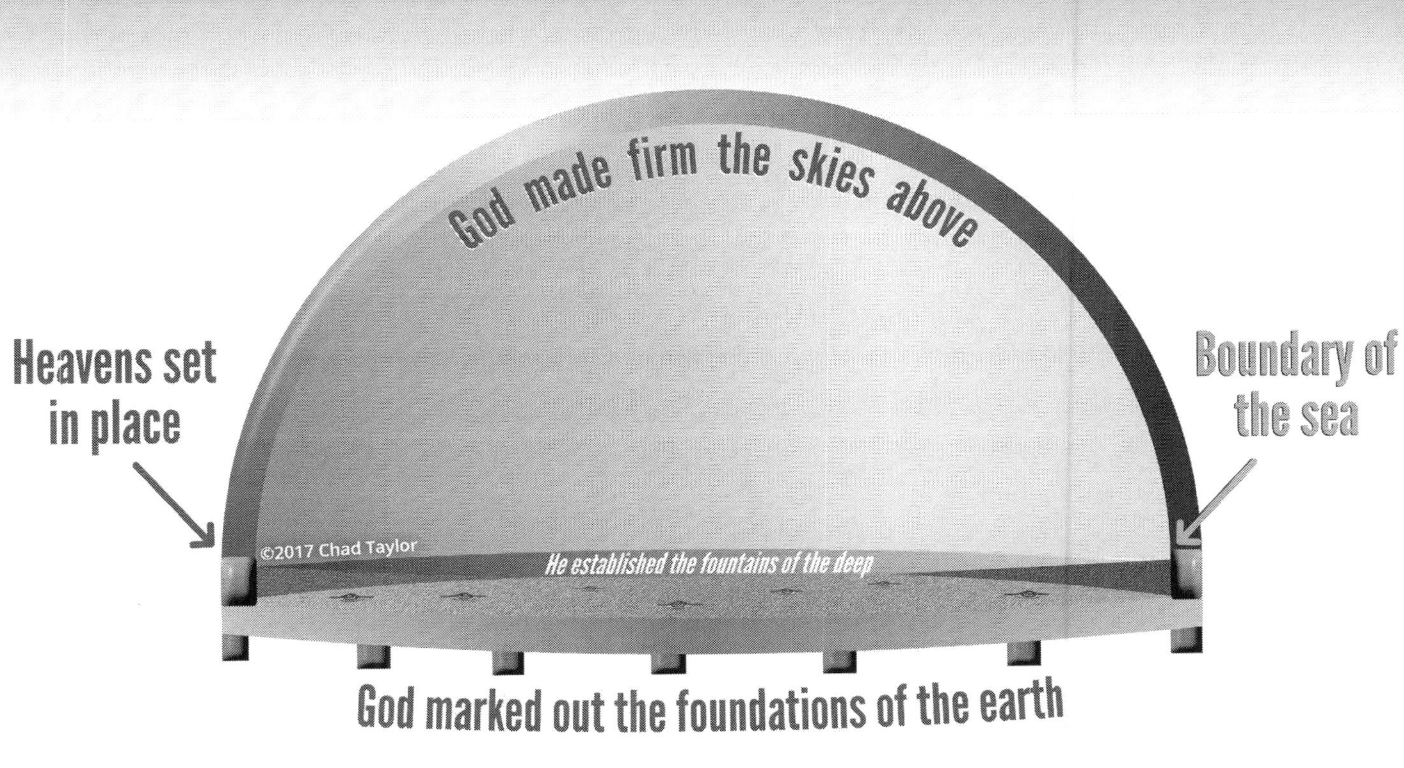

God made firm the skies above

Heavens set in place

Boundary of the sea

He established the fountains of the deep

©2017 Chad Taylor

God marked out the foundations of the earth

Ecclesiastes 1:5-7

[5] The sun also <u>ariseth</u>, and the sun goeth <u>down</u>, and hasteth to <u>his</u> place where <u>he</u> arose. [6] The wind goeth toward the south, and turneth about unto the north; it whirleth about continually, and the wind <u>returneth</u> again according to his <u>circuits</u>. [7] All the rivers run into the sea; yet the sea is not full; unto the place from whence the rivers come, thither they <u>return</u> <u>again</u>. Ecclesiastes 1:5-7 (KJV)

[5] The sun rises and the sun sets, and hurries back to where it rises. [6] The wind blows to the south and turns to the north; round and round it goes, ever returning on its course. [7] All streams flow into the sea, yet the sea is never full. To the place the streams come from, there they return again. Ecclesiastes 1:5-7 (NIV)

[5] The sun <u>rises</u>, and the sun goes <u>down</u>, and hastens to the place where it rises. [6] The wind blows to the south and goes around to the north; <u>around</u> and <u>around</u> goes the wind, and on its <u>circuits</u> the wind <u>returns</u>. [7] All streams run to the sea, but the sea is not full; to the place where the streams flow, there they flow <u>again</u>. Ecclesiastes 1:5-7 (ESV)

[5] The sun <u>rises</u> and the sun goes <u>down</u>, and hurries to the place where it <u>rises</u>. [6] The wind blows to the south, and goes <u>around</u> to the north; <u>round</u> and <u>round</u> goes the wind, and on its <u>circuits</u> the wind <u>returns</u>. [7] All streams run to the sea, but the sea is not full; to the place where the streams flow, there they continue to flow. Ecclesiastes 1:5-7 (NRSV)

[5] The sun <u>rises</u> and the sun <u>sets</u>, then hurries <u>around</u> to <u>rise</u> <u>again</u>. [6] The wind blows south, and then turns north. <u>Around</u> and <u>around</u> it goes, blowing in <u>circles</u>. [7] Rivers run into the sea, but the sea is never full. Then the water <u>returns</u> <u>again</u> to the rivers and flows out <u>again</u> to the sea. Ecclesiastes 1:5-7 (NLT)

- **Rises / Ariseth:** to appear above the horizon (p. 290)

- **Sets:** to pass below the horizon / go down (p. 291)

- **Back:** to, toward, or in the place where someone or something was previously (p. 288)

- **Return(s/eth/ing):** to come or go to a place again (p. 290)

- **Again:** for another time (p. 288)

- **Down:** below the horizon (p. 289)

- **Round:** encircle, encompass (p. 290)

- **Around:** in a circle (p. 288)

- **Circles:** a path that goes around a central point (p. 288)

- **Circuits:** the route traveled (p. 288)

- **Course:** the path or direction that something or someone moves along (p. 289)

Downward View:

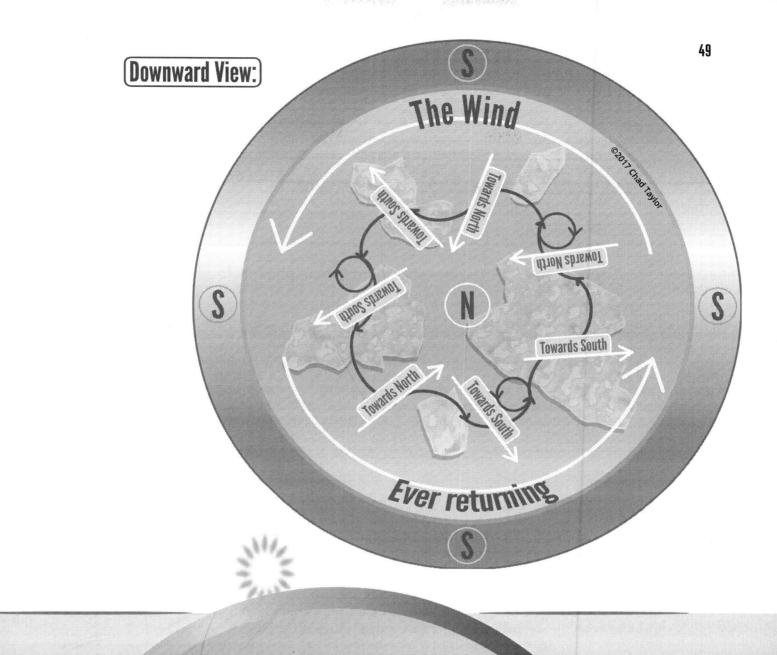

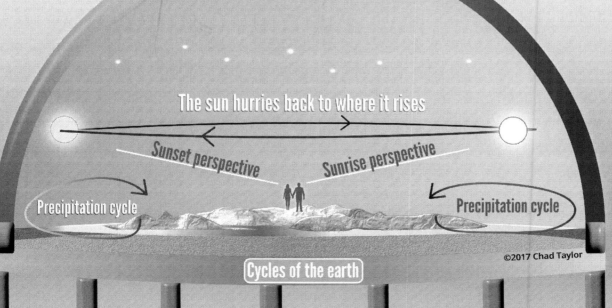

Isaiah 40:22

²² It is he that sitteth <u>upon</u> the <u>circle</u> of the earth, and the inhabitants thereof are as grasshoppers; that <u>stretcheth out</u> the heavens as a <u>curtain</u>, and <u>spreadeth</u> them out as a <u>tent</u> to dwell <u>in</u>: Isaiah 40:22 (KJV)

²² He sits enthroned above the circle of the earth, and its people are like grasshoppers. He stretches out the heavens like a canopy, and spreads them out like a tent to live in. Isaiah 40:22 (NIV)

²² It is he who sits <u>above</u> the <u>circle</u> of the earth, and its inhabitants are like grasshoppers; who <u>stretches out</u> the heavens like a <u>curtain</u>, and <u>spreads</u> them like a <u>tent</u> to dwell <u>in</u>; Isaiah 40:22 (ESV)

²² It is he who sits <u>above</u> the <u>circle</u> of the earth, and its inhabitants are like grasshoppers; who <u>stretches out</u> the heavens like a <u>curtain</u>, and <u>spreads</u> them like a <u>tent</u> to live <u>in</u>; Isaiah 40:22 (NRSV)

²² God sits <u>above</u> the <u>circle</u> of the earth. The people <u>below</u> seem like grasshoppers to him! He <u>spreads out</u> the heavens like a <u>curtain</u> and makes his <u>tent</u> from them. Isaiah 40:22 (NLT)

- **Upon, (on):** touching and being supported by the top surface of (something) (p. 291)
- **Above:** in or to a higher place (p. 288)
- **Circle:** a closed plane curve every point of which is equidistant from a fixed point within the curve (p. 288)
- **Below:** in or to a lower place (p. 288)
- **Stretches out:** the act of stretching out / the state of being stretched out (p. 291)
- **Spreads:** to open or expand over a larger area (p. 291)
- **Curtain:** a piece of cloth or other material that is hung to protect or hide something/ a hanging screen usually capable of being drawn back or up (p. 289)
- **Canopy:** something that hangs or spreads out over an area (p. 288)
- **Tent:** something that resembles a tent or that serves as a shelter (p. 291)
- **In:** used to indicate location or position within something (p. 290)

The heavens stretched out like a tent to live in

From above the circle of the earth
we seem small like grasshoppers

©2017 Chad Taylor

God sits above the circle of the earth... Isaiah 40:22 (NLT)

Downward View:

Circle of the earth

©2017 Chad Taylor

Circle of the earth

Isaiah 42:5

⁵ Thus saith God the Lᴏʀᴅ, **he that created the heavens, and** <u>stretched</u> them <u>out</u>; he that <u>spread forth</u> **the earth,** and that which cometh out of it; he that giveth breath unto the people upon it, and spirit to them that walk therein: Isaiah 42:5 (KJV)

⁵ This is what God the Lᴏʀᴅ says—the Creator of the heavens, who stretches them out, who spreads out the earth with all that springs from it, who gives breath to its people, and life to those who walk on it: Isaiah 42:5 (NIV)

⁵ Thus says God, the Lord, **who created the heavens and** <u>stretched</u> them <u>out</u>, who <u>spread out</u> **the earth** and what comes from it, who gives breath to the people on it and spirit to those who walk in it: Isaiah 42:5 (ESV)

⁵ Thus says God, the Lᴏʀᴅ, **who created the heavens and** <u>stretched</u> them <u>out</u>, who <u>spread out</u> **the earth** and what comes from it, who gives breath to the people upon it and spirit to those who walk in it: Isaiah 42:5 (NRSV)

Isaiah 44:24

²⁴ Thus saith the Lᴏʀᴅ, thy redeemer, and he that formed thee from the womb, **I am the Lᴏʀᴅ that** **maketh** <u>all</u> **things; that** <u>stretcheth forth</u> **the heavens** <u>alone</u>**; that** <u>spreadeth</u> <u>abroad</u> **the earth by** <u>myself</u>**;** Isaiah 44:24 (KJV)

²⁴ "This is what the Lᴏʀᴅ says—your Redeemer, who formed you in the womb: I am the Lᴏʀᴅ, the Maker of all things, who stretches out the heavens, who spreads out the earth by myself, Isaiah 44:24 (NIV)

²⁴ Thus says the Lord, your Redeemer, who formed you from the womb: **"I am the Lord, who made** <u>all</u> **things, who** <u>alone</u> <u>stretched out</u> **the heavens, who** <u>spread out</u> **the earth by** <u>myself</u>, Isaiah 44:24 (ESV)

²⁴ Thus says the Lᴏʀᴅ, your Redeemer, who formed you in the womb: **I am the Lᴏʀᴅ, who made** <u>all</u> **things, who** <u>alone</u> <u>stretched out</u> **the heavens, who by** <u>myself</u> <u>spread out</u> **the earth;** Isaiah 44:24 (NRSV)

⌣ **Stretched(es):** to extend in length (p. 291)

⌣ **Out:** away from a particular place (p. 290)

⌣ **Spread(s) out:** to open, arrange, or place (something) over a large area (p. 291)

⌣ **Spread:** to open or expand over a larger area (p. 291)

⌣ **Forth:** onward or forward in time or place (p. 289)

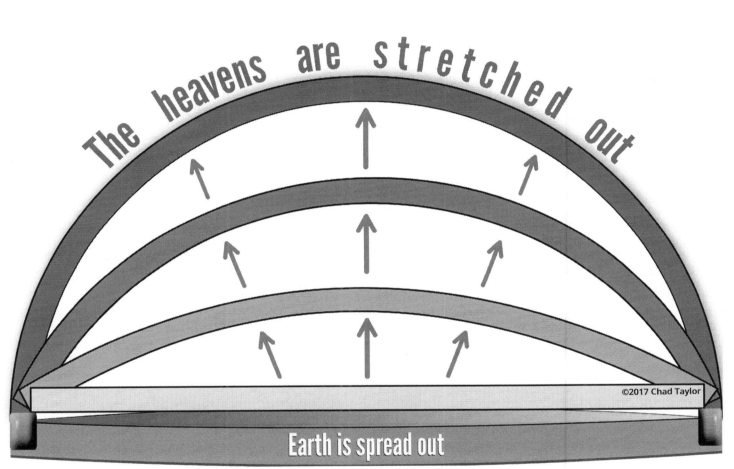

(See also p.4)

⌣ **All:** the whole, entire, total amount, quantity, or extent of (p. 288)

⌣ **Stretched(es) out:** the act of stretching out / the state of being stretched out (p. 291)

⌣ **Alone:** without anyone or anything else (p. 288)

⌣ **Spread(eth):** to open or expand over a larger area (p. 291)

⌣ **Abroad:** over a wide area (p. 288)

⌣ **Spread(s) out:** to open, arrange, or place (something) over a large area (p. 291)

⌣ **Myself:** Alone (p. 290)

Isaiah 48:12-13

¹² Hearken unto me, O Jacob and Israel, my called; **I am he; I am the first, I also am the last.** ¹³ Mine hand also hath <u>laid</u> the <u>foundation</u> of the earth, and my right hand hath <u>spanned</u> the heavens: when I call unto them, they <u>stand up</u> together. Isaiah 48:12-13 (KJV)

¹² "Listen to me, Jacob, Israel, whom I have called: I am he; I am the first and I am the last. ¹³ My own hand laid the foundations of the earth, and my right hand spread out the heavens; when I summon them, they all stand up together. Isaiah 48:12-13 (NIV)

¹² "Listen to me, O Jacob, and Israel, whom I called! **I am he; I am the first, and I am the last.** ¹³ My hand <u>laid</u> the <u>foundation</u> of the earth, and my right hand <u>spread out</u> the heavens; when I call to them, they stand forth together. Isaiah 48:12-13 (ESV)

¹² Listen to me, O Jacob, and Israel, whom I called: **I am He; I am the first, and I am the last.** ¹³ My hand <u>laid</u> the <u>foundation</u> of the earth, and my right hand <u>spread out</u> the heavens; when I summon them, they <u>stand</u> at <u>attention</u>. Isaiah 48:12-13 (NRSV)

¹² "Listen to me, O family of Jacob, Israel my chosen one! **I <u>alone</u> am God, the First and the Last.** ¹³ It was my hand that <u>laid</u> the <u>foundations</u> of the earth, my right hand that <u>spread out</u> the heavens <u>above</u>. When I call out the stars, they all appear in order." Isaiah 48:12-13 (NLT)

☐ **Alone:** without anyone or anything else (p. 288)

☐ **Laid:** to put or set down (p. 290)

☐ **Foundation(s):** the natural or prepared ground or base on which some structure rests (p. 289)

☐ **Spanned:** to form an arch over (p. 291)

☐ **Spread out:** to open, arrange, or place (something) over a large area (p. 291)

☐ **Stand up:** to rise to a standing position (p. 291)

☐ **Above:** in the sky / overhead (p. 288)

☐ **Stand:** to be in an upright position (p. 291)

☐ **Attention:** the way a soldier stands with the body stiff and straight, heels together, and arms at the sides
(p. 288)

God spread out the heavens above

Heaven: throne   earth: footstool

God laid the foundations of the earth

©2017 Chad Taylor

Isaiah 66:1

¹ Thus saith the LORD, **The heaven is my <u>throne</u>, and the earth is my <u>footstool</u>:** where is the house that ye build unto me? and where is the place of my rest? Isaiah 66:1 (KJV)

¹ This is what the LORD says: "Heaven is my throne, and the earth is my footstool. Where is the house you will build for me? Where will my resting place be? Isaiah 66:1 (NIV)

¹ Thus says the Lord: **"Heaven is my <u>throne</u>, and the earth is my <u>footstool</u>;** what is the house that you would build for me, and what is the place of my rest? Isaiah 66:1 (ESV)

¹ Thus says the LORD: **Heaven is my <u>throne</u> and the earth is my <u>footstool</u>;** what is the house that you would build for me, and what is my resting place? Isaiah 66:1 (NRSV)

Throne: the position of king or queen / the special chair for a king, queen, or other powerful person (p. 291)

Footstool: a low stool used to support the feet (p. 289)

Jeremiah 10:10-13

¹⁰ But the LORD is the true God, he is the living God, and an everlasting king: **at his wrath the earth shall tremble,** and the nations shall not be able to abide his indignation. ¹¹ Thus shall ye say unto them, The gods that have not made the heavens and the earth, even they shall perish from the earth, **and from <u>under</u> these heavens.** ¹² He hath made the earth by his power, he hath established the world by his wisdom, and **hath <u>stretched out</u> the heavens by his discretion.** ¹³ When he uttereth his voice, there is a multitude of waters in the heavens, and **he causeth the vapours to <u>ascend</u>** from the <u>ends</u> of the earth; he maketh lightnings with rain, and bringeth forth the wind out of his treasures. Jeremiah 10:10-13 (KJV)

¹⁰ But the LORD is the true God; he is the living God, the eternal King. When he is angry, the earth trembles; the nations cannot endure his wrath. ¹¹ "Tell them this: 'These gods, who did not make the heavens and the earth, will perish from the earth and from under the heavens.'" ¹² But God made the earth by his power; he founded the world by his wisdom and stretched out the heavens by his understanding. ¹³ When he thunders, the waters in the heavens roar; he makes clouds rise from the ends of the earth. He sends lightning with the rain and brings out the wind from his storehouses. Jeremiah 10:10-13 (NIV)

¹⁰ But the Lord is the true God; he is the living God and the everlasting King. **At his wrath the earth quakes,** and the nations cannot endure his indignation. ¹¹ Thus shall you say to them: "The gods who did not make the heavens and the earth shall perish from the earth **and from <u>under</u> the heavens.**" ¹² It is he who made the earth by his power, who established the world by his wisdom, and **by his understanding <u>stretched out</u> the heavens.** ¹³ When he utters his voice, there is a tumult of waters in the heavens, and **he makes the mist <u>rise</u> from the <u>ends</u> of the earth.** He makes lightning for the rain, and he brings forth the wind from his storehouses. Jeremiah 10:10-13 (ESV)

¹⁰ But the LORD is the true God; he is the living God and the everlasting King. **At his wrath the earth quakes,** and the nations cannot endure his indignation. ¹¹ Thus shall you say to them: The gods who did not make the heavens and the earth shall perish from the earth **and from <u>under</u> the heavens.** ¹² It is he who made the earth by his power, who established the world by his wisdom, and **by his understanding <u>stretched out</u> the heavens.** ¹³ When he utters his voice, there is a tumult of waters in the heavens, and **he makes the mist <u>rise</u> from the <u>ends</u> of the earth.** He makes lightnings for the rain, and he brings out the wind from his storehouses. Jeremiah 10:10-13 (NRSV)

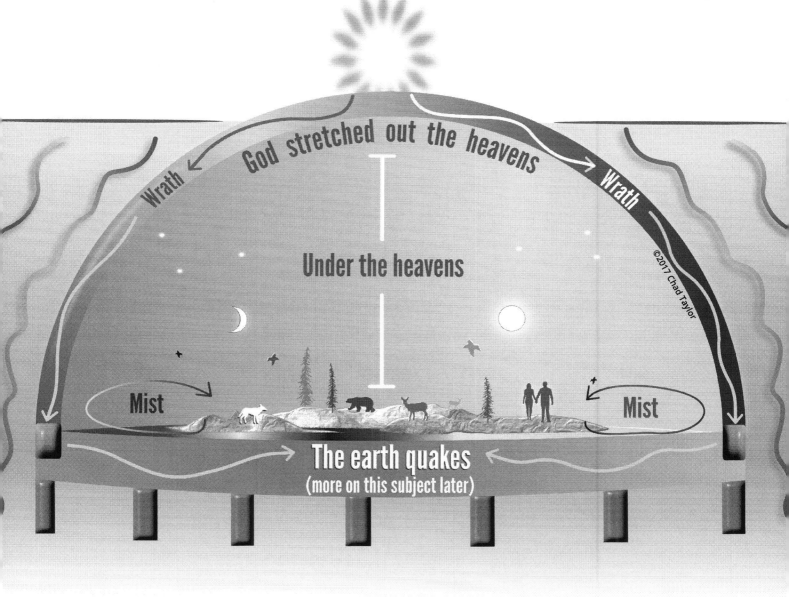

☐ **Tremble(s):** the act or a period of shaking (p. 291)

☐ **Quakes:** to shake violently (p. 290)

☐ **Under:** in or into a position below or beneath something (p. 291)

☐ **Stretched out:** the act of stretching out / the state of being stretched out (p. 291)

☐ **Ascend:** to move upward (p. 288)

☐ **Rise:** to move upward (p. 290)

☐ **Ends:** the part at the edge or limit of an area (p. 289)

Jeremiah 31:37

[37] Thus saith the LORD; **If heaven <u>above</u> can be measured, and the <u>foundations</u> of the earth searched out <u>beneath</u>,** I will also cast off all the seed of Israel for all that they have done, saith the LORD. Jeremiah 31:37 (KJV)

[37] This is what the LORD says: "Only if the heavens above can be measured and the foundations of the earth below be searched out will I reject all the descendants of Israel because of all they have done," declares the LORD. Jeremiah 31:37 (NIV)

[37] Thus says the Lord: **"If the heavens <u>above</u> can be measured, and the <u>foundations</u> of the earth <u>below</u> can be explored,** then I will cast off all the offspring of Israel for all that they have done, declares the Lord." Jeremiah 31:37 (ESV)

[37] Thus says the LORD: **If the heavens <u>above</u> can be measured, and the <u>foundations</u> of the earth <u>below</u> can be explored,** then I will reject all the offspring of Israel because of all they have done, says the LORD. Jeremiah 31:37 (NRSV)

[37] This is what the LORD says: **"Just as the heavens <u>cannot</u> be measured and the <u>foundations</u> of the earth <u>cannot</u> be explored,** so I will not consider casting them away for the evil they have done. I, the LORD, have spoken! Jeremiah 31:37 (NLT)

⌐⌐ **Above:** in the sky / overhead (p. 288)

⌐⌐ **Cannot:** can not (p. 288)

⌐⌐ **Foundations:** the natural or prepared ground or base on which some structure rests (p. 289)

⌐⌐ **Beneath:** in or to a lower position (p. 288)

⌐⌐ **Below:** in or to a lower place (p. 288)

Amos 9:6

⁶ **It is he that buildeth his stories in the heaven, and hath founded his troop in the earth;** he that calleth for the waters of the sea, and poureth them out **upon the <u>face</u> of the earth:** The LORD is his name.
Amos 9:6 (KJV)

⁶ he builds his lofty palace in the heavens and sets its foundation on the earth; he calls for the waters of the sea and pours them out over the face of the land—the LORD is his name. Amos 9:6 (NIV)

⁶ **who builds his upper chambers in the heavens and <u>founds</u> his <u>vault</u> <u>upon</u> the earth;** who calls for the waters of the sea and pours them out **<u>upon</u> the surface of the earth**—the Lord is his name. Amos 9:6 (ESV)

⁶ **who builds his upper chambers in the heavens, and <u>founds</u> his <u>vault</u> <u>upon</u> the earth;** who calls for the waters of the sea, and pours them out **<u>upon</u> the surface of the earth**—the LORD is his name. Amos 9:6 (NRSV)

- ☐ **Sets:** to put or fix in a place or condition (p. 291)
- ☐ **Founds:** to set or ground on something solid (p. 289)
- ☐ **Foundation:** the natural or prepared ground or base on which some structure rests (p. 289)
- ☐ **Vault:** an arched structure of masonry usually forming a ceiling or roof (p. 291)
- ☐ **On/upon:** touching and being supported by the top surface of (something) (p. 290)
- ☐ **Face:** any of the plane surfaces that bound a geometric solid / an inscribed, printed, or marked side (p. 289)

God's palace

The heavens above can not be measured

God's
vault founded
upon the earth

heaven's foundation
is on the earth

©2017 Chad Taylor

Earth's foundations cannot be explored

Ephesians 1:19-23

¹⁹ And what is the exceeding greatness of his power to us-ward who believe, according to the working of his mighty power, ²⁰ **Which he wrought in Christ, when he <u>raised</u> him from the dead, and set him <u>at</u> his own right hand <u>in</u> the heavenly places,** ²¹ **<u>Far</u> <u>above</u> <u>all</u> principality, and power, and might, and dominion, and every name that is named, not only in this world, but also in that which is to come:** ²² And hath put all things under his feet, and gave him to be the head over all things to the church, ²³ Which is his body, the fulness of him that filleth all in all. Ephesians 1:19-23 (KJV)

¹⁹ and his incomparably great power for us who believe. That power is the same as the mighty strength ²⁰ he exerted when he raised Christ from the dead and seated him at his right hand in the heavenly realms, ²¹ far above all rule and authority, power and dominion, and every name that is invoked, not only in the present age but also in the one to come. ²² And God placed all things under his feet and appointed him to be head over everything for the church, ²³ which is his body, the fullness of him who fills everything in every way. Ephesians 1:19-23 (NIV)

¹⁹ and what is the immeasurable greatness of his power toward us who believe, according to the working of his great might ²⁰ that he worked in Christ **when he <u>raised</u> him from the dead and seated him <u>at</u> his right hand <u>in</u> the heavenly places,** ²¹ **<u>far</u> <u>above</u> <u>all</u> rule and authority and power and dominion, and <u>above</u> every name that is named, not only in this age but also in the one to come.** ²² And he put all things under his feet and gave him as head over all things to the church, ²³ which is his body, the fullness of him who fills all in all. Ephesians 1:19-23 (ESV)

¹⁹ and what is the immeasurable greatness of his power for us who believe, according to the working of his great power. ²⁰ God put this power to work in Christ **when he <u>raised</u> him from the dead and seated him <u>at</u> his right hand <u>in</u> the heavenly places,** ²¹ **<u>far</u> <u>above</u> <u>all</u> rule and authority and power and dominion, and <u>above</u> every name that is named, not only in this age but also in the age to come.** ²² And he has put all things under his feet and has made him the head over all things for the church, ²³ which is his body, the fullness of him who fills all in all. Ephesians 1:19-23 (NRSV)

- **Raised:** to lift up (p. 290)
- **At:** used to indicate the place where someone or something is (p. 288)
- **In:** within a particular place (p. 290)
- **Far:** to a great extent (p. 289)
- **Above:** in or to a higher place (p. 288)
- **All:** the whole, entire, total amount, quantity, or extent of (p. 288)

At his right hand in the heavenly places

Far above all...

©2017 Chad Taylor

Ephesians 6:12

[12] For we wrestle not against flesh and blood, but against <u>principalities</u>, against <u>powers</u>, against the <u>rulers</u> of the darkness of this world, against spiritual wickedness <u>in</u> <u>high</u> places. Ephesians 6:12 (KJV)

[12] For our struggle is not against flesh and blood, but against the rulers, against the authorities, against the powers of this dark world and against the spiritual forces of evil in the heavenly realms.   Ephesians 6:12 (NIV)

[12] For we do not wrestle against flesh and blood, but against the <u>rulers</u>, against the <u>authorities</u>, against the <u>cosmic</u> <u>powers</u> over this present darkness, against the spiritual <u>forces</u> of evil in the <u>heavenly</u> places. Ephesians 6:12 (ESV)

[12] For our struggle is not against enemies of blood and flesh, but against the <u>rulers</u>, against the <u>authorities</u>, against the <u>cosmic</u> <u>powers</u> of this present darkness, against the spiritual <u>forces</u> of evil <u>in</u> the <u>heavenly</u> places. Ephesians 6:12 (NRSV)

- **Principalities:** the state, office, or authority of a prince (p. 290)

- **Rulers:** a person (such as a king or queen) who rules a country, area, group, etc. (p. 290)

- **Authorities:** persons in command; specifically : government (p. 288)

- **Powers:** a person or organization that has a lot of control and influence over other people or organizations (p. 290)

- **Forces:** a body of persons available for a particular end (p. 289)

- **In:** used to indicate location or position within something (p. 290)

- **High:** located far above the ground or another surface (p. 289)

- **Heavenly:** appearing or occurring in the sky (p. 289)

- **Cosmic:** of or relating to the cosmos, the extraterrestrial vastness, or the universe in contrast to the earth alone (p. 288)

- **Realms:** kingdom (p. 290)

Note: see also page 114 and Daniel 10:12-13 (not in this book)

Spiritual forces of evil in heavenly places

Cosmic powers of this present darkness

©2017 Chad Taylor

James 1:17

[17] <u>Every</u> good gift and <u>every</u> perfect gift is <u>from</u> <u>above</u>, and cometh <u>down</u> <u>from</u> the Father of lights, with whom is no variableness, neither shadow of turning. James 1:17 (KJV)

[17] Every good and perfect gift is from above, coming down from the Father of the heavenly lights, who does not change like shifting shadows. James 1:17 (NIV)

[17] <u>Every</u> good gift and <u>every</u> perfect gift is <u>from</u> <u>above</u>, coming <u>down</u> <u>from</u> the Father of lights, with whom there is no variation or shadow due to change. James 1:17 (ESV)

[17] <u>Every</u> generous act of giving, with <u>every</u> perfect gift, is <u>from</u> <u>above</u>, coming <u>down</u> <u>from</u> the Father of lights, with whom there is no variation or shadow due to change. James 1:17 (NRSV)

[17] Whatever is good and perfect is a gift coming <u>down</u> to us <u>from</u> God our Father, who created <u>all</u> the lights <u>in</u> the heavens. He never changes or casts a shifting shadow. James 1:17 (NLT)

- **Every:** including each of a group or series without leaving out any (p. 289)

- **From:** used to indicate the starting point of a physical movement or action (p. 289)

- **Above:** in or to a higher place (p. 288)

- **Down:** from a higher to a lower place or position (p. 289)

- **All:** the whole, entire, total amount, quantity, or extent of (p. 288)

- **In:** used to indicate location or position within something (p. 290)

Coming down to us from God our Father

From above

Every good and perfect gift

©2017 Chad Taylor

PART THREE

Clues about Earth
in Biblical Stories

*All things were made by him; and without him
was not any thing made that was made.*

- John 1:3 (KJV)

Genesis 7:11-12

[11] In the six hundredth year of Noah's life, in the second month, the seventeenth day of the month, the same day were **all the <u>fountains</u> of the great deep broken up, <u>and</u> the <u>windows</u> of heaven were <u>opened</u>.** [12] **And the rain was upon the earth** forty days and forty nights. Genesis 7:11-12 (KJV)

[11] In the six hundredth year of Noah's life, on the seventeenth day of the second month—on that day all the springs of the great deep burst forth, and the floodgates of the heavens were opened. [12] And rain fell on the earth forty days and forty nights. Genesis 7:11-12 (NIV)

[11] In the six hundredth year of Noah's life, in the second month, on the seventeenth day of the month, on that day **all the <u>fountains</u> of the great deep burst forth, <u>and</u> the <u>windows</u> of the heavens were <u>opened</u>.** [12] **And rain fell upon the earth** forty days and forty nights. Genesis 7:11-12 (ESV)

[11] In the six hundredth year of Noah's life, in the second month, on the seventeenth day of the month, on that day **all the <u>fountains</u> of the great deep burst forth, <u>and</u> the <u>windows</u> of the heavens were <u>opened</u>.** [12] **The rain fell on the earth** forty days and forty nights. Genesis 7:11-12 (NRSV)

- **All:** the whole, entire, total amount, quantity, or extent of (p. 288)

- **And:** plus (p. 288)

- **Fountains:** the source from which something proceeds or is supplied (p. 289)

- **Springs:** a source of supply (p. 291)

- **Windows:** an opening especially in the wall of a building for admission of light and air that is usually closed by casements or sashes containing transparent material (as glass) and capable of being opened and shut (p. 291)

- **Floodgates:** a gate for controlling the flow of water from a lake, river, reservoir, etc. (p. 289)

- **Opened:** to cause (something) to no longer be covered, sealed, or blocked (p. 290)

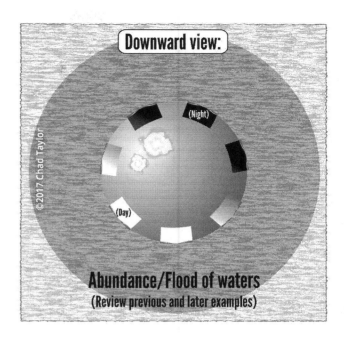

Downward view:

(Night)

(Day)

Abundance/Flood of waters
(Review previous and later examples)

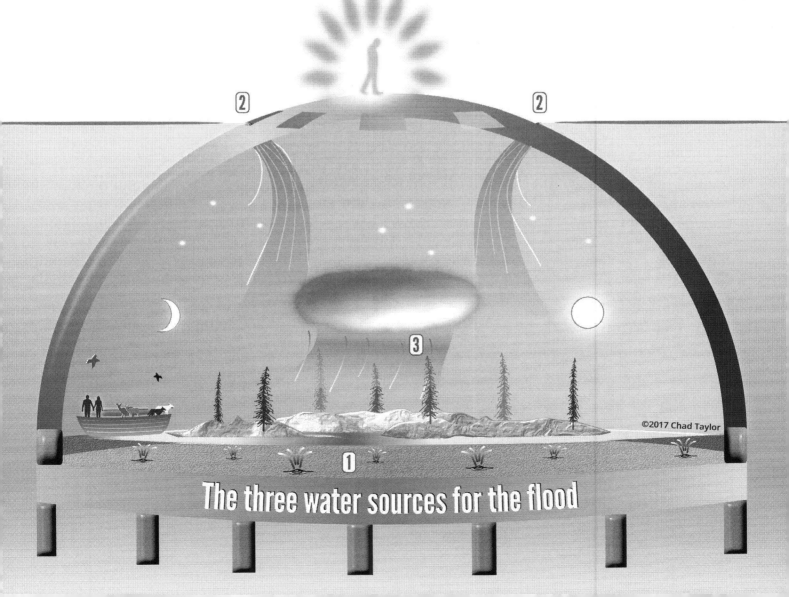

2 2

3

1

The three water sources for the flood

Genesis 7:17-20

[17] And the flood was forty days upon the earth; and the waters increased, and bare up the ark, and it was **lift up <u>above</u> the earth.** [18] **And the waters <u>prevailed</u>,** and were increased greatly upon the earth; and the ark went **upon the <u>face</u> of the waters.** [19] **And the waters <u>prevailed</u> exceedingly** upon the earth; and **<u>all</u> the high hills, that were <u>under</u> the <u>whole</u> heaven, were covered.** [20] **Fifteen cubits <u>upward</u>** did the waters <u>prevail</u>; and the mountains were covered. Genesis 7:17-20 (KJV)

[17] For forty days the flood kept coming on the earth, and as the waters increased they lifted the ark high above the earth. [18] The waters rose and increased greatly on the earth, and the ark floated on the surface of the water. [19] They rose greatly on the earth, and all the high mountains under the entire heavens were covered. [20] The waters rose and covered the mountains to a depth of more than fifteen cubits. Genesis 7:17-20 (NIV)

[17] The flood continued forty days on the earth. The waters increased and bore up the ark, and **it <u>rose</u> high <u>above</u> the earth.** [18] **The waters <u>prevailed</u> and increased greatly on the earth, and the ark floated on the <u>face</u> of the waters.** [19] And the waters prevailed so mightily on the earth that **<u>all</u> the high mountains <u>under</u> the <u>whole</u> heaven were covered.** [20] The waters prevailed above the mountains, covering them fifteen cubits deep. Genesis 7:17-20 (ESV)

[17] The flood continued forty days on the earth; and the waters increased, and bore up the ark, and **it <u>rose</u> high <u>above</u> the earth.** [18] The waters swelled and increased greatly **<u>on</u> the earth;** and the ark floated **on the <u>face</u> of the waters.** [19] The waters swelled so mightily on the earth that **<u>all</u> the high mountains <u>under</u> the <u>whole</u> heaven were covered;** [20] the waters swelled above the mountains, covering them fifteen cubits deep. Genesis 7:17-20 (NRSV)

- **Above:** in or to a higher place (p. 288)

- **Rose:** to move upward (p. 290)

- **Upward:** toward the ceiling, sky, etc. (p. 291)

- **On:** to a position that is supported by (p. 290)

- **Face:** any of the plane surfaces that bound a geometric solid / an inscribed, printed, or marked side (p. 289)

- **Prevail(ed):** to gain ascendancy through strength or superiority (p. 290)

- **Under:** in or into a position below or beneath something (p. 291)

- **Whole:** not lacking or leaving out any part (p. 291)

- **Entire:** having no element or part left out (p. 289)

- **All:** the whole, entire, total amount, quantity, or extent of (p. 288)

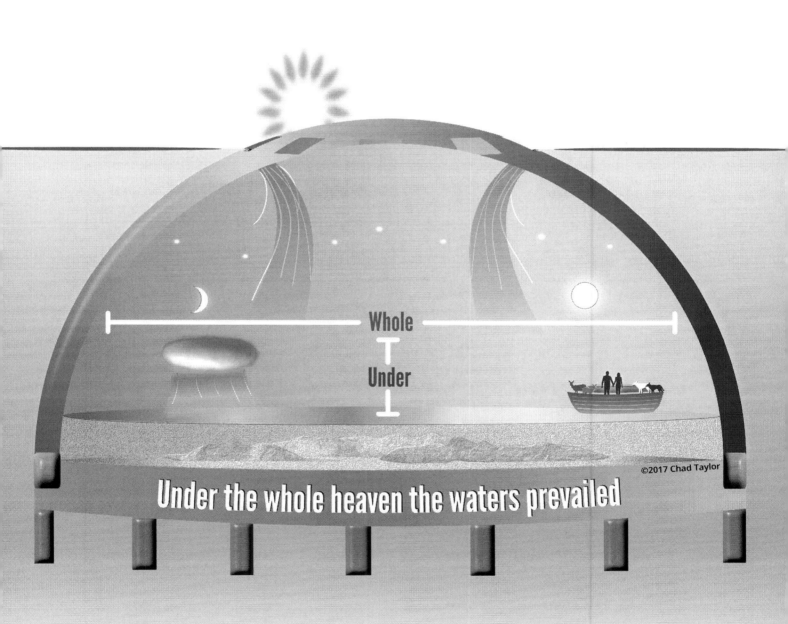

Whole

Under

©2017 Chad Taylor

Under the whole heaven the waters prevailed

Genesis 9:11-15

[11] And I will establish my covenant with you, **neither shall all flesh be cut off any more by the waters of a flood; neither shall there any more be a flood to destroy the earth.** [12] And God said, **This is the <u>token</u>** of the covenant which I make between me and you and every living creature that is with you, for perpetual generations: [13] **I do set my <u>bow</u> in the cloud, and it shall be for a <u>token</u>** of a covenant between me and the earth. [14] And it shall come to pass, when I bring a cloud over the earth, **that the <u>bow</u> shall be seen in the cloud:** [15] And I will remember my covenant, which is between me and you and every living creature of all flesh; and **the waters shall no more become a flood to destroy <u>all</u> flesh.**   Genesis 9:11-15 (KJV)

[11] I establish my covenant with you: Never again will all life be destroyed by the waters of a flood; never again will there be a flood to destroy the earth." [12] And God said, "This is the sign of the covenant I am making between me and you and every living creature with you, a covenant for all generations to come: [13] I have set my rainbow in the clouds, and it will be the sign of the covenant between me and the earth. [14] Whenever I bring clouds over the earth and the rainbow appears in the clouds, [15] I will remember my covenant between me and you and all living creatures of every kind. Never again will the waters become a flood to destroy all life. Genesis 9:11-15 (NIV)

[11] I establish my covenant with you, that **never again shall <u>all</u> flesh be cut off by the waters of the flood, and never again shall there be a flood to destroy the earth."** [12] And God said, "This is the <u>sign</u> of the covenant that I make between me and you and every living creature that is with you, **for <u>all</u> future generations:** [13] **I have set my <u>bow</u> in the cloud, and it shall be a <u>sign</u> of the covenant between me and the earth.** [14] When I bring clouds over the earth and **the <u>bow</u> is seen in the clouds,** [15] I will remember my covenant that is between me and you and every living creature of all flesh. And **the waters shall never again become a flood to destroy <u>all</u> flesh.** Genesis 9:11-15 (ESV)

[11] I establish my covenant with you, **that never again shall <u>all</u> flesh be cut off by the waters of a flood, and never again shall there be a flood to destroy the earth."** [12] God said, "This is the <u>sign</u> of the covenant that I make between me and you and every living creature that is with you, **for <u>all</u> future generations:** [13] I have set **my <u>bow</u> in the clouds, and it shall be a <u>sign</u>** of the covenant between me and the earth. [14] When I bring clouds over the earth and **the <u>bow</u> is seen in the clouds,** [15] I will remember my covenant that is between me and you and every living creature of all flesh; and **the waters shall never again become a flood to destroy <u>all</u> flesh.** Genesis 9:11-15 (NRSV)

⌐⌐   **All:** the whole, entire, total amount, quantity, or extent of (p. 288)

⌐⌐   **Token:** something that is a symbol of a feeling, event, etc. (p. 291)

⌐⌐   **Sign:** something material or external that stands for or signifies something spiritual (p. 291)

⌐⌐   **Bow:** something bent into a simple curve (p. 288)

⌐⌐   **Rainbow:** a curved line of different colors that sometimes appears in the sky when the sun shines through rain
(p. 290)

©2017 Chad Taylor

This is the sign

Ever wonder why a rainbow is shaped the way it is?

Genesis 11:4-9

⁴And they said, Go to, let us build us a city and a tower, **whose <u>top</u> may <u>reach</u> <u>unto</u> heaven;** and let us make us a name, lest we be **scattered <u>abroad</u>** upon the <u>face</u> of the <u>whole</u> **earth.** ⁵And the Lᴏʀᴅ came <u>down</u> to see the city and the tower, which the children of men builded. ⁶And the Lᴏʀᴅ said, Behold, the people is one, and they have all one language; and this they begin to do: and now nothing will be restrained from them, which they have imagined to do. ⁷Go to, **let <u>us</u> go <u>down</u>,** and there confound their language, that they may not understand one another's speech. ⁸So the Lᴏʀᴅ scattered them **<u>abroad</u> from thence upon the <u>face</u> of <u>all</u> the earth:** and they left off to build the city. Genesis 11:4-9 (KJV)

⁴Then they said, "Come, let us build ourselves a city, with a tower that reaches to the heavens, so that we may make a name for ourselves; otherwise we will be scattered over the face of the whole earth." ⁵But the Lᴏʀᴅ came down to see the city and the tower the people were building. ⁶The Lᴏʀᴅ said, "If as one people speaking the same language they have begun to do this, then nothing they plan to do will be impossible for them. ⁷Come, let us go down and confuse their language so they will not understand each other." ⁸So the Lᴏʀᴅ scattered them from there over all the earth, and they stopped building the city. ⁹That is why it was called Babel—because there the Lᴏʀᴅ confused the language of the whole world. From there the Lᴏʀᴅ scattered them over the face of the whole earth. Genesis 11:4-9 (NIV)

⁴Then they said, "Come, let us build ourselves a city **and a tower with its <u>top</u> in the heavens,** and let us make a name for ourselves, lest we be dispersed **over the <u>face</u> of the <u>whole</u> earth."** ⁵**And the Lord came <u>down</u>** to see the city and the tower, which the children of man had built. ⁶And the Lord said, "Behold, they are one people, and they have all one language, and this is only the beginning of what they will do. And nothing that they propose to do will now be impossible for them. ⁷**Come, let <u>us</u> go <u>down</u> and there** confuse their language, so that they may not understand one another's speech." ⁸So the Lord dispersed them from there **over the <u>face</u> of <u>all</u> the earth,** and they left off building the city. ⁹Therefore its name was called Babel, because there the Lord confused the language of all the earth. And from there **the Lord dispersed them over the <u>face</u> of <u>all</u> the earth.** Genesis 11:4-9 (ESV)

⁴Then they said, "Come, let us build ourselves a city, and **a tower with its <u>top</u> in the heavens,** and let us make a name for ourselves; otherwise we shall be **scattered <u>abroad</u>** upon the <u>face</u> of the <u>whole</u> earth." ⁵**The Lᴏʀᴅ came <u>down</u>** to see the city and the tower, which mortals had built. ⁶And the Lᴏʀᴅ said, "Look, they are one people, and they have all one language; and this is only the beginning of what they will do; nothing that they propose to do will now be impossible for them. ⁷Come, **let <u>us</u> go <u>down</u>,** and confuse their language there, so that they will not understand one another's speech." ⁸So the Lᴏʀᴅ scattered them **<u>abroad</u> from there over the <u>face</u> of <u>all</u> the earth,** and they left off building the city. ⁹Therefore it was called Babel, because there the Lᴏʀᴅ confused the language of all the earth; and from there the Lᴏʀᴅ **scattered them <u>abroad</u> over the <u>face</u> of <u>all</u> the earth.** Genesis 11:4-9 (NRSV)

Top: the highest point, level, or part of something (p. 291)

Reach: to extend to   (p. 290)

Unto: To   (p. 291)

Abroad: over a wide area   (p. 288)

Face: any of the plane surfaces that bound a geometric solid / an inscribed, printed, or marked side (p. 289)

Whole: not lacking or leaving out any part   (p. 291)

Us: I and at least one other   (p. 291)

Down: from a higher to a lower place or position   (p. 289)

All: the whole, entire, total amount, quantity, or extent of (p. 288)

Genesis 17:22

[22] And he left off talking with him, and **God <u>went</u> <u>up</u>** from Abraham. Genesis 17:22 (KJV)

[22] When he had finished speaking with Abraham, God went up from him. Genesis 17:22 (NIV)

[22] When he had finished talking with him, **God <u>went</u> <u>up</u>** from Abraham. Genesis 17:22 (ESV)

[22] And when he had finished talking with him, **God <u>went</u> <u>up</u>** from Abraham. Genesis 17:22 (NRSV)

Went: to move on a course (p. 291)

Up: from a lower to a higher place or position (p. 291)

Up

God went up from Abraham

©2017 Chad Taylor

Genesis 19:24-25

²⁴Then the Lord <u>rained</u> <u>upon</u> Sodom and <u>upon</u> Gomorrah brimstone and fire <u>from</u> the Lord <u>out</u> of heaven; ²⁵And he overthrew those cities, and all the plain, and all the inhabitants of the cities, and that which grew upon the ground. Genesis 19:24-25 (KJV)

²⁴Then the Lord rained down burning sulfur on Sodom and Gomorrah—from the Lord out of the heavens. ²⁵Thus he overthrew those cities and the entire plain, destroying all those living in the cities—and also the vegetation in the land. Genesis 19:24-25 (NIV)

²⁴Then the Lord <u>rained</u> <u>on</u> Sodom and Gomorrah sulfur and fire <u>from</u> the Lord <u>out</u> of heaven. ²⁵And he overthrew those cities, and all the valley, and all the inhabitants of the cities, and what grew on the ground. Genesis 19:24-25 (ESV)

²⁴Then the Lord <u>rained</u> <u>on</u> Sodom and Gomorrah sulfur and fire <u>from</u> the Lord <u>out</u> of heaven; ²⁵and he overthrew those cities, and all the Plain, and all the inhabitants of the cities, and what grew on the ground. Genesis 19:24-25 (NRSV)

- **Rained:** to cause (something) to fall in large amounts (p. 290)

- **Upon:** On (p. 291)

- **On:** used to indicate the location of something (p. 290)

- **From:** used to indicate the starting point of a physical movement or action (p. 289)

- **Out:** away from a particular place (p. 290)

- **Down:** from a higher to a lower place or position (p. 289)

Rained down from the Lord out of heaven

©2017 Chad Taylor

Genesis 28:12-13 & 17

[12] **And he dreamed, and behold a ladder set up on the earth, and the <u>top</u> of it reached to heaven:** and behold the angels of God <u>ascending</u> and <u>descending</u> on it. [13] And, behold, **the LORD <u>stood</u> <u>above</u> it,** and said, I am the LORD God of Abraham thy father, and the God of Isaac: the land whereon thou liest, to thee will I give it, and to thy seed; [14...] [15...] [16...] [17] And he was afraid, and said, How dreadful is this place! **this is none other but the house of God, and this is the <u>gate</u> of heaven.**   Genesis 28:12-13 & 17 (KJV)

[12] He had a dream in which he saw a stairway resting on the earth, with its top reaching to heaven, and the angels of God were ascending and descending on it. [13] There above it stood the LORD, and he said: "I am the LORD, the God of your father Abraham and the God of Isaac. I will give you and your descendants the land on which you are lying. [14...] [15...] [16...] [17] He was afraid and said, "How awesome is this place! This is none other than the house of God; this is the gate of heaven."   Genesis 28:12-13 & 17 (NIV)

[12] **And he dreamed, and behold, there was a ladder set up on the earth, and the <u>top</u> of it reached to heaven.** And behold, the angels of God were <u>ascending</u> and <u>descending</u> on it! [13] And behold, **the Lord <u>stood</u> <u>above</u> it** and said, "I am the Lord, the God of Abraham your father and the God of Isaac. The land on which you lie I will give to you and to your offspring. [14...] [15...] [16...] [17] And he was afraid and said, "How awesome is this place! **This is none other than the house of God, and this is the <u>gate</u> of heaven."**   Genesis 28:12-13 & 17 (ESV)

[12] **And he dreamed that there was a ladder set up on the earth, the <u>top</u> of it reaching to heaven;** and the angels of God were <u>ascending</u> and <u>descending</u> on it. [13] And the LORD stood beside him and said, "I am the LORD, the God of Abraham your father and the God of Isaac; the land on which you lie I will give to you and to your offspring; [14...] [15...] [16...] [17] And he was afraid, and said, "How awesome is this place! **This is none other than the house of God, and this is the <u>gate</u> of heaven."**   Genesis 28:12-13 & 17 (NRSV)

⌐⌐   **Top:** the highest point, level, or part of something (p. 291)

⌐⌐   **Ascending:** rising or increasing to higher levels, values, or degrees (p. 288)

⌐⌐   **Descending:** to go or move from a higher to a lower place or level (p. 289)

⌐⌐   **Stood:** to be in an upright position with all of your weight on your feet (p. 291)

⌐⌐   **Above:** in or to a higher place than / over (p. 288)

⌐⌐   **Gate:** a means of entrance or exit (p. 289)

A ladder whose top reached to the Lord and heaven above

©2017 Chad Taylor

Genesis 35:13

[13] And **God <u>went</u> <u>up</u>** from him in the place where he talked with him. Genesis 35:13 (KJV)

[13] Then God went up from him at the place where he had talked with him. Genesis 35:13 (NIV)

[13] Then **God <u>went</u> <u>up</u>** from him in the place where he had spoken with him. Genesis 35:13 (ESV)

[13] Then **God <u>went</u> <u>up</u>** from him at the place where he had spoken with him. Genesis 35:13 (NRSV)

Went: to move on a course (p. 291)

Up: from a lower to a higher place or position (p. 291)

©2017 Chad Taylor

Exodus 2:23-25

[23] And it came to pass in process of time, that the king of Egypt died: and the children of Israel sighed by reason of the bondage, and they cried, and **their cry <u>came</u> <u>up</u> <u>unto</u> God** by reason of the bondage. [24] And God heard their groaning, and God remembered his covenant with Abraham, with Isaac, and with Jacob. [25] And **God looked upon** the children of Israel, and God had respect unto them. Exodus 2:23-25 (KJV)

[23] During that long period, the king of Egypt died. The Israelites groaned in their slavery and cried out, and their cry for help because of their slavery went up to God. [24] God heard their groaning and he remembered his covenant with Abraham, with Isaac and with Jacob. [25] So God looked on the Israelites and was concerned about them. Exodus 2:23-25 (NIV)

[23] During those many days the king of Egypt died, and the people of Israel groaned because of their slavery and cried out for help. Their cry for rescue from slavery **<u>came</u> <u>up</u> <u>to</u> God.** [24] And God heard their groaning, and God remembered his covenant with Abraham, with Isaac, and with Jacob. [25] **God saw the people of Israel**—and God knew. Exodus 2:23-25 (ESV)

[23] After a long time the king of Egypt died. The Israelites groaned under their slavery, and cried out. Out of the slavery their cry for help **<u>rose</u> <u>up</u> <u>to</u> God.** [24] God heard their groaning, and God remembered his covenant with Abraham, Isaac, and Jacob. [25] **God looked upon the Israelites,** and God took notice of them. Exodus 2:23-25 (NRSV)

⌐ **Rose:** to move upward (p. 290)

⌐ **Came:** to move toward something (p. 288)

⌐ **Went:** to move on a course (p. 291)

⌐ **Up:** from a lower to a higher place or position (p. 291)

⌐ **Unto:** To (p. 291)

⌐ **To:** in the direction of (p. 291)

©2017 Chad Taylor

Exodus 19:20

^{20} And the Lord came <u>down</u> upon mount Sinai, on the <u>top</u> of the mount: and the Lord called Moses <u>up</u> to the <u>top</u> of the mount; and Moses went <u>up</u>. Exodus 19:20 (KJV)

^{20} The Lord descended to the top of Mount Sinai and called Moses to the top of the mountain. So Moses went up Exodus 19:20 (NIV)

^{20} The Lord came <u>down</u> on Mount Sinai, to the <u>top</u> of the mountain. And the Lord called Moses to the <u>top</u> of the mountain, and Moses went <u>up</u>. Exodus 19:20 (ESV)

^{20} When the Lord <u>descended</u> upon Mount Sinai, to the <u>top</u> of the mountain, the Lord summoned Moses to the <u>top</u> of the mountain, and Moses went <u>up</u>. Exodus 19:20 (NRSV)

⌐⌐ **Down:** from a higher to a lower place or position (p. 289)

⌐⌐ **Descended:** to go or move from a higher to a lower place or level (p. 289)

⌐⌐ **Top:** the highest point, level, or part of something (p. 291)

⌐⌐ **Up:** from a lower to a higher place or position (p. 291)

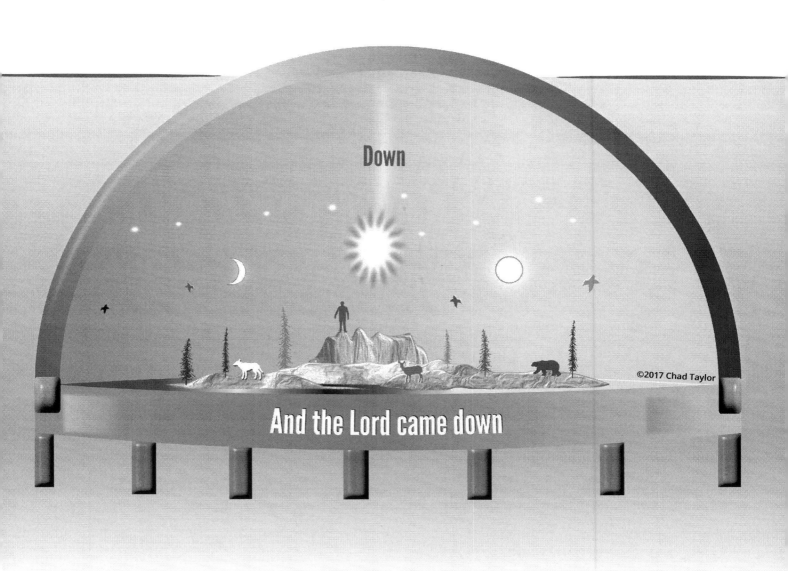

Down

And the Lord came down

©2017 Chad Taylor

Numbers 11:25

[25] **And the LORD <u>came</u> <u>down</u> <u>in</u> a cloud, and spake unto him,** and took of the spirit that was upon him, and gave it unto the seventy elders: and it came to pass, that, when the spirit rested upon them, they prophesied, and did not cease. Numbers 11:25 (KJV)

[25] Then the LORD came down in the cloud and spoke with him, and he took some of the power of the Spirit that was on him and put it on the seventy elders. When the Spirit rested on them, they prophesied—but did not do so again. Numbers 11:25 (NIV)

[25] **Then the Lord <u>came</u> <u>down</u> <u>in</u> the cloud and spoke to him,** and took some of the Spirit that was on him and put it on the seventy elders. And as soon as the Spirit rested on them, they prophesied. But they did not continue doing it. Numbers 11:25 (ESV)

[25] **Then the LORD <u>came</u> <u>down</u> <u>in</u> the cloud and spoke to him,** and took some of the spirit that was on him and put it on the seventy elders; and when the spirit rested upon them, they prophesied. But they did not do so again. Numbers 11:25 (NRSV)

Came: to move toward something (p. 288)

Down: from a higher to a lower place or position (p. 289)

In: used to indicate location or position within something (p. 290)

Down

The Lord came down in a cloud

©2017 Chad Taylor

Numbers 12:5-8

⁵ **And the LORD came down in the pillar of the cloud, and stood in the door of the tabernacle,** and called Aaron and Miriam: and they both came forth. ⁶ And he said, Hear now my words: If there be a prophet among you, I the LORD will make myself known unto him in a vision, and will speak unto him in a dream. ⁷ My servant Moses is not so, who is faithful in all mine house. ⁸ **With him will I speak mouth to mouth,** even apparently, and not in dark speeches; and the similitude of the LORD shall he behold: wherefore then were ye not afraid to speak against my servant Moses? Numbers 12:5-8 (KJV)

⁵ Then the LORD came down in a pillar of cloud; he stood at the entrance to the tent and summoned Aaron and Miriam. When the two of them stepped forward, ⁶ he said, "Listen to my words: "When there is a prophet among you, I, the LORD, reveal myself to them in visions, I speak to them in dreams. ⁷ But this is not true of my servant Moses; he is faithful in all my house. ⁸ With him I speak face to face, clearly and not in riddles; he sees the form of the LORD. Why then were you not afraid to speak against my servant Moses?" Numbers 12:5-8 (NIV)

⁵ **And the Lord came down in a pillar of cloud and stood at the entrance of the tent** and called Aaron and Miriam, and they both came forward. ⁶ And he said, "Hear my words: If there is a prophet among you, I the Lord make myself known to him in a vision; I speak with him in a dream. ⁷ Not so with my servant Moses. He is faithful in all my house. ⁸ **With him I speak mouth to mouth, clearly, and not in riddles, and he beholds the form of the Lord.** Why then were you not afraid to speak against my servant Moses?" Numbers 12:5-8 (ESV)

⁵ **Then the LORD came down in a pillar of cloud, and stood at the entrance of the tent,** and called Aaron and Miriam; and they both came forward. ⁶ And he said, "Hear my words: When there are prophets among you, I the LORD make myself known to them in visions; I speak to them in dreams. ⁷ Not so with my servant Moses; he is entrusted with all my house. ⁸ **With him I speak face to face— clearly, not in riddles; and he beholds the form of the LORD.** Why then were you not afraid to speak against my servant Moses?" Numbers 12:5-8 (NRSV)

⌐⌐   **Came:** to move toward something (p. 288)

⌐⌐   **Down:** from a higher to a lower place or position (p. 289)

⌐⌐   **In:** used to indicate location or position within something (p. 290)

Down

The Lord came down in a pillar of cloud

©2017 Chad Taylor

There is currently a debate about the shape of the tent/tabernacle in the wilderness. Some say it was a rectangular shape, others say it was a dome shape. Both are shown above.

Deuteronomy 4:19

¹⁹ **And lest thou lift up thine eyes unto heaven,** and when thou seest the sun, and the moon, and the stars, even all the **host of heaven,** shouldest be driven to worship them, and serve them, which the LORD thy God hath divided unto **all** nations **under** the **whole** heaven. Deuteronomy 4:19 (KJV)

¹⁹ And when you look up to the sky and see the sun, the moon and the stars—all the heavenly array—do not be enticed into bowing down to them and worshiping things the LORD your God has apportioned to all the nations under heaven. Deuteronomy 4:19 (NIV)

¹⁹ **And beware lest you raise your eyes to heaven,** and when you see the sun and the moon and the stars, **all the host of heaven,** you be drawn away and bow down to them and serve them, things that the Lord your God has **allotted to all** the peoples **under** the **whole** heaven. Deuteronomy 4:19 (ESV)

¹⁹ **And when you look up to the heavens** and see the sun, the moon, and the stars, **all the host of heaven,** do not be led astray and bow down to them and serve them, things that the LORD your God has allotted to **all the peoples everywhere under** heaven. Deuteronomy 4:19 (NRSV)

- **Up:** toward the sky or ceiling (p. 291)
- **Unto:** To (p. 291)
- **Raise:** to lift up (p. 290)
- **To:** in the direction of (p. 291)
- **Host:** Army / a great number / multitude (p. 289)
- **All:** the whole, entire, total amount, quantity, or extent of (p. 288)
- **Under:** in or into a position below or beneath something (p. 291)
- **Whole:** not lacking or leaving out any part (p. 291)

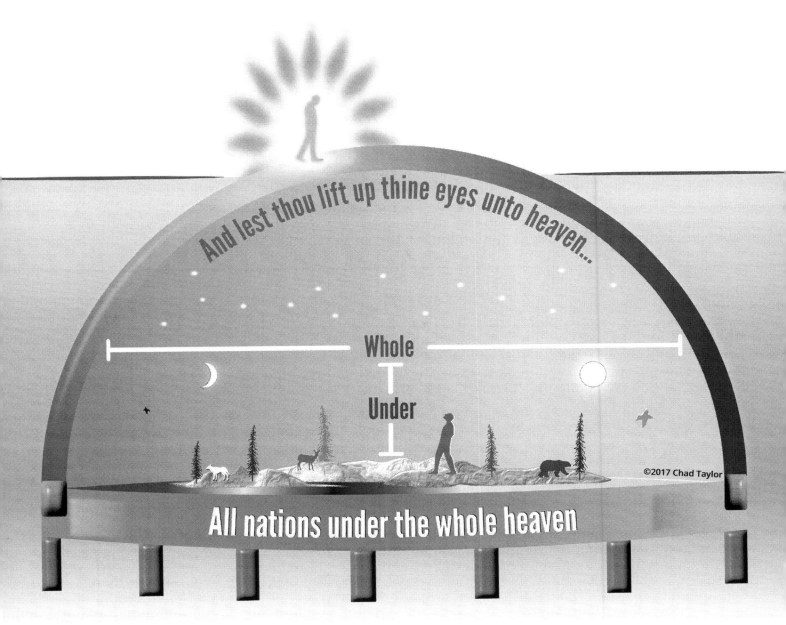

And lest thou lift up thine eyes unto heaven...

Whole

Under

©2017 Chad Taylor

All nations under the whole heaven

Joshua 10:11-13

¹¹ And it came to pass, as they fled from before Israel, and were in the going down to Bethhoron, that **the Lord cast <u>down</u> great stones <u>from</u> heaven upon them** unto Azekah, and they died: they were more which died with hailstones than they whom the children of Israel slew with the sword. ¹² Then spake Joshua to the Lord in the day when the Lord delivered up the Amorites before the children of Israel, and he said in the sight of Israel, **Sun, stand thou <u>still</u> <u>upon</u> Gibeon; and thou, Moon, <u>in</u> the valley of Ajalon.** ¹³ **And the sun stood <u>still</u>, and the moon <u>stayed</u>, until the people had avenged themselves upon their enemies. Is not this written in the book of Jasher? So the sun stood <u>still</u> <u>in</u> the <u>midst</u> of heaven, and hasted not to go down about a whole day.** Joshua 10:11-13 (KJV)

¹¹ As they fled before Israel on the road down from Beth Horon to Azekah, the Lord hurled large hailstones down on them, and more of them died from the hail than were killed by the swords of the Israelites. ¹² On the day the Lord gave the Amorites over to Israel, Joshua said to the Lord in the presence of Israel: "Sun, stand still over Gibeon, and you, moon, over the Valley of Aijalon." ¹³ So the sun stood still, and the moon stopped, till the nation avenged itself on its enemies, as it is written in the Book of Jashar. The sun stopped in the middle of the sky and delayed going down about a full day. Joshua 10:11-13 (NIV)

¹¹ And as they fled before Israel, while they were going down the ascent of Beth-horon, **the Lord threw <u>down</u> large stones <u>from</u> heaven on them** as far as Azekah, and they died. There were more who died because of the hailstones than the sons of Israel killed with the sword. ¹² At that time Joshua spoke to the Lord in the day when the Lord gave the Amorites over to the sons of Israel, and he said in the sight of Israel, **"Sun, stand <u>still</u> <u>at</u> Gibeon, and moon, <u>in</u> the Valley of Aijalon."** ¹³ **And the sun stood <u>still</u>, and the moon <u>stopped</u>, until the nation took vengeance on their enemies. Is this not written in the Book of Jashar? The sun <u>stopped</u> in the <u>midst</u> of heaven and did not hurry to set for about a whole day.** Joshua 10:11-13 (ESV)

¹¹ As they fled before Israel, while they were going down the slope of Beth-horon, **the Lord threw <u>down</u> huge stones <u>from</u> heaven on them** as far as Azekah, and they died; there were more who died because of the hailstones than the Israelites killed with the sword. ¹² On the day when the Lord gave the Amorites over to the Israelites, Joshua spoke to the Lord; and he said in the sight of Israel, **"Sun, stand <u>still</u> <u>at</u> Gibeon, and Moon, <u>in</u> the valley of Aijalon."** ¹³ **And the sun stood <u>still</u>, and the moon <u>stopped</u>, until the nation took vengeance on their enemies. Is this not written in the Book of Jashar? The sun <u>stopped</u> <u>in</u> midheaven, and did not hurry to set for about a whole day.** Joshua 10:11-13 (NRSV)

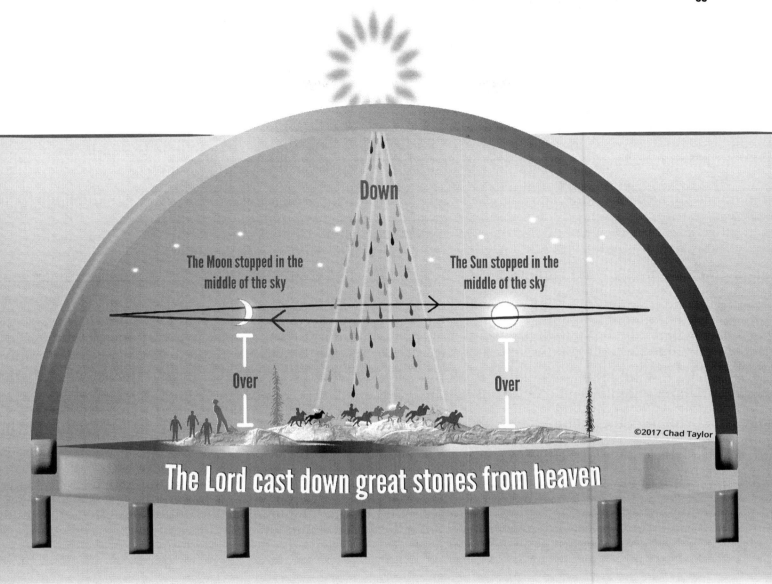

Down

The Moon stopped in the middle of the sky

The Sun stopped in the middle of the sky

Over

Over

©2017 Chad Taylor

The Lord cast down great stones from heaven

⌣ **Down:** from a higher to a lower place or position (p. 289)

⌣ **From:** used to indicate the starting point of a physical movement or action (p. 289)

⌣ **Still:** not moving (p. 291)

⌣ **At:** used to indicate the place where someone or something is (p. 288)

⌣ **Upon:** on (p. 291)

⌣ **Stayed:** the state of being stopped (p. 291)

⌣ **Stopped:** to cease moving especially temporarily or for a purpose (p. 291)

⌣ **Delayed:** a situation in which something happens later than it should (p. 289)

⌣ **Over:** Above (p. 290)

⌣ **In:** used to indicate location or position within something (p. 290)

⌣ **Midst:** the middle or central part (p. 290)

⌣ **Middle:** the part, point, or position that is equally distant from the ends or opposite sides (p. 290)

2 Samuel 22:8-16

[8] Then the earth shook and trembled; the <u>foundations</u> of heaven moved and shook, because he was **wroth.** [9] There went up a smoke out of his nostrils, and fire out of his mouth devoured: coals were kindled by it. [10] **He** <u>bowed</u> **the heavens also, and** <u>came</u> <u>down</u>**;** and darkness was under his feet. [11] And he rode upon a cherub, and did fly: and he was seen upon the wings of the wind. [12] And he made darkness pavilions round about him, dark waters, and thick clouds of the skies. [13] Through the brightness before him were coals of fire kindled. [14] **The** L ORD **thundered** <u>from</u> **heaven, and the** <u>most</u> <u>High</u> **uttered his voice.** [15] And he sent out arrows, and scattered them; lightning, and discomfited them. [16] **And the** <u>channels</u> **of the sea appeared, the** <u>foundations</u> **of the world were** <u>discovered</u>**,** at the rebuking of the L ORD, at the blast of the breath of his nostrils. 2 Samuel 22:8-16 (KJV)

[8] The earth trembled and quaked, the foundations of the heavens shook; they trembled because he was angry. [9] Smoke rose from his nostrils; consuming fire came from his mouth, burning coals blazed out of it. [10] He parted the heavens and came down; dark clouds were under his feet. [11] He mounted the cherubim and flew; he soared on the wings of the wind. [12] He made darkness his canopy around him—the dark rain clouds of the sky. [13] Out of the brightness of his presence bolts of lightning blazed forth. [14] The L ORD thundered from heaven; the voice of the Most High resounded. [15] He shot his arrows and scattered the enemy, with great bolts of lightning he routed them. [16] The valleys of the sea were exposed and the foundations of the earth laid bare at the rebuke of the L ORD, at the blast of breath from his nostrils. 2 Samuel 22:8-16 (NIV)

[8] "Then the earth reeled and rocked; the <u>foundations</u> of the heavens trembled and quaked, because he was angry. [9] Smoke went up from his nostrils, and devouring fire from his mouth; glowing coals flamed forth from him. [10] He <u>bowed</u> the heavens and <u>came</u> <u>down</u>; thick darkness was under his feet. [11] He rode on a cherub and flew; he was seen on the wings of the wind. [12] He made darkness around him his canopy, thick clouds, a gathering of water. [13] Out of the brightness before him coals of fire flamed forth. [14] **The Lord thundered** <u>from</u> **heaven, and the** <u>Most</u> <u>High</u> **uttered his voice.** [15] And he sent out arrows and scattered them; lightning, and routed them. [16] **Then the** <u>channels</u> **of the sea were seen; the** <u>foundations</u> **of the world were** <u>laid</u> <u>bare</u>**,** at the rebuke of the Lord, at the blast of the breath of his nostrils. 2 Samuel 22:8-16 (ESV)

[8] Then the earth reeled and rocked; the <u>foundations</u> of the heavens trembled and quaked, because he was angry. [9] Smoke went up from his nostrils, and devouring fire from his mouth; glowing coals flamed forth from him. [10] He <u>bowed</u> the heavens, and <u>came</u> <u>down</u>; thick darkness was under his feet. [11] He rode on a cherub, and flew; he was seen upon the wings of the wind. [12] He made darkness around him a canopy, thick clouds, a gathering of water. [13] Out of the brightness before him coals of fire flamed forth. [14] **The** L ORD **thundered** <u>from</u> **heaven; the** <u>Most</u> <u>High</u> **uttered his voice.** [15] He sent out arrows, and scattered them—lightning, and routed them. [16] **Then the** <u>channels</u> **of the sea were seen, the** <u>foundations</u> **of the world were** <u>laid</u> <u>bare</u> at the rebuke of the L ORD, at the blast of the breath of his nostrils. 2 Samuel 22:8-16 (NRSV)

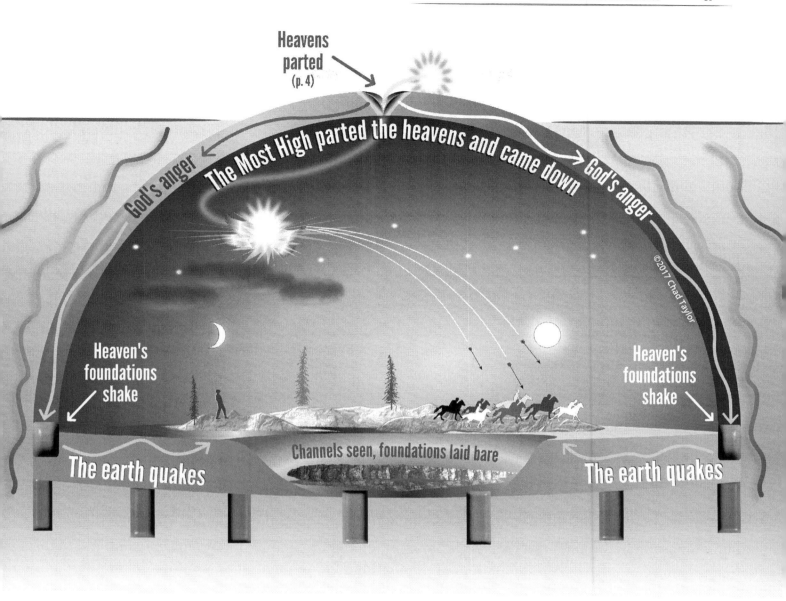

⊏⊐ **Bowed:** to stop resisting / yield (p. 288)

⊏⊐ **Parted:** divided into parts (p. 290)

⊏⊐ **Came:** to move toward something (p. 288)

⊏⊐ **Down:** from a higher to a lower place or position (p. 289)

⊏⊐ **From:** used to indicate the starting point of a physical movement or action (p. 289)

⊏⊐ **Most:** greatest in amount or degree (p. 290)

⊏⊐ **High:** located far above the ground or another surface (p. 289)

⊏⊐ **Foundations:** the natural or prepared ground or base on which some structure rests (p. 289)

⊏⊐ **Discovered:** to see, find, or become aware of (something) for the first time (p. 289)

⊏⊐ **Channels:** the bed where a natural stream of water runs (p. 288)

⊏⊐ **Laid:** to bring to a specified condition (p. 290)

⊏⊐ **Bare:** open to view / exposed (p. 288)

1 Kings 8:27

²⁷ But will God indeed dwell on the earth? **behold, the heaven and heaven of heavens cannot contain thee;** how much less this house that I have builded? 1 Kings 8:27 (KJV)

²⁷ "But will God really dwell on earth? The heavens, even the highest heaven, cannot contain you. How much less this temple I have built! 1 Kings 8:27 (NIV)

²⁷ "But will God indeed dwell on the earth? **Behold, heaven and the <u>highest</u> heaven cannot contain you;** how much less this house that I have built! 1 Kings 8:27 (ESV)

²⁷ "But will God indeed dwell on the earth? **Even heaven and the <u>highest</u> heaven cannot contain you,** much less this house that I have built! 1 Kings 8:27 (NRSV)

Highest: a high or the highest point, place, or level; peak   (p. 289)

Even the highest heaven cannot contain God

©2017 Chad Taylor

Job 9:6-8

⁶ Which shaketh the earth out of her place, and the <u>pillars</u> thereof tremble. ⁷ Which commandeth the sun, and it riseth not; and sealeth up the stars. ⁸ Which <u>alone</u> <u>spreadeth out</u> the heavens, and treadeth upon the waves of the sea. Job 9:6-8 (KJV)

⁶ He shakes the earth from its place and makes its pillars tremble. ⁷ He speaks to the sun and it does not shine; he seals off the light of the stars. ⁸ He alone stretches out the heavens and treads on the waves of the sea. Job 9:6-8 (NIV)

⁶ who shakes the earth out of its place, and its <u>pillars</u> tremble; ⁷ who commands the sun, and it does not rise; who seals up the stars; ⁸ who <u>alone</u> <u>stretched out</u> the heavens and trampled the waves of the sea; Job 9:6-8 (ESV)

⁶ who shakes the earth out of its place, and its <u>pillars</u> tremble; ⁷ who commands the sun, and it does not rise; who seals up the stars; ⁸ who <u>alone</u> <u>stretched out</u> the heavens and trampled the waves of the Sea; Job 9:6-8 (NRSV)

- **Pillars:** a firm upright support for a superstructure (p. 290)
- **Stretches(ed) out:** the act of stretching out / the state of being stretched out (p. 291)
- **Spread(eth) out:** to open, arrange, or place (something) over a large area (p. 291)
- **Alone:** without anyone or anything else (p. 288)

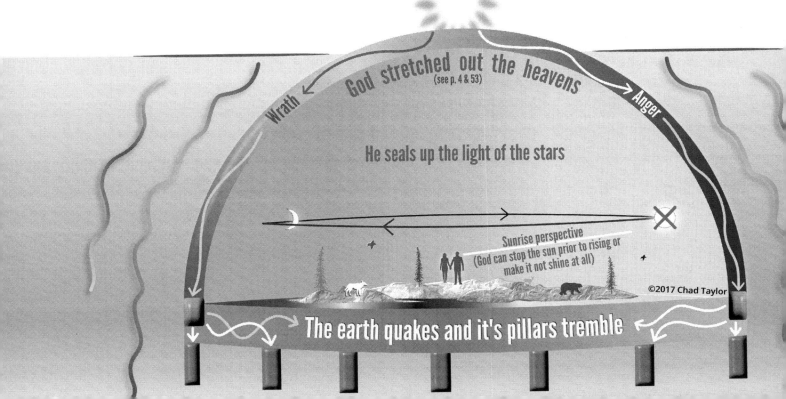

God stretched out the heavens (see p. 4 & 53)

Wrath   Anger

He seals up the light of the stars

Sunrise perspective
(God can stop the sun prior to rising or make it not shine at all)

©2017 Chad Taylor

The earth quakes and it's pillars tremble

Job 37:1-3

¹ At this also my heart trembleth, and is moved out of his place. ² Hear attentively the noise of his voice, and the sound that goeth out of his mouth. ³ He directeth it **under** the **whole** heaven, and his lightning unto the **ends** of the earth. Job 37:1-3 (KJV)

¹ "At this my heart pounds and leaps from its place. ² Listen! Listen to the roar of his voice, to the rumbling that comes from his mouth. ³ He unleashes his lightning beneath the whole heaven and sends it to the ends of the earth. Job 37:1-3 (NIV)

¹ "At this also my heart trembles and leaps out of its place. ² Keep listening to the thunder of his voice and the rumbling that comes from his mouth. ³ **Under** the **whole** heaven he lets it go, and his lightning to the **corners** of the earth. Job 37:1-3 (ESV)

¹ "At this also my heart trembles, and leaps out of its place. ² Listen, listen to the thunder of his voice and the rumbling that comes from his mouth. ³ **Under** the **whole** heaven he lets it loose, and his lightning to the **corners** of the earth. Job 37:1-3 (NRSV)

⌐⌐   **Under:** in or into a position below or beneath something   (p. 291)

⌐⌐   **Beneath:** in or to a lower position   (p. 288)

⌐⌐   **Whole:** not lacking or leaving out any part   (p. 291)

⌐⌐   **Ends:** the part at the edge or limit of an area   (p. 289)

⌐⌐   **Corners:** a private, secret, or remote place   (p. 288)

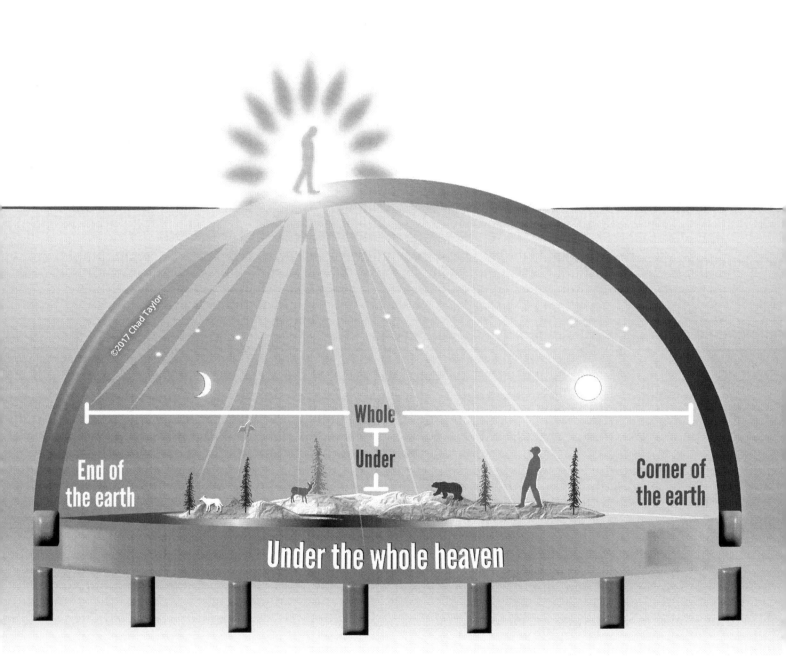

Job 38:12-14

[12] Hast thou commanded the morning since thy days; and caused the dayspring to know his place; [13] That it might take hold of **the ends of the earth,** that the wicked might be shaken out of it? [14] It is turned **as clay to the seal;** and they stand as a garment. Job 38:12-14 (KJV)

[12] "Have you ever given orders to the morning, or shown the dawn its place, [13] that it might take the earth by the edges and shake the wicked out of it? [14] The earth takes shape like clay under a seal; its features stand out like those of a garment. Job 38:12-14 (NIV)

[12] "Have you commanded the morning since your days began, and caused the dawn to know its place, [13] that it might take hold of **the skirts of the earth,** and the wicked be shaken out of it? [14] **It is changed like clay under the seal,** and its features stand out like a garment. Job 38:12-14 (ESV)

[12] "Have you commanded the morning since your days began, and caused the dawn to know its place, [13] so that it might take hold of **the skirts of the earth,** and the wicked be shaken out of it? [14] **It is changed like clay under the seal,** and it is dyed like a garment. Job 38:12-14 (NRSV)

- **Ends:** the part at the edge or limit of an area (p. 289)
- **Edges:** the line or part where an object or area begins or ends (p. 289)
- **Skirts:** the rim, periphery, or environs of an area (p. 291)
- **Under:** in or into a position below or beneath something (p. 291)
- **Seal:** a medallion or ring face bearing such a device incised so that it can be impressed on wax or moist clay (p. 291)

Edge of the earth

The earth takes shape like clay pressed beneath a seal

Skirt of the earth

Proverbs 25:2-3

[2] It is the glory of God to conceal a thing: but the honour of kings is to search out a matter. [3] **The heaven for <u>height</u>, <u>and</u> the earth for <u>depth</u>, <u>and</u> the heart of kings is <u>unsearchable</u>.** Proverbs 25:2-3 (KJV)

[2] It is the glory of God to conceal a matter; to search out a matter is the glory of kings. [3] As the heavens are high and the earth is deep, so the hearts of kings are unsearchable. Proverbs 25:2-3 (NIV)

[2] It is the glory of God to conceal things, but the glory of kings is to search things out. [3] **<u>As</u> the heavens for <u>height</u>, <u>and</u> the earth for <u>depth</u>, <u>so</u> the heart of kings is <u>unsearchable</u>.** Proverbs 25:2-3 (ESV)

[2] It is the glory of God to conceal things, but the glory of kings is to search things out. [3] **<u>Like</u> the heavens for <u>height</u>, <u>like</u> the earth for <u>depth</u>, <u>so</u> the mind of kings is <u>unsearchable</u>.** Proverbs 25:2-3 (NRSV)

[2] It is God's privilege to conceal things and the king's privilege to discover them. [3] **<u>No one</u> can <u>comprehend</u> the <u>height</u> of heaven, the <u>depth</u> of the earth, or all that goes on in the king's mind!** Proverbs 25:2-3 (NLT)

- **Like:** similar to (p. 290)
- **As:** in the way that (p. 288)
- **No one:** no person (p. 290)
- **Comprehend:** to understand fully (p. 288)
- **So:** to a degree that is suggested or stated (p. 291)
- **And:** plus (p. 288)
- **Height:** distance upward (p. 289)
- **High:** rising or extending upward a great distance (p. 289)
- **Deep:** extending far downward (p. 289)
- **Depth:** the perpendicular measurement downward from a surface (p. 289)
- **Unsearchable:** not capable of being searched or explored (p. 291)

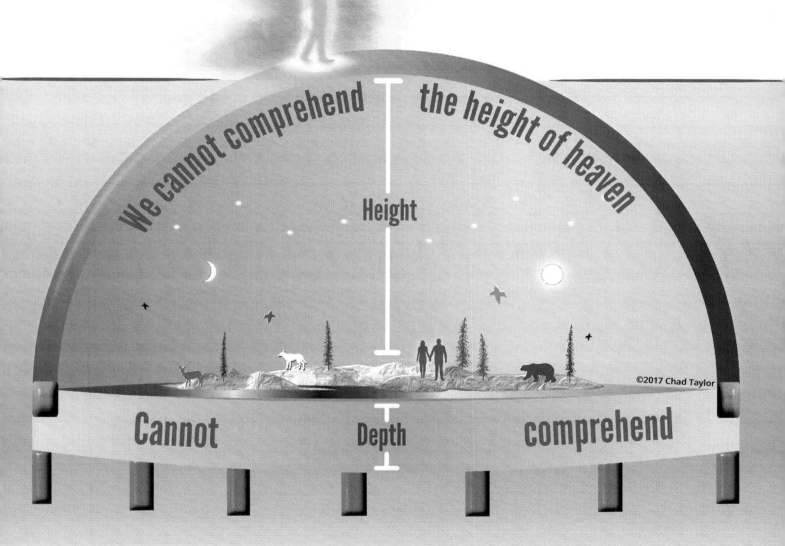

©2017 Chad Taylor

Ecclesiastes 1:9

[9] The thing that hath been, it is that which shall be; and that which is done is that which shall be done: and there is **no new thing <u>under</u>** the sun. Ecclesiastes 1:9 (KJV)

[9] What has been will be again, what has been done will be done again; there is nothing new under the sun. Ecclesiastes 1:9 (NIV)

[9] What has been is what will be, and what has been done is what will be done, and there is **nothing new <u>under</u>** the sun. Ecclesiastes 1:9 (ESV)

[9] What has been is what will be, and what has been done is what will be done; **there is nothing new <u>under</u> the sun.** Ecclesiastes 1:9 (NRSV)

[9] History merely repeats itself. It has all been done before. **Nothing <u>under</u> the sun is truly new.** Ecclesiastes 1:9 (NLT)

Under: in or into a position below or beneath something   (p. 291)

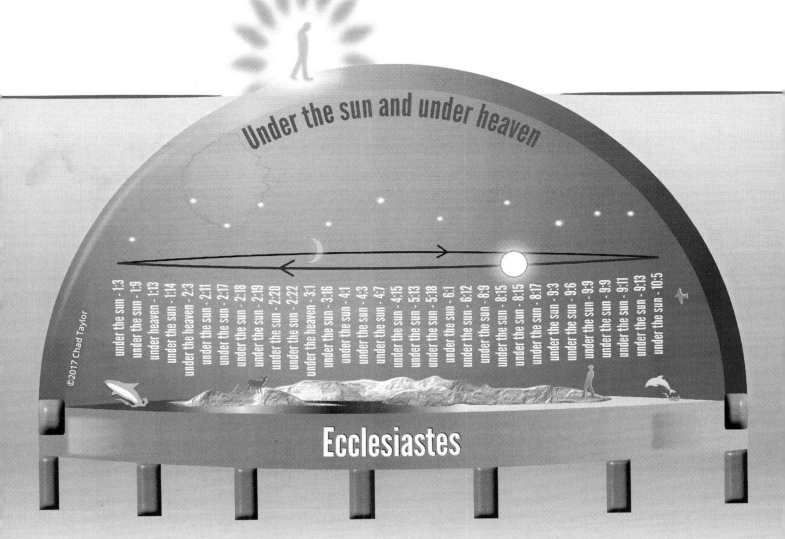

©2017 Chad Taylor

Under the sun and under heaven

under the sun - 1:3
under the sun - 1:9
under heaven - 1:13
under the sun - 1:14
under the heaven - 2:3
under the sun - 2:11
under the sun - 2:17
under the sun - 2:18
under the sun - 2:19
under the sun - 2:20
under the sun - 2:22
under the heaven - 3:1
under the sun - 3:16
under the sun - 4:1
under the sun - 4:3
under the sun - 4:7
under the sun - 4:15
under the sun - 5:13
under the sun - 5:18
under the sun - 6:1
under the sun - 6:12
under the sun - 8:9
under the sun - 8:15
under the sun - 8:15
under the sun - 8:17
under the sun - 9:3
under the sun - 9:6
under the sun - 9:9
under the sun - 9:9
under the sun - 9:11
under the sun - 9:13
under the sun - 10:5

Ecclesiastes

In the King James Version of Ecclesiastes, "under the sun" is used 29 times, "under the heaven" is used twice and "under heaven" is used once.

Isaiah 11:12

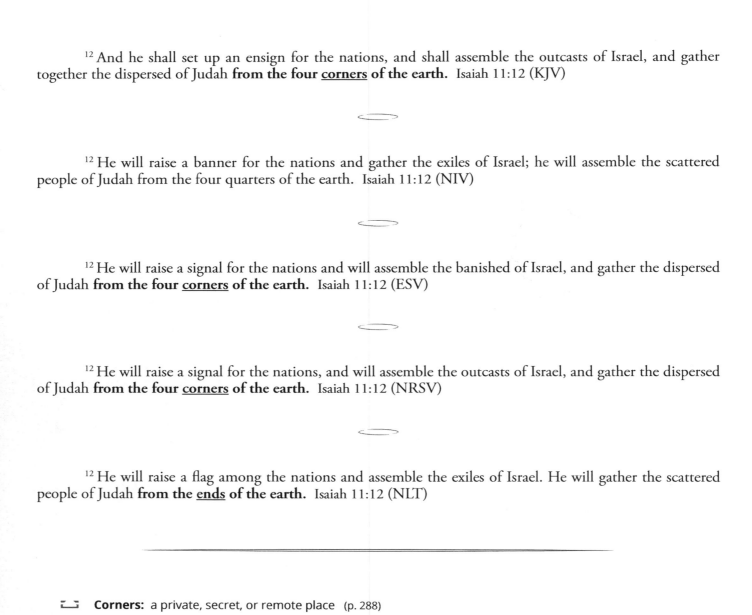

^{12} And he shall set up an ensign for the nations, and shall assemble the outcasts of Israel, and gather together the dispersed of Judah **from the four <u>corners</u> of the earth.** Isaiah 11:12 (KJV)

^{12} He will raise a banner for the nations and gather the exiles of Israel; he will assemble the scattered people of Judah from the four quarters of the earth. Isaiah 11:12 (NIV)

^{12} He will raise a signal for the nations and will assemble the banished of Israel, and gather the dispersed of Judah **from the four <u>corners</u> of the earth.** Isaiah 11:12 (ESV)

^{12} He will raise a signal for the nations, and will assemble the outcasts of Israel, and gather the dispersed of Judah **from the four <u>corners</u> of the earth.** Isaiah 11:12 (NRSV)

^{12} He will raise a flag among the nations and assemble the exiles of Israel. He will gather the scattered people of Judah **from the <u>ends</u> of the earth.** Isaiah 11:12 (NLT)

Corners: a private, secret, or remote place (p. 288)

Quarters: any of various units of length or area equal to one fourth of some larger unit (p. 290)

Ends: the part at the edge or limit of an area (p. 289)

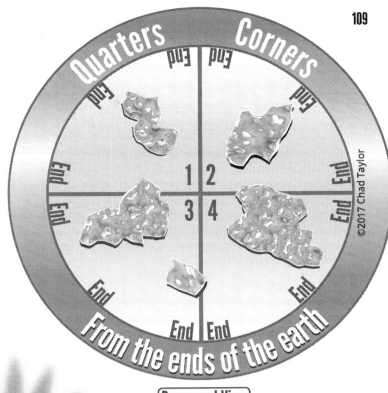

Quarters

Corners

End End

End

End

End

End

1 2

3 4

End

End

End End

End

End

End End

From the ends of the earth

©2017 Chad Taylor

Downward View

©2017 Chad Taylor

End of
the earth

Corner of
the earth

1 2

3 4

From the four quarters of the earth

Isaiah 13:9-13

⁹ Behold, the day of the LORD cometh, cruel both with wrath and fierce anger, to lay the land desolate: and he shall destroy the sinners thereof out of it. ¹⁰ **For the stars of heaven and the constellations thereof shall not <u>give</u> their light: the sun shall be darkened in <u>his</u> going forth, and the moon shall not cause <u>her</u> light to shine.** ¹¹ And I will punish the world for their evil, and the wicked for their iniquity; and I will cause the arrogancy of the proud to cease, and will lay low the haughtiness of the terrible. ¹² I will make a man more precious than fine gold; even a man than the golden wedge of Ophir. ¹³ **Therefore I will <u>shake</u> the heavens, and the earth shall remove out of <u>her</u> <u>place</u>, in the wrath of the LORD of <u>hosts</u>, and in the day of his fierce anger.** Isaiah 13:9-13 (KJV)

⁹ See, the day of the LORD is coming—a cruel day, with wrath and fierce anger—to make the land desolate and destroy the sinners within it. ¹⁰ The stars of heaven and their constellations will not show their light. The rising sun will be darkened and the moon will not give its light. ¹¹ I will punish the world for its evil, the wicked for their sins. I will put an end to the arrogance of the haughty and will humble the pride of the ruthless. ¹² I will make people scarcer than pure gold, more rare than the gold of Ophir. ¹³ Therefore I will make the heavens tremble; and the earth will shake from its place at the wrath of the LORD Almighty, in the day of his burning anger. Isaiah 13:9-13 (NIV)

⁹ Behold, the day of the Lord comes, cruel, with wrath and fierce anger, to make the land a desolation and to destroy its sinners from it. ¹⁰ **For the stars of the heavens and their constellations will not <u>give</u> their light; the sun will be dark at its rising, and the moon will not <u>shed</u> <u>its</u> light.** ¹¹ I will punish the world for its evil, and the wicked for their iniquity; I will put an end to the pomp of the arrogant, and lay low the pompous pride of the ruthless. ¹² I will make people more rare than fine gold, and mankind than the gold of Ophir. ¹³ **Therefore I will make the heavens <u>tremble</u>, and the earth will be <u>shaken</u> out of <u>its</u> place, at the wrath of the Lord of <u>hosts</u> in the day of his fierce anger.** Isaiah 13:9-13 (ESV)

⁹ See, the day of the LORD comes, cruel, with wrath and fierce anger, to make the earth a desolation, and to destroy its sinners from it. ¹⁰ **For the stars of the heavens and their constellations will not <u>give</u> their light; the sun will be dark at its rising, and the moon will not <u>shed</u> <u>its</u> light.** ¹¹ I will punish the world for its evil, and the wicked for their iniquity; I will put an end to the pride of the arrogant, and lay low the insolence of tyrants. ¹² I will make mortals more rare than fine gold, and humans than the gold of Ophir. ¹³ **Therefore I will make the heavens <u>tremble</u>, and the earth will be <u>shaken</u> out of <u>its</u> <u>place</u>, at the wrath of the LORD of <u>hosts</u> in the day of his fierce anger.** Isaiah 13:9-13 (NRSV)

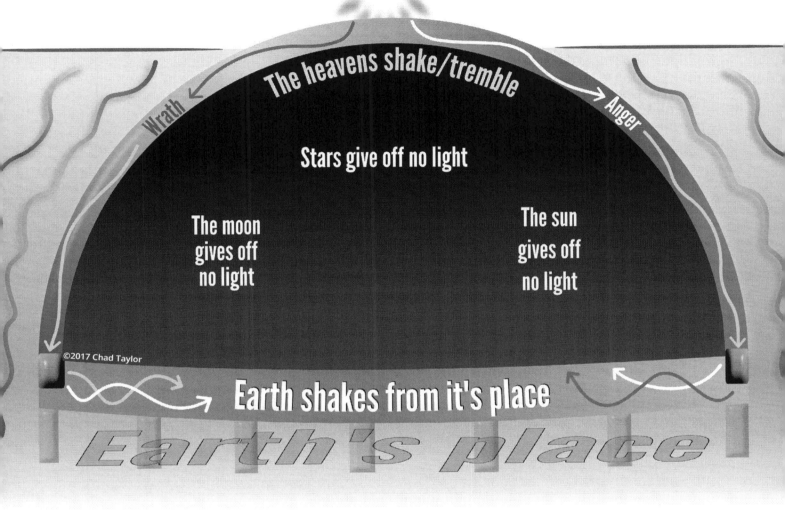

The heavens shake/tremble

Wrath

Anger

Stars give off no light

The moon gives off no light

The sun gives off no light

©2017 Chad Taylor

Earth shakes from it's place

Earth's place

- **Give:** to make a present of / to yield as a product, consequence, or effect (p. 289)

- **Shed:** to give off or out (p. 291)

- **Dark:** having very little or no light (p. 289)

- **Darkened:** to make dark (p. 289)

- **His:** that which belongs to him (p. 289)

- **Her:** of or relating to her or herself especially as possessor, agent, or object of an action (p. 289)

- **Shake(n):** to move sometimes violently back and forth or up and down with short, quick movements (p. 291)

- **Tremble:** the act or a period of shaking (p. 291)

- **Its:** relating to or belonging to it or itself (p. 290)

- **Place: Out of Place:** not in the proper or usual location (p. 290)

- **Hosts:** Army / a great number / multitude (p. 289)

Isaiah 14:12-15

¹² How art thou **fallen** **from** heaven, O **Lucifer**, son of the morning! how art thou **cut** **down** **to** the **ground**, which didst weaken the nations! ¹³ For thou hast said in thine heart, **I will** **ascend** **into** heaven, I will exalt my throne **above** the stars of God: I will sit also **upon** the **mount** of the **congregation**, in the sides of the **north**: ¹⁴ I will **ascend** **above** the **heights** of the clouds; I will be like the **most** **High**. ¹⁵ Yet thou shalt be brought **down** **to** hell, to the sides of the pit. Isaiah 14:12-15 (KJV)

¹² How you have fallen from heaven, morning star, son of the dawn! You have been cast down to the earth, you who once laid low the nations! ¹³ You said in your heart, "I will ascend to the heavens; I will raise my throne above the stars of God; I will sit enthroned on the mount of assembly, on the utmost heights of Mount Zaphon. ¹⁴ I will ascend above the tops of the clouds; I will make myself like the Most High." ¹⁵ But you are brought down to the realm of the dead, to the depths of the pit. Isaiah 14:12-15 (NIV)

¹² "How you are **fallen** **from** heaven, O Day Star, son of Dawn! How you are **cut** **down** **to** the ground, you who laid the nations low! ¹³ You said in your heart, 'I will **ascend** **to** heaven; **above** the stars of God I will **set** my throne on **high**; I will sit on the **mount** of **assembly** in the **far** reaches of the north; ¹⁴ I will **ascend** **above** the **heights** of the clouds; I will make myself like the **Most** **High**.' ¹⁵ But you are brought **down** **to** Sheol, to the **far** reaches of the pit. Isaiah 14:12-15 (ESV)

¹² How you are **fallen** **from** heaven, O Day Star, son of Dawn! How you are **cut** **down** **to** the ground, you who laid the nations low! ¹³ You said in your heart, "I will **ascend** **to** heaven; I will **raise** my throne **above** the stars of God; I will sit **on** the **mount** of **assembly** **on** the **heights** of Zaphon; ¹⁴ I will **ascend** to the **tops** of the clouds, I will make myself like the **Most** **High**." ¹⁵ But you are brought **down** **to** Sheol, **to** the **depths** of the **Pit**. Isaiah 14:12-15 (NRSV)

¹² "How you are **fallen** **from** heaven, O shining star, son of the morning! You have been **thrown** **down** **to** the earth, you who destroyed the nations of the world. ¹³ For you said to yourself, 'I will **ascend** **to** heaven and **set** my throne **above** God's stars. I will preside **on** the mountain of the gods **far** away in the north. ¹⁴ I will climb to the **highest** heavens and be like the **Most** **High**.' ¹⁵ Instead, you will be brought **down** **to** the place of the dead, **down** **to** its lowest **depths**. Isaiah 14:12-15 (NLT)

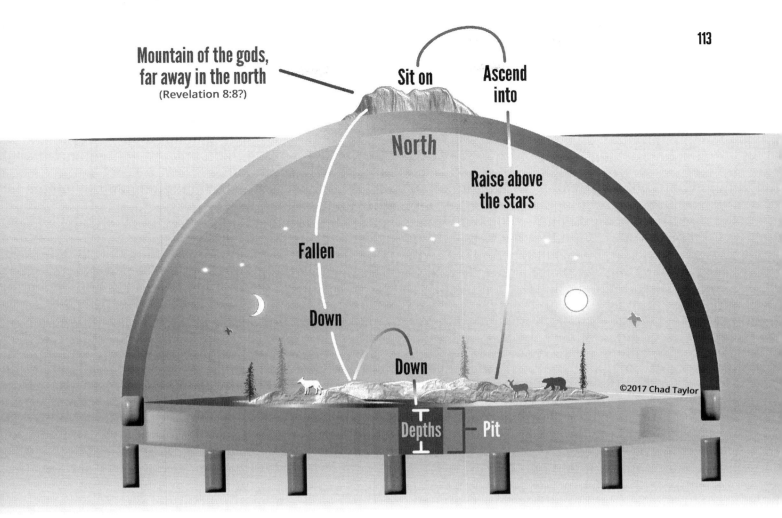

Mountain of the gods, far away in the north (Revelation 8:8?)

Sit on

Ascend into

North

Raise above the stars

Fallen

Down

Down

Depths — Pit

©2017 Chad Taylor

- **Fallen:** to come or go down quickly from a high place or position (p. 289)
- **From:** used to indicate the starting point of a physical movement or action (p. 289)
- **Down:** from a higher to a lower place or position (p. 289)
- **To:** in the direction of (p. 291)
- **Ascend:** to move upward (p. 288)
- **Into:** used as a function word to indicate entry, introduction, insertion, superposition, or inclusion (p. 290)
- **Raise:** to lift up (p. 290)
- **Above:** in or to a higher place (p. 288)
- **Tops:** the highest point, level, or part of something (p. 291)
- **On/upon:** to a position that is supported by (p. 290)
- **Utmost:** the highest point or degree that can be reached (p. 291)
- **Far:** to a great extent (p. 289)
- **Mount:** a high hill / mountain (p. 290)
- **Congregation:** an assembly of persons / gathering; *especially* : an assembly of persons met for worship and religious instruction (p. 288)
- **Assembly:** a company of persons collected together in one place usually for some common purpose (p. 288)
- **Heights:** distance upward (p. 289)
- **Highest:** a high or the highest point, place, or level; peak: (p. 289)
- **Most:** greatest in amount or degree (p. 290)
- **Set:** to place with care or deliberate purpose and with relative stability (p. 291)
- **High:** located far above the ground or another surface (p. 289)
- **Depths:** the perpendicular measurement downward from a surface (p. 289)

Isaiah 24:18-21

¹⁸ And it shall come to pass, that he who fleeth from the noise of the fear shall fall into the pit; and he that cometh up out of the midst of the pit shall be taken in the snare: for **the** <u>windows</u> **from on** <u>high</u> **are** <u>open</u>, **and the** <u>foundations</u> **of the earth do** <u>shake</u>. ¹⁹ The earth is utterly broken down, the earth is clean <u>dissolved</u>, the earth is moved exceedingly. ²⁰ The earth shall <u>reel</u> to and fro like a drunkard, and shall be removed like a <u>cottage</u>; and the transgression thereof shall be heavy upon it; and it shall fall, and not rise again. ²¹ And it shall come to pass in that day, that the LORD shall <u>punish</u> the <u>host</u> of the <u>high</u> ones that are on <u>high</u>, <u>and</u> the kings of the earth upon the earth. Isaiah 24:18-21 (KJV)

¹⁸ Whoever flees at the sound of terror will fall into a pit; whoever climbs out of the pit will be caught in a snare. The floodgates of the heavens are opened, the foundations of the earth shake. ¹⁹ The earth is broken up, the earth is split asunder, the earth is violently shaken. ²⁰ The earth reels like a drunkard, it sways like a hut in the wind; so heavy upon it is the guilt of its rebellion that it falls—never to rise again. ²¹ In that day the LORD will punish the powers in the heavens above and the kings on the earth below. Isaiah 24:18-21 (NIV)

¹⁸ He who flees at the sound of the terror shall fall into the pit, and he who climbs out of the pit shall be caught in the snare. For **the** <u>windows</u> **of heaven are** <u>opened</u>, **and the** <u>foundations</u> **of the earth** <u>tremble</u>. ¹⁹ The earth is utterly broken, the earth is split apart, the earth is violently <u>shaken</u>. ²⁰ The earth staggers like a drunken man; it <u>sways</u> like a <u>hut</u>; its transgression lies heavy upon it, and it falls, and will not rise again. ²¹ **On that day the Lord will** <u>punish</u> **the** <u>host</u> **of heaven,** <u>in</u> **heaven,** <u>and</u> **the kings of the earth, on the earth.** Isaiah 24:18-21 (ESV)

¹⁸ Whoever flees at the sound of the terror shall fall into the pit; and whoever climbs out of the pit shall be caught in the snare. For **the** <u>windows</u> **of heaven are** <u>opened</u>, **and the** <u>foundations</u> **of the earth** <u>tremble</u>. ¹⁹ The earth is utterly broken, the earth is torn asunder, the earth is violently <u>shaken</u>. ²⁰ The earth staggers like a drunkard, it <u>sways</u> like a <u>hut</u>; its transgression lies heavy upon it, and it falls, and will not rise again. ²¹ **On that day the LORD will** <u>punish</u> **the** <u>host</u> **of heaven** <u>in</u> **heaven,** <u>and</u> **on earth the kings of the earth.** Isaiah 24:18-21 (NRSV)

¹⁸ Those who flee in terror will fall into a trap, and those who escape the trap will be caught in a snare. **Destruction falls like rain from the heavens; the** <u>foundations</u> **of the earth** <u>shake</u>. ¹⁹ The earth has broken up. It **has utterly collapsed; it is violently** <u>shaken</u>. ²⁰ The earth staggers like a drunk. It <u>trembles</u> **like a** <u>tent</u> **in a storm. It falls and will not rise again, for the guilt of its rebellion is very heavy.** ²¹ **In that day the LORD will** <u>punish</u> **the gods** <u>in</u> **the heavens** <u>and</u> **the proud rulers of the nations on earth.** Isaiah 24:18-21 (NLT)

- **Windows:** anything likened to a window in appearance or function... (p. 291)
- **Floodgates:** a gate for controlling the flow of water from a lake, river, reservoir, etc. (p. 289)
- **High:** located far above the ground or another surface (p. 289)
- **Open(ed):** to move (as a door) from a closed position (p. 290)
- **Foundations:** the natural or prepared ground or base on which some structure rests (p. 289)
- **Shake(n):** to move sometimes violently back and forth or up and down with short, quick movements (p. 291)
- **Tremble(s):** the act or a period of shaking (p. 291)
- **Reel(s):** to behave in a violent disorderly manner (p. 290)
- **Sways:** to swing slowly back and forth or from side to side (p. 291)
- **Dissolved:** break up, disperse (p. 289)
- **Punish:** to impose a penalty on for a fault, offense, or violation (p. 290)
- **Host:** Army / a great number / multitude (p. 289)
- **Powers:** a person or organization that has a lot of control and influence over other people or organizations (p. 290)
- **In:** used to indicate location or position within something (p. 290)
- **Above:** in the sky / overhead (p. 288)
- **And:** plus (p. 288)
- **Below:** in or to a lower place (p. 288)
- **Cottage:** a small house, usually of only one story (p. 288)
- **Hut:** a small and simple house or building (p. 289)
- **Tent:** something that resembles a tent or that serves as a shelter (p. 291)

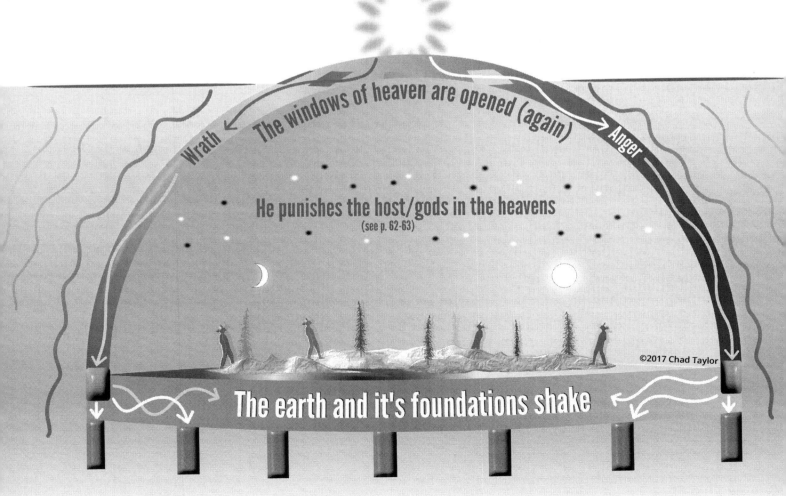

Wrath

The windows of heaven are opened (again)

Anger

He punishes the host/gods in the heavens
(see p. 62-63)

The earth and it's foundations shake

©2017 Chad Taylor

Isaiah 34:4-5

[4] And **all** the **host** of heaven shall be dissolved, and the heavens shall be **rolled** together as a **scroll**: and **all** their **host** shall **fall down**, as the leaf **falleth** off from the vine, and as a **falling** fig from the fig tree. [5] For my sword shall be bathed **in** heaven: behold, it shall come **down** upon Idumea, and upon the people of my curse, to judgment. Isaiah 34:4-5 (KJV)

[4] All the stars in the sky will be dissolved and the heavens rolled up like a scroll; all the starry host will fall like withered leaves from the vine, like shriveled figs from the fig tree. [5] My sword has drunk its fill in the heavens; see, it descends in judgment on Edom, the people I have totally destroyed. Isaiah 34:4-5 (NIV)

[4] **All** the **host** of heaven shall rot away, and the skies **roll** up like a **scroll**. **All** their **host** shall **fall**, as leaves **fall** from the vine, like leaves **falling** from the fig tree. [5] For my sword has drunk its fill **in** the heavens; behold, it **descends** for judgment upon Edom, upon the people I have devoted to destruction. Isaiah 34:4-5 (ESV)

[4] **All** the host of heaven shall rot away, and the skies **roll** up like a **scroll**. **All** their host shall wither like a leaf withering on a vine, or fruit withering on a fig tree. [5] When my sword has drunk its fill **in** the heavens, lo, it will **descend** upon Edom, upon the people I have doomed to judgment. Isaiah 34:4-5 (NRSV)

- **Above:** in the sky / overhead (p. 288)
- **All:** the whole, entire, total amount, quantity, or extent of (p. 288)
- **Host(s):** Army / a great number / multitude (p. 289)
- **Fall(eth/ing):** to descend freely by the force of gravity (p. 289)
- **Down:** from a higher to a lower place or position (p. 289)
- **Roll(ed):** to wrap round on itself (p. 290)
- **Scroll:** a long piece of paper that rolls around one or two cylinders and that usually has something written or drawn on it (p. 290)
- **In:** within a particular place (p. 290)
- **Descend(s):** to go or move from a higher to a lower place or level (p. 289)

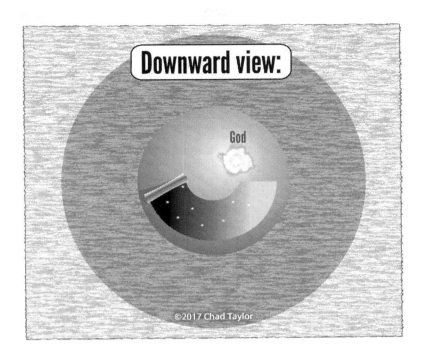

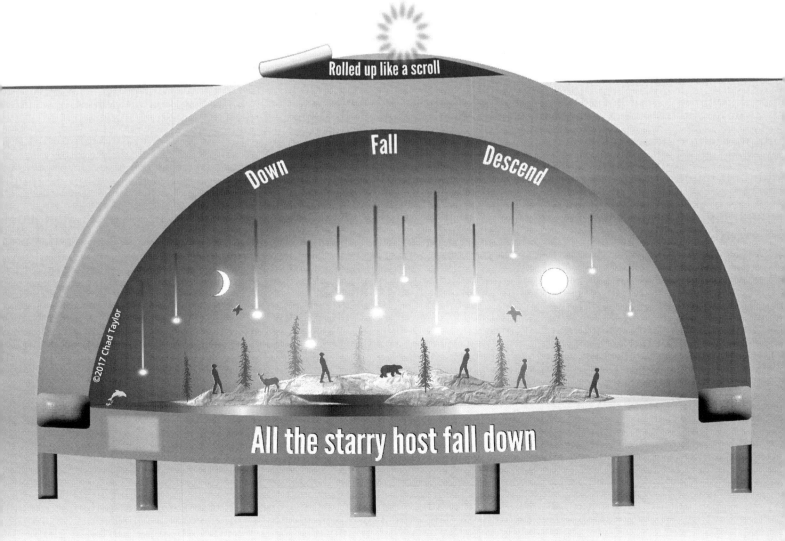

Isaiah 38:7-8

[7] And this shall be a sign unto thee from the LORD, that the LORD will do this thing that he hath spoken; **[8] Behold, I will bring <u>again</u> the shadow of the degrees, which is gone down in the sun dial of Ahaz, ten degrees <u>backward</u>. So the sun <u>returned</u> ten degrees, by which degrees it was gone down.** Isaiah 38:7-8 (KJV)

[7] "'This is the LORD's sign to you that the LORD will do what he has promised: [8] I will make the shadow cast by the sun go back the ten steps it has gone down on the stairway of Ahaz.'" So the sunlight went back the ten steps it had gone down. Isaiah 38:7-8 (NIV)

[7] "This shall be the sign to you from the Lord, that the Lord will do this thing that he has promised: **[8] Behold, I will make the shadow cast by the declining sun on the dial of Ahaz turn <u>back</u> ten steps.** So the sun turned <u>back</u> on the dial the ten steps by which it had declined. Isaiah 38:7-8 (ESV)

[7] "This is the sign to you from the LORD, that the LORD will do this thing that he has promised: **[8] See, I will make the shadow cast by the declining sun on the dial of Ahaz turn <u>back</u> ten steps."** So the sun turned <u>back</u> on the dial the ten steps by which it had declined. Isaiah 38:7-8 (NRSV)

- **Again:** for another time (p. 288)

- **Backward:** in a reverse or contrary direction or way (p. 288)

- **Returned:** happening or done for the second time (p. 290)

- **Back:** to, toward, or in the place where someone or something was previously (p. 288)

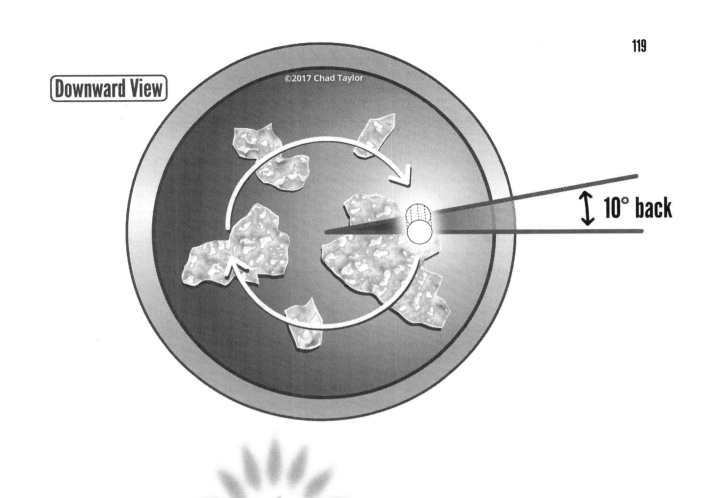

Downward View

10° back

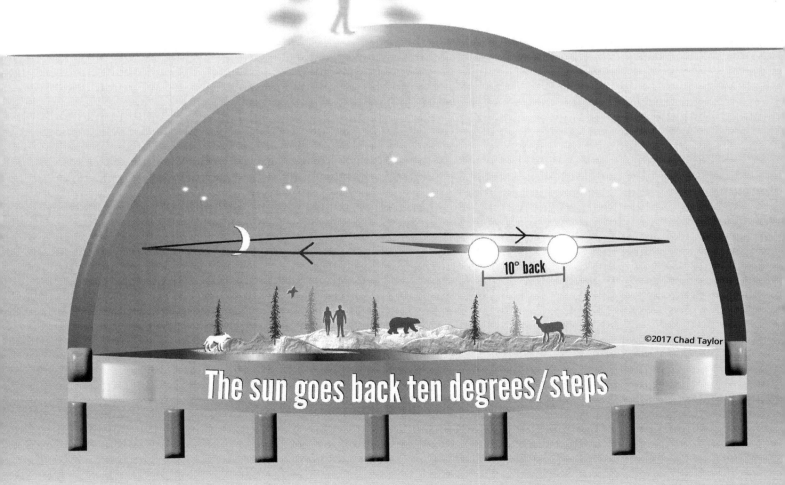

10° back

The sun goes back ten degrees/steps

Isaiah 38:14

¹⁴ Like a crane or a swallow, so did I chatter: I did mourn as a dove: **mine eyes fail with looking <u>upward</u>:** O Lᴏʀᴅ, I am oppressed; undertake for me.   Isaiah 38:14 (KJV)

---

¹⁴ I cried like a swift or thrush, I moaned like a mourning dove.   My eyes grew weak as I looked to the heavens.   I am being threatened; Lord, come to my aid!"   Isaiah 38:14 (NIV)

---

¹⁴ Like a swallow or a crane I chirp; I moan like a dove. **My eyes are weary with looking <u>upward</u>.** O Lord, I am oppressed; be my pledge of safety!   Isaiah 38:14 (ESV)

---

¹⁴ Like a swallow or a crane I clamor, I moan like a dove.   **My eyes are weary with looking <u>upward</u>.** O Lord, I am oppressed; be my security!   Isaiah 38:14 (NRSV)

---

¹⁴ Delirious, I chattered like a swallow or a crane, and then I moaned like a mourning dove.   **My eyes grew tired of looking <u>to</u> heaven** for help.   I am in trouble, Lord. Help me!"   Isaiah 38:14 (NLT)

Upward: toward the ceiling, sky, etc.   (p. 291)

To: in the direction of   (p. 291)

©2017 Chad Taylor

Looking upward to heaven and the starry host

Isaiah 40:26

²⁶ **Lift up your eyes on high,** and behold who hath created these things, that bringeth out **their host by number: he calleth them all by names by the greatness of his might,** for that he is strong in power; not one faileth.   Isaiah 40:26 (KJV)

²⁶ Lift up your eyes and look to the heavens: Who created all these? He who brings out the starry host one by one and calls forth each of them by name. Because of his great power and mighty strength, not one of them is missing. Isaiah 40:26 (NIV)

²⁶ **Lift up your eyes on high and see:** who created these? He who brings out **their host by number, calling them all by name;** by the greatness of his might and because he is strong in power, not one is missing. Isaiah 40:26 (ESV)

²⁶ **Lift up your eyes on high and see:** Who created these? He who brings out **their host and numbers them, calling them all by name;** because he is great in strength, mighty in power, not one is missing. Isaiah 40:26 (NRSV)

²⁶ **Look up into the heavens. Who created all the stars? He brings them out like an army, one after another, calling each by its name.** Because of his great power and incomparable strength, not a single one is missing. Isaiah 40:26 (NLT)

- ⌐⌐ **Up:** toward the sky or ceiling (p. 291)
- ⌐⌐ **High:** located far above the ground or another surface (p. 289)
- ⌐⌐ **Host:** Army / a great number / multitude (p. 289)
- ⌐⌐ **All:** the whole, entire, total amount, quantity, or extent of (p. 288)
- ⌐⌐ **Each:** every one of two or more people or things considered separately (p. 289)

Isaiah 60:19-20

[19] **The sun shall be no more thy light by day; neither for brightness shall the moon <u>give</u> light** unto thee: but **the Lord shall be unto thee an <u>everlasting</u> light, and thy God thy glory.** [20] Thy sun shall no more go down; neither shall thy moon withdraw itself: for **the Lord shall be thine <u>everlasting</u> light,** and the days of thy mourning shall be ended. Isaiah 60:19-20 (KJV)

[19] The sun will no more be your light by day, nor will the brightness of the moon shine on you, for the Lord will be your everlasting light, and your God will be your glory. [20] Your sun will never set again, and your moon will wane no more; the Lord will be your everlasting light, and your days of sorrow will end. Isaiah 60:19-20 (NIV)

[19] **The sun shall be no more your light by day, nor for brightness shall the moon give you light; but the Lord will be your <u>everlasting</u> light, and your God will be your glory.** [20] Your sun shall no more go down, nor your moon withdraw itself; for **the Lord will be your <u>everlasting</u> light,** and your days of mourning shall be ended. Isaiah 60:19-20 (ESV)

[19] **The sun shall no longer be your light by day, nor for brightness shall the moon <u>give</u> light to you by night; but the Lord will be your <u>everlasting</u> light, and your God will be your glory.** [20] Your sun shall no more go down, or your moon withdraw itself; for **the Lord will be your <u>everlasting</u> light,** and your days of mourning shall be ended. Isaiah 60:19-20 (NRSV)

Give: to make a present of / to yield as a product, consequence, or effect (p. 289)

Everlasting: lasting forever (p. 289)

©2017 Chad Taylor

The Lord will be your everlasting light

Isaiah 64:1

[1] Oh that thou wouldest **rend the heavens, that thou wouldest <u>come down</u>,** that the mountains might flow down at thy presence, Isaiah 64:1 (KJV)

[1] Oh, that you would rend the heavens and come down, that the mountains would tremble before you! Isaiah 64:1 (NIV)

[1] Oh that you would **<u>rend</u> the heavens and <u>come down</u>,** that the mountains might quake at your presence— Isaiah 64:1 (ESV)

[1] O that you would **<u>tear open</u> the heavens and <u>come down</u>,** so that the mountains would quake at your presence— Isaiah 64:1 (NRSV)

[1] Oh, that you would **<u>burst from</u> the heavens and <u>come down</u>**! How the mountains would quake in your presence! Isaiah 64:1 (NLT)

- **Rend:** to become torn or split (p. 290)
- **Burst:** to open suddenly (p. 288)
- **From:** used to indicate the starting point of a physical movement or action (p. 289)
- **Tear:** to separate parts of or pull apart by force (p. 291)
- **Open:** to cause (something) to no longer be covered, sealed, or blocked (p. 290)
- **Come:** to move toward (p. 288)
- **Down:** from a higher to a lower place or position (p. 289)

©2017 Chad Taylor

Jeremiah 49:36

[36] **And upon Elam will I <u>bring</u> the four winds <u>from</u> the four <u>quarters</u> of heaven,** and will scatter them toward all those winds; and there shall be no nation whither the outcasts of Elam shall not come. Jeremiah 49:36 (KJV)

[36] I will bring against Elam the four winds from the four quarters of heaven; I will scatter them to the four winds, and there will not be a nation where Elam's exiles do not go. Jeremiah 49:36 (NIV)

[36] **And I will <u>bring</u> upon Elam the four winds <u>from</u> the four <u>quarters</u> of heaven.** And I will scatter them to all those winds, and there shall be no nation to which those driven out of Elam shall not come. Jeremiah 49:36 (ESV)

[36] and **I will <u>bring</u> upon Elam the four winds <u>from</u> the four <u>quarters</u> of heaven;** and I will scatter them to all these winds, and there shall be no nation to which the exiles from Elam shall not come. Jeremiah 49:36 (NRSV)

Bring: to cause (something or someone) to come (p. 288)

From: used to indicate the starting point of a physical movement or action (p. 289)

Quarters: any of various units of length or area equal to one fourth of some larger unit (p. 290)

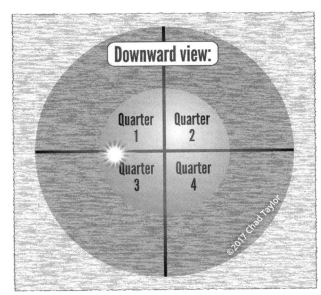

Downward view:

Quarter 1 | Quarter 2
Quarter 3 | Quarter 4

©2017 Chad Taylor

From the four quarters of heaven

©2017 Chad Taylor

Ezekiel 1:4-5 & 22-28

⁴And I looked, and, behold, a whirlwind **came out of the north,** a great cloud, and a fire infolding itself, and a brightness was about it, and out of the midst thereof as the colour of amber, out of the midst of the fire. ⁵Also out of the midst thereof came the likeness of four living creatures. And this was their appearance; they had the likeness of a man. ⁶..7..8..9..10..11..12..13..14..15..16..17..18..19..20..21..22And the likeness of **the firmament** upon the heads of **the living creature** was as the colour of the terrible <u>crystal</u>, <u>stretched</u> forth <u>over</u> their heads <u>above</u>. ²³And <u>under the firmament</u> were their wings straight, the one toward the other: every one had two, which covered on this side, and every one had two, which covered on that side, their bodies. ²⁴And when they went, I heard the noise of their wings, like the noise of great waters, as the voice of the Almighty, the voice of speech, **as the noise of an host: when they <u>stood</u>,** they let down their wings. ²⁵And there was a voice **from the firmament that was <u>over</u> their heads, when they <u>stood</u>,** and had let down their wings. ²⁶And <u>above</u> the <u>firmament</u> that was <u>over</u> their heads was the likeness of a <u>throne</u>, **as the appearance of a sapphire stone: and <u>upon</u> the likeness of the <u>throne</u> was the likeness as the appearance of a man <u>above</u> <u>upon</u> it.** ²⁷And I saw as the colour of amber, as the appearance of fire round about within it, from the appearance of his loins even upward, and from the appearance of his loins even downward, I saw as it were the appearance of fire, and it had brightness round about. ²⁸As the appearance of the bow that is in the cloud in the day of rain, so was the appearance of the brightness round about. This was the appearance of the likeness of the glory of the LORD. And when I saw it, I fell upon my face, and I heard a voice of one that spake. Ezekiel 1:4-5 & 22-28 (KJV)

⁴I looked, and I saw a windstorm coming out of the north—an immense cloud with flashing lightning and surrounded by brilliant light. The center of the fire looked like glowing metal, ⁵and in the fire was what looked like four living creatures. In appearance their form was human, ⁶..7..8..9..10..11..12..13..14..15..16..17..18..19..20..21.. ²²Spread out above the heads of the living creatures was what looked something like a vault, sparkling like crystal, and awesome. ²³Under the vault their wings were stretched out one toward the other, and each had two wings covering its body. ²⁴When the creatures moved, I heard the sound of their wings, like the roar of rushing waters, like the voice of the Almighty, like the tumult of an army. When they stood still, they lowered their wings. ²⁵Then there came a voice from above the vault over their heads as they stood with lowered wings. ²⁶Above the vault over their heads was what looked like a throne of lapis lazuli, and high above on the throne was a figure like that of a man. ²⁷I saw that from what appeared to be his waist up he looked like glowing metal, as if full of fire, and that from there down he looked like fire; and brilliant light surrounded him. ²⁸Like the appearance of a rainbow in the clouds on a rainy day, so was the radiance around him. This was the appearance of the likeness of the glory of the LORD. When I saw it, I fell facedown, and I heard the voice of one speaking. Ezekiel 1:4-5 & 22-28 (NIV)

- **Crystal:** made of or being like a clear colorless glass of very good quality (p. 289)
- **Spread out:** to open, arrange, or place (something) over a large area (p. 291)
- **Firmament:** the vault or arch of the sky (p. 289)
- **Dome:** a large rounded roof or ceiling that is shaped like half of a ball / a large hemispherical roof or ceiling (p. 289)
- **Stretched:** to extend in length (p. 291)
- **Forth:** onward or forward in time or place (p. 289)
- **Over:** Above (p. 290)

⁴ As I looked, behold, a stormy wind **came out of the north,** and a great cloud, with brightness around it, and fire flashing forth continually, and in the midst of the fire, as it were gleaming metal. ⁵ And from the midst of it came the likeness of four living creatures. And this was their appearance: they had a human likeness,⁶⁻⁷⁻⁸⁻⁹⁻¹⁰⁻¹¹⁻¹²⁻¹³⁻¹⁴⁻¹⁵⁻¹⁶⁻¹⁷⁻¹⁸⁻¹⁹⁻²⁰⁻²¹⁻²²⁻²² **Over the heads of the living creatures there was the likeness of an expanse, shining like awe-inspiring <u>crystal</u>, <u>spread out</u> <u>above</u> their heads.** ²³ And <u>under</u> the <u>expanse</u> their wings were stretched out straight, one toward another. And each creature had two wings covering its body. ²⁴ And when they went, I heard the sound of their wings like the sound of many waters, like the sound of the Almighty, **a sound of tumult like the sound of an army.** When they stood still, they let down their wings. ²⁵ And **there came a voice from <u>above</u> the <u>expanse</u> <u>over</u> their heads. When they <u>stood</u> <u>still</u>,** they let down their wings. ²⁶ And <u>above</u> **the <u>expanse</u> <u>over</u> their heads there was the likeness of a <u>throne</u>, in appearance like sapphire; and seated <u>above</u> the likeness of a <u>throne</u> was a likeness with a human appearance.** ²⁷ And upward from what had the appearance of his waist I saw as it were gleaming metal, like the appearance of fire enclosed all around. And downward from what had the appearance of his waist I saw as it were the appearance of fire, and there was brightness around him. ²⁸ Like the appearance of the bow that is in the cloud on the day of rain, so was the appearance of the brightness all around. Such was the appearance of the likeness of the glory of the Lᴏʀᴅ. And when I saw it, I fell on my face, and I heard the voice of one speaking. Ezekiel 1:4-5 & 22-28 (ESV)

⁴ As I looked, a stormy wind **came out of the north:** a great cloud with brightness around it and fire flashing forth continually, and in the middle of the fire, something like gleaming amber. ⁵ In the middle of it was something like four living creatures. This was their appearance: they were of human form. ⁶⁻⁷⁻⁸⁻⁹⁻¹⁰⁻¹¹⁻¹²⁻¹³⁻¹⁴⁻¹⁵⁻¹⁶⁻¹⁷⁻¹⁸⁻¹⁹⁻²⁰⁻²¹⁻²² **Over the heads of the living creatures there was something like a <u>dome</u>, shining like <u>crystal</u>, <u>spread out</u> <u>above</u> their heads.** ²³ **<u>Under</u> the <u>dome</u>** their wings were stretched out straight, one toward another; and each of the creatures had two wings covering its body. ²⁴ When they moved, I heard the sound of their wings like the sound of mighty waters, like the thunder of the Almighty, **a sound of tumult like the sound of an army; when they stopped,** they let down their wings. ²⁵ And there came **a voice from <u>above</u> the <u>dome</u> <u>over</u> their heads;** when they stopped, they let down their wings. ²⁶ And <u>above</u> the <u>dome</u> <u>over</u> their heads **there was something like a <u>throne</u>, in appearance like sapphire; and seated <u>above</u> the likeness of a <u>throne</u> was something that seemed like a human form.** ²⁷ Upward from what appeared like the loins I saw something like gleaming amber, something that looked like fire enclosed all around; and downward from what looked like the loins I saw something that looked like fire, and there was a splendor all around. ²⁸ Like the bow in a cloud on a rainy day, such was the appearance of the splendor all around. This was the appearance of the likeness of the glory of the Lᴏʀᴅ. When I saw it, I fell on my face, and I heard the voice of someone speaking.
Ezekiel 1:4-5 & 22-28 (NRSV)

☐ **High:** located far above the ground or another surface (p. 289)

☐ **Above:** in or to a higher place (p. 288)

☐ **Under:** in or into a position below or beneath something (p. 291)

☐ **Upon/On:** touching and being supported by the top surface of (something) (p. 291)

☐ **Expanse:** Firmament / great extent of something spread out (p. 289)

☐ **Vault:** an arched structure of masonry usually forming a ceiling or roof (p. 291)

☐ **Throne:** the position of king or queen / the special chair for a king, queen, or other powerful person (p. 291)

☐ **Host:** Army / a great number / multitude (p. 289)

☐ **Stood:** to maintain one's position / to remain stationary or inactive (p. 291)

☐ **Still:** not moving (p. 291)

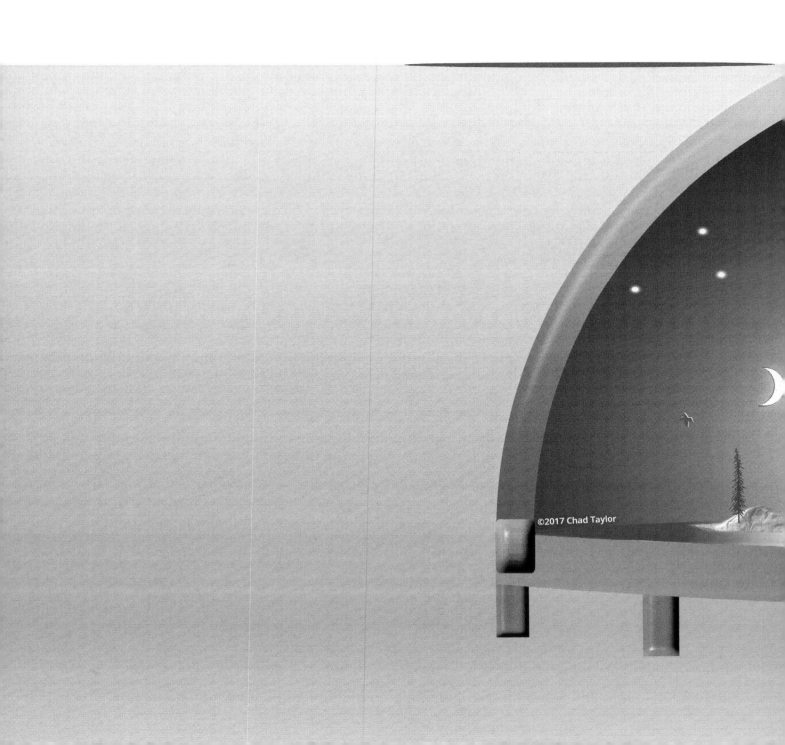

©2017 Chad Taylor

North

©2017 Chad Taylor

A dome shining like crystal over their heads

Ezekiel 8:2-4

² Then I beheld, and lo a likeness as the appearance of fire: from the appearance of his loins even downward, fire; and from his loins even upward, as the appearance of brightness, as the colour of amber. ³ **And he put forth the form of an hand, and took me by a lock of mine head; and the spirit <u>lifted</u> me <u>up</u> <u>between</u> the earth and the heaven, and brought me in the visions of God to Jerusalem,** to the door of the inner gate that looketh toward the north; where was the seat of the image of jealousy, which provoketh to jealousy. ⁴ And, behold, **the <u>glory</u> of the God of Israel was there,** according to the vision that I saw in the plain. Ezekiel 8:2-4 (KJV)

² I looked, and I saw a figure like that of a man. From what appeared to be his waist down he was like fire, and from there up his appearance was as bright as glowing metal. ³ He stretched out what looked like a hand and took me by the hair of my head. The Spirit lifted me up between earth and heaven and in visions of God he took me to Jerusalem, to the entrance of the north gate of the inner court, where the idol that provokes to jealousy stood. ⁴ And there before me was the glory of the God of Israel, as in the vision I had seen in the plain. Ezekiel 8:2-4 (NIV)

² Then I looked, and behold, a form that had the appearance of a man. Below what appeared to be his waist was fire, and above his waist was something like the appearance of brightness, like gleaming metal. ³ **He put out the form of a hand and took me by a lock of my head, and the Spirit <u>lifted</u> me <u>up</u> <u>between</u> earth and heaven and brought me in visions of God to Jerusalem,** to the entrance of the gateway of the inner court that faces north, where was the seat of the image of jealousy, which provokes to jealousy. ⁴ And behold, **the <u>glory</u> of the God of Israel was there,** like the vision that I saw in the valley. Ezekiel 8:2-4 (ESV)

² I looked, and there was a figure that looked like a human being; below what appeared to be its loins it was fire, and above the loins it was like the appearance of brightness, like gleaming amber. ³ **It stretched out the form of a hand, and took me by a lock of my head; and the spirit <u>lifted</u> me <u>up</u> <u>between</u> earth and heaven, and brought me in visions of God to Jerusalem,** to the entrance of the gateway of the inner court that faces north, to the seat of the image of jealousy, which provokes to jealousy. ⁴ And **the <u>glory</u> of the God of Israel was there,** like the vision that I had seen in the valley. Ezekiel 8:2-4 (NRSV)

   Lifted: to raise from a lower to a higher position (p. 290)

   Up: from a lower to a higher place or position (p. 291)

   Between: in the space that separates (two things or people) (p. 288)

   Glory: brilliance, splendor (p. 289)

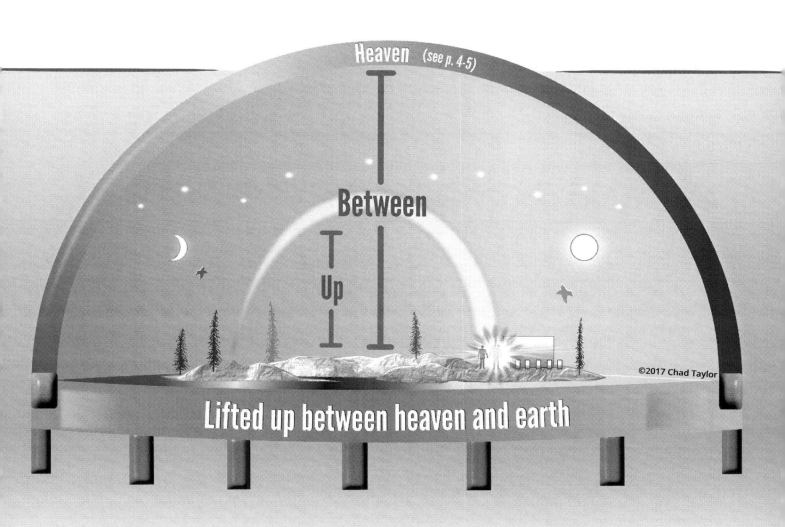

Heaven (see p. 4-5)

©2017 Chad Taylor

Ezekiel 32:7-8

⁷ And when I shall put thee out, **I will <u>cover</u> the heaven, and make the stars thereof dark; I will <u>cover</u> the sun with a cloud, and the moon shall not <u>give</u> <u>her</u> light.** ⁸ <u>All</u> **the bright lights of heaven will I make dark <u>over</u> thee,** and set darkness upon thy land, saith the Lord God. Ezekiel 32:7-8 (KJV)

⁷ When I snuff you out, I will cover the heavens and darken their stars; I will cover the sun with a cloud, and the moon will not give its light. ⁸ All the shining lights in the heavens I will darken over you; I will bring darkness over your land, declares the Sovereign Lord. Ezekiel 32:7-8 (NIV)

⁷ When I blot you out, **I will <u>cover</u> the heavens and make their stars dark; I will <u>cover</u> the sun with a cloud, and the moon shall not <u>give</u> <u>its</u> light.** ⁸ <u>All</u> **the bright lights of heaven will I make dark <u>over</u> you,** and put darkness on your land, declares the Lord God. Ezekiel 32:7-8 (ESV)

⁷ When I blot you out, **I will <u>cover</u> the heavens, and make their stars dark; I will <u>cover</u> the sun with a cloud, and the moon shall not <u>give</u> <u>its</u> light.** ⁸ <u>All</u> **the shining lights of the heavens I will darken <u>above</u> you,** and put darkness on your land, says the Lord God. Ezekiel 32:7-8 (NRSV)

- ☐ **Cover:** to put something over, on top of, or in front of (something else) especially in order to protect, hide, or close it (p. 289)

- ☐ **Give:** to make a present of / to yield as a product, consequence, or effect (p. 289)

- ☐ **Her:** of or relating to her or herself especially as possessor, agent, or object of an action (p. 289)

- ☐ **Its:** relating to or belonging to it or itself (p. 290)

- ☐ **All:** the whole, entire, total amount, quantity, or extent of (p. 288)

- ☐ **In:** used to indicate location or position within something (p. 290)

- ☐ **Above:** in the sky / overhead (p. 288)

- ☐ **Over:** Above (p. 290)

God makes the stars dark overhead

The moon gives off no light

The sun is covered with a cloud

©2017 Chad Taylor

All the lights above will be darkened

Daniel 4:10-13

¹⁰ Thus were the visions of mine head in my bed; I saw, and behold **a tree in the <u>midst</u> of the earth, and the <u>height</u> thereof was great.** ¹¹ The tree grew, and was strong, and **the <u>height</u> thereof reached <u>unto</u> heaven, and the <u>sight</u> thereof to the <u>end</u> of <u>all</u> the earth:** ¹² The leaves thereof were fair, and the fruit thereof much, and in it was meat for all: the beasts of the field had shadow under it, and the fowls of the heaven dwelt in the boughs thereof, and all flesh was fed of it. ¹³ I saw in the visions of my head upon my bed, and, behold, **a watcher and an holy one came <u>down</u> <u>from</u> heaven;** Daniel 4:10-13 (KJV)

¹⁰ These are the visions I saw while lying in bed: I looked, and there before me stood a tree in the middle of the land. Its height was enormous. ¹¹ The tree grew large and strong and its top touched the sky; it was visible to the ends of the earth. ¹² Its leaves were beautiful, its fruit abundant, and on it was food for all. Under it the wild animals found shelter, and the birds lived in its branches; from it every creature was fed. ¹³ "In the visions I saw while lying in bed, I looked, and there before me was a holy one, a messenger, coming down from heaven. Daniel 4:10-13 (NIV)

¹⁰ The visions of my head as I lay in bed were these: I saw, and behold, **a tree in the <u>midst</u> of the earth, and its <u>height</u> was great.** ¹¹ The tree grew and became strong, and its <u>top</u> reached <u>to</u> heaven, and it was <u>visible</u> to the <u>end</u> of the <u>whole</u> earth. ¹² Its leaves were beautiful and its fruit abundant, and in it was food for all. The beasts of the field found shade under it, and the birds of the heavens lived in its branches, and all flesh was fed from it. ¹³ "I saw in the visions of my head as I lay in bed, and behold, **a watcher, a holy one, came <u>down</u> <u>from</u> heaven.** Daniel 4:10-13 (ESV)

¹⁰ Upon my bed this is what I saw; there was **a tree at the <u>center</u> of the earth, and its <u>height</u> was great.** ¹¹ The tree grew great and strong, its <u>top</u> reached <u>to</u> heaven, and it was <u>visible</u> to the <u>ends</u> of the <u>whole</u> earth. ¹² Its foliage was beautiful, its fruit abundant, and it provided food for all. The animals of the field found shade under it, the birds of the air nested in its branches, and from it all living beings were fed. ¹³ "I continued looking, in the visions of my head as I lay in bed, and there was **a holy watcher, coming <u>down</u> <u>from</u> heaven.** Daniel 4:10-13 (NRSV)

(see p. 4-5)

Sky

Heaven

©2017 Chad Taylor

Visible

Visible

End of the earth

End of the earth

A tree touching the sky / heaven

- **Midst:** the middle or central part (p. 290)
- **Middle:** the part, point, or position that is equally distant from the ends or opposite sides (p. 290)
- **Center:** the middle point or part of something (p. 288)
- **Height:** distance upward (p. 289)
- **Top:** the highest point, level, or part of something (p. 291)
- **Unto:** To (p. 291)
- **To:** used as a function word to indicate contact or proximity (p. 291)
- **Touched:** to be in contact with (something) (p. 291)
- **Sight:** something that is seen (p. 291)
- **Visible:** able to be seen (p. 291)
- **End(s):** the part at the edge or limit of an area (p. 289)
- **All:** the whole, entire, total amount, quantity, or extent of (p. 288)
- **Whole:** not lacking or leaving out any part (p. 291)
- **Down:** from a higher to a lower place or position (p. 289)
- **From:** used to indicate the starting point of a physical movement or action (p. 289)

Joel 2:10-11

[10] The earth shall <u>quake</u> <u>before</u> them; the heavens shall <u>tremble</u>: the sun and the moon shall be <u>dark</u>, and the stars shall withdraw their shining: [11] And the Lord shall utter his voice <u>before</u> his army: for his camp is very great: for he is strong that executeth his word: for **the day of the Lord** is great and very terrible; and who can abide it? Joel 2:10-11 (KJV)

[10] Before them the earth shakes, the heavens tremble, the sun and moon are darkened, and the stars no longer shine. [11] The Lord thunders at the head of his army; his forces are beyond number, and mighty is the army that obeys his command. The day of the Lord is great; it is dreadful. Who can endure it? Joel 2:10-11 (NIV)

[10] The earth <u>quakes</u> <u>before</u> them; the heavens <u>tremble</u>. The sun and the moon are <u>darkened</u>, and the stars withdraw their shining. [11] The Lord utters his voice <u>before</u> his army, for his camp is exceedingly great; he who executes his word is powerful. For **the day of the Lord** is great and very awesome; who can endure it? Joel 2:10-11 (ESV)

[10] The earth <u>quakes</u> <u>before</u> them, the heavens <u>tremble</u>. The sun and the moon are <u>darkened</u>, and the stars withdraw their shining. [11] The Lord utters his voice at the <u>head</u> of his army; how vast is his <u>host</u>! Numberless are those who obey his command. Truly the day of the Lord is great; terrible indeed—who can endure it? Joel 2:10-11 (NRSV)

⌐⌐ **Quake(s):** to shake violently (p. 290)

⌐⌐ **Shakes:** to move sometimes violently back and forth or up and down with short, quick movements (p. 291)

⌐⌐ **Before:** forward of / in front of (p. 288)

⌐⌐ **Tremble:** the act or a period of shaking (p. 291)

⌐⌐ **Host:** Army / a great number / multitude (p. 289)

⌐⌐ **Dark:** having very little or no light (p. 289)

⌐⌐ **Darkened:** to make dark (p. 289)

⌐⌐ **Head:** to be the leader of (something) (p. 289)

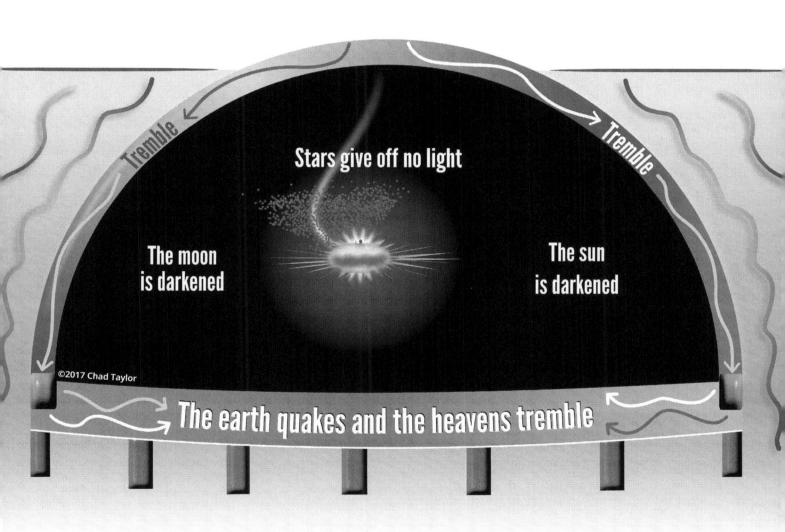

Habakkuk 3:11

[11] **The sun and moon <u>stood</u> <u>still</u> <u>in</u> their <u>habitation</u>:** at the light of thine arrows they went, and at the shining of thy glittering spear. Habakkuk 3:11 (KJV)

[11] Sun and moon stood still in the heavens at the glint of your flying arrows, at the lightning of your flashing spear. Habakkuk 3:11 (NIV)

[11] **The sun and moon <u>stood</u> <u>still</u> <u>in</u> their place** at the light of your arrows as they sped, at the flash of your glittering spear. Habakkuk 3:11 (ESV)

[11] **the moon <u>stood</u> <u>still</u> <u>in</u> its exalted place,** at the light of your arrows speeding by, at the gleam of your flashing spear. Habakkuk 3:11 (NRSV)

[11] **The sun and moon <u>stood</u> <u>still</u> <u>in</u> the sky** as your brilliant arrows flew and your glittering spear flashed. Habakkuk 3:11 (NLT)

Stood: to maintain one's position / to remain stationary or inactive (p. 291)

Still: not moving (p. 291)

In: within a particular place (p. 290)

Habitation: a place to live (p. 289)

The Moon stood still

The Sun stood still

©2017 Chad Taylor

The sun and moon stood still

Matthew 2:1-2 & 9-10

[1] Now when Jesus was born in Bethlehem of Judaea in the days of Herod the king, behold, there came wise men from the east to Jerusalem, [2] Saying, Where is he that is born King of the Jews? for **we have seen his star in the east,** and are come to worship him. [3..4..5..6..7..8..9] When they had heard the king, they departed; and, lo, **the star, which they saw in the east, <u>went</u> before them, till it came and <u>stood</u> <u>over</u> where the young child was.** [10] **When they saw the star, they rejoiced with exceeding great joy.** Matthew 2:1-2 & 9-10 (KJV)

[1] After Jesus was born in Bethlehem in Judea, during the time of King Herod, Magi from the east came to Jerusalem [2] and asked, "Where is the one who has been born king of the Jews? We saw his star when it rose and have come to worship him." [3..4..5..6..7..8..9] After they had heard the king, they went on their way, and the star they had seen when it rose went ahead of them until it stopped over the place where the child was. [10] When they saw the star, they were overjoyed. Matthew 2:1-2 & 9-10 (NIV)

[1] Now after Jesus was born in Bethlehem of Judea in the days of Herod the king, behold, wise men from the east came to Jerusalem, [2] saying, "Where is he who has been born king of the Jews? For **we saw his star when it rose** and have come to worship him." [3..4..5..6..7..8..9] After listening to the king, they went on their way. And behold, **the star that they had seen when it rose <u>went</u> before them until it came to <u>rest</u> <u>over</u> the place where the child was.** [10] **When they saw the star, they rejoiced exceedingly with great joy.** Matthew 2:1-2 & 9-10 (ESV)

[1] In the time of King Herod, after Jesus was born in Bethlehem of Judea, wise men from the East came to Jerusalem, [2] asking, "Where is the child who has been born king of the Jews? For **we observed his star at its rising,** and have come to pay him homage." [3..4..5..6..7..8..9] When they had heard the king, they set out; and there, **<u>ahead</u> of them, <u>went</u> the star that they had seen at its rising, until it <u>stopped</u> <u>over</u> the <u>place</u> where the child was.** [10] **When they saw that the star had <u>stopped</u>, they were overwhelmed with joy.** Matthew 2:1-2 & 9-10 (NRSV)

- **Went:** to move on a course (p. 291)

- **Before:** forward of / in front of (p. 288)

- **Ahead:** in a forward direction or position (p. 288)

- **Stood:** an act of stopping or staying in one place (p. 291)

- **Stopped:** to cease moving especially temporarily or for a purpose (p. 291)

- **Rest:** to cease from action or motion (p. 290)

- **Over:** Above (p. 290)

- **Place:** a building, part of a building, or area occupied as a home (p. 290)

©2017 Chad Taylor

The star stopped over where the child was

Matthew 4:8-9

[8] Again, the devil taketh him **up into an exceeding high mountain, and sheweth him all the kingdoms of the world,** and the glory of them; [9] And saith unto him, **All these things will I give thee,** if thou wilt fall down and worship me. Matthew 4:8-9 (KJV)

[8] Again, the devil took him to a very high mountain and showed him all the kingdoms of the world and their splendor. [9] "All this I will give you," he said, "if you will bow down and worship me." Matthew 4:8-9 (NIV)

[8] Again, the devil took him **to a very high mountain and showed him all the kingdoms of the world** and their glory. [9] And he said to him, **"All these I will give you,** if you will fall down and worship me." Matthew 4:8-9 (ESV)

[8] Again, the devil took him **to a very high mountain and showed him all the kingdoms of the world** and their splendor; [9] and he said to him, **"All these I will give you,** if you will fall down and worship me." Matthew 4:8-9 (NRSV)

Up: from a lower to a higher place or position (p. 291)

High: rising or extending upward a great distance (p. 289)

All: the whole, entire, total amount, quantity, or extent of (p. 288)

He showed him all the kingdoms of the world

Matthew 24:29-31

[29] **Immediately** <u>after</u> the tribulation of those days shall the sun be <u>darkened</u>, and the moon shall not <u>give</u> <u>her</u> light, and the stars shall <u>fall</u> <u>from</u> heaven, and the <u>powers</u> of the heavens shall be shaken: [30] And <u>then</u> shall appear the <u>sign</u> of the Son of man <u>in</u> heaven: and <u>then</u> shall <u>all</u> the tribes of the earth mourn, and they shall <u>see</u> the Son of man coming in the clouds of heaven with power and great glory. [31] And he shall send his angels with a great sound of a trumpet, and they shall gather together his elect from the four winds, from one <u>end</u> of heaven to the other.   Matthew 24:29-31 (KJV)

[29] "Immediately after the distress of those days "'the sun will be darkened, and the moon will not give its light; the stars will fall from the sky, and the heavenly bodies will be shaken.' [30] "Then will appear the sign of the Son of Man in heaven. And then all the peoples of the earth will mourn when they see the Son of Man coming on the clouds of heaven, with power and great glory. [31] And he will send his angels with a loud trumpet call, and they will gather his elect from the four winds, from one end of the heavens to the other.
Matthew 24:29-31 (NIV)

[29] "<u>Immediately</u> <u>after</u> the tribulation of those days the sun will be <u>darkened</u>, and the moon will not <u>give</u> <u>its</u> light, and the stars will <u>fall</u> <u>from</u> heaven, and the <u>powers</u> of the heavens will be shaken. [30] <u>Then</u> will appear <u>in</u> heaven the <u>sign</u> of the Son of Man, and <u>then</u> <u>all</u> the tribes of the earth will mourn, and they will <u>see</u> the Son of Man coming <u>on</u> the clouds of heaven with power and great glory. [31] And he will send out his angels with a loud trumpet call, and they will gather his elect from the four winds, from one <u>end</u> of heaven to the other.
Matthew 24:29-31 (ESV)

[29] "<u>Immediately</u> <u>after</u> the suffering of those days the sun will be <u>darkened</u>, and the moon will not <u>give</u> <u>its</u> light; the stars will <u>fall</u> <u>from</u> heaven, and the <u>powers</u> of heaven will be shaken. [30] <u>Then</u> the <u>sign</u> of the Son of Man will appear <u>in</u> heaven, and <u>then</u> <u>all</u> the tribes of the earth will mourn, and they will see 'the Son of Man coming <u>on</u> the clouds of heaven' with power and great glory. [31] And he will send out his angels with a loud trumpet call, and they will gather his elect from the four winds, from one <u>end</u> of heaven to the other.
Matthew 24:29-31 (NRSV)

©2017 Chad Taylor

☐   **Immediately:** without any delay (p. 289)

☐   **After:** later in time (p. 288)

☐   **Darkened:** to make dark (p. 289)

☐   **Give:** to make a present of / to yield as a product, consequence, or effect (p. 289)

☐   **Her:** of or relating to her or herself especially as possessor, agent, or object of an action (p. 289)

☐   **Its:** relating to or belonging to it or itself (p. 290)

☐   **Fall:** to descend freely by the force of gravity (p. 289)

☐   **From:** used to indicate the starting point of a physical movement or action (p. 289)

☐   **Powers:** a person or organization that has a lot of control and influence over other people or organizations (p. 290)

☐   **Then:** next in order of time (p. 291)

☐   **Sign:** something (such as an action or event) which shows that something else exists, is true, or will happen (p. 291)

☐   **In:** within a particular place (p. 290)

☐   **On:** to a position that is supported by (p. 290)

☐   **All:** the whole, entire, total amount, quantity, or extent of (p. 288)

☐   **See:** to perceive by the eye (p. 291)

☐   **End:** the part at the edge or limit of an area (p. 289)

End of
heaven

©2017 Chad Taylor

End of
heaven

©2017 Chad Taylor

The Son of Man returns on the clouds

Luke 2:9-15

⁹ And, lo, **the angel** of the Lord came upon them, and **the glory of the Lord shone** round **about** them: and they were sore **afraid**. ¹⁰ **And the angel** said unto them, Fear not: for, behold, I bring you good tidings of great joy, which shall be **to all people.** ¹¹ For unto you is born this day in the city of David a Saviour, which is Christ the Lord. ¹² And this shall be a sign unto you; Ye shall find the babe wrapped in swaddling clothes, lying in a manger. ¹³ And **suddenly there was with the angel a multitude of the heavenly host praising God, and saying,** ¹⁴ **Glory to God in the highest, and on earth peace, good will toward men.** ¹⁵ **And it came to pass, as the angels were gone away from them into heaven,** the shepherds said one to another, Let us now go even unto Bethlehem, and see this thing which is come to pass, which the Lord hath made known unto us. Luke 2:9-15 (KJV)

⁹ An angel of the Lord appeared to them, and the glory of the Lord shone around them, and they were terrified. ¹⁰ But the angel said to them, "Do not be afraid. I bring you good news that will cause great joy for all the people. ¹¹ Today in the town of David a Savior has been born to you; he is the Messiah, the Lord. ¹² This will be a sign to you: You will find a baby wrapped in cloths and lying in a manger." ¹³ Suddenly a great company of the heavenly host appeared with the angel, praising God and saying, ¹⁴ "Glory to God in the highest heaven, and on earth peace to those on whom his favor rests." ¹⁵ When the angels had left them and gone into heaven, the shepherds said to one another, "Let's go to Bethlehem and see this thing that has happened, which the Lord has told us about." Luke 2:9-15 (NIV)

⁹ And **an angel** of the Lord appeared to them, and **the glory of the Lord shone around them, and they were filled with great fear.** ¹⁰ **And the angel** said to them, "Fear not, for behold, I bring you good news of great joy that will be **for all the people.** ¹¹ For unto you is born this day in the city of David a Savior, who is Christ the Lord. ¹² And this will be a sign for you: you will find a baby wrapped in swaddling cloths and lying in a manger." ¹³ **And suddenly there was with the angel a multitude of the heavenly host praising God and saying,** ¹⁴ **"Glory to God in the highest, and on earth peace among those with whom he is pleased!"** ¹⁵ **When the angels went away from them into heaven,** the shepherds said to one another, "Let us go over to Bethlehem and see this thing that has happened, which the Lord has made known to us." Luke 2:9-15 (ESV)

⁹ Then **an angel** of the Lord stood before them, and **the glory of the Lord shone around them, and they were terrified.** ¹⁰ But the angel said to them, "Do not be afraid; for see—I am bringing you good news of great joy **for all the people:** ¹¹ to you is born this day in the city of David a Savior, who is the Messiah, the Lord. ¹² This will be a sign for you: you will find a child wrapped in bands of cloth and lying in a manger." ¹³ And **suddenly there was with the angel a multitude of the heavenly host, praising God and saying,** ¹⁴ **"Glory to God in the highest heaven, and on earth peace among those whom he favors!"** ¹⁵ **When the angels had left them and gone into heaven,** the shepherds said to one another, "Let us go now to Bethlehem and see this thing that has taken place, which the Lord has made known to us." Luke 2:9-15 (NRSV)

⁹ Suddenly, **an angel** of the Lord appeared among them, and **the radiance of the Lord's glory surrounded them. They were terrified,** ¹⁰ but the angel reassured them. "Don't be afraid!" he said. "I bring you good news that will bring great joy **to all people.** ¹¹ The Savior—yes, the Messiah, the Lord—has been born today in Bethlehem, the city of David! ¹² And you will recognize him by this sign: You will find a baby wrapped snugly in strips of cloth, lying in a manger." ¹³ **Suddenly, the angel was joined by a vast host of others—the armies of heaven—praising God and saying,** ¹⁴ **"Glory to God in highest heaven, and peace on earth to those with whom God is pleased."** ¹⁵ **When the angels had returned to heaven,** the shepherds said to each other, "Let's go to Bethlehem! Let's see this thing that has happened, which the Lord has told us about." Luke 2:9-15 (NLT)

Highest heaven

©2017 Chad Taylor

Joined by the armies of heaven

☐ **Glory:** brilliance, splendor (p. 289)

☐ **Radiance:** warm or vivid brightness (p. 290)

☐ **Shone:** to give off light (p. 291)

☐ **About:** on every side of (p. 288)

☐ **Around:** on all or various sides / in every or any direction (p. 288)

☐ **Surrounded:** to be on every side of (someone or something) (p. 291)

☐ **Afraid:** filled with fear (p. 288)

☐ **Terrified:** to cause (someone) to be extremely afraid (p. 291)

☐ **All:** the whole, entire, total amount, quantity, or extent of (p. 288)

☐ **Company:** a body of soldiers (p. 288)

☐ **Vast:** very great in size, amount, or extent (p. 291)

☐ **Host:** Army / a great number / multitude (p. 289)

☐ **Multitude:** a great number / host (p. 290)

☐ **Highest:** a high or the highest point, place, or level; peak (p. 289)

☐ **Returned:** the act of coming or going back to the place you started from or to a place where you were before (p. 290)

☐ **Into:** in the direction of (something) (p. 290)

Luke 3:21-22

[21] Now when all the people were baptized, it came to pass, that Jesus also being baptized, and praying, **the heaven was <u>opened</u>,** [22] **And the Holy Ghost <u>descended</u>** in a bodily shape like a dove **<u>upon</u> him, and a voice came <u>from</u> heaven,** which said, Thou art my beloved Son; in thee I am well pleased. Luke 3:21-22 (KJV)

[21] When all the people were being baptized, Jesus was baptized too. And as he was praying, heaven was opened [22] and the Holy Spirit descended on him in bodily form like a dove. And a voice came from heaven: "You are my Son, whom I love; with you I am well pleased." Luke 3:21-22 (NIV)

[21] Now when all the people were baptized, and when Jesus also had been baptized and was praying, **the heavens were <u>opened</u>,** [22] **and the Holy Spirit <u>descended</u> on him in bodily form, like a dove; and a voice came <u>from</u> heaven,** "You are my beloved Son; with you I am well pleased." Luke 3:21-22 (ESV)

[21] Now when all the people were baptized, and when Jesus also had been baptized and was praying, **the heaven was <u>opened</u>,** [22] **and the Holy Spirit <u>descended</u> <u>upon</u> him in bodily form like a dove. And a voice came <u>from</u> heaven,** "You are my Son, the Beloved; with you I am well pleased." Luke 3:21-22 (NRSV)

John 1:51

[51] And he saith unto him, Verily, verily, I say unto you, Hereafter **ye shall <u>see</u> heaven <u>open</u>, and the angels of God <u>ascending</u> and <u>descending</u> <u>upon</u> the Son of man.** John 1:51 (KJV)

[51] He then added, "Very truly I tell you, you will see 'heaven open, and the angels of God ascending and descending on' the Son of Man." John 1:51 (NIV)

[51] And he said to him, "Truly, truly, I say to you, **you will <u>see</u> heaven <u>opened</u>, and the angels of God <u>ascending</u> and <u>descending</u> on the Son of Man."** John 1:51 (ESV)

[51] And he said to him, "Very truly, I tell you, **you will <u>see</u> heaven <u>opened</u> and the angels of God <u>ascending</u> and <u>descending</u> <u>upon</u> the Son of Man."** John 1:51 (NRSV)

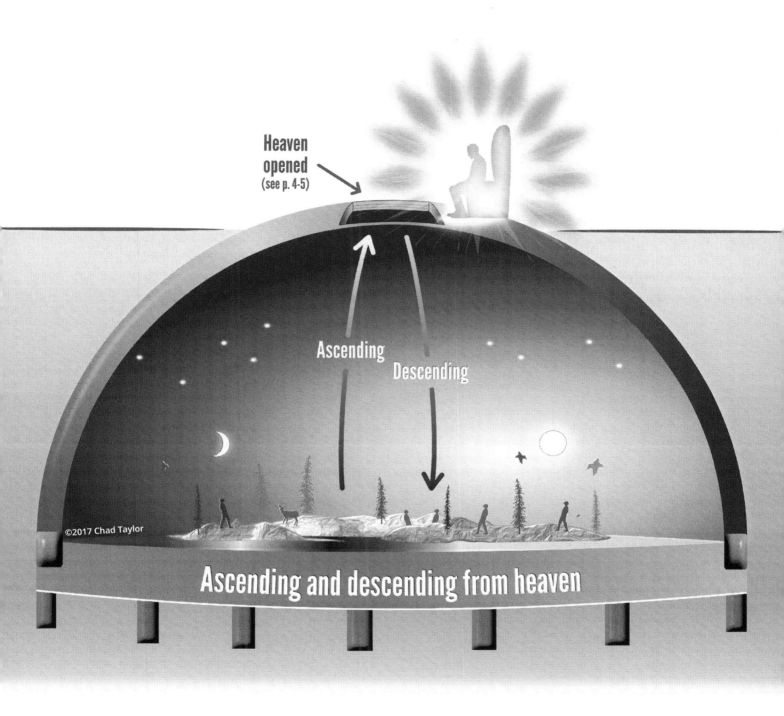

Heaven opened (see p. 4-5)

Ascending

Descending

©2017 Chad Taylor

Ascending and descending from heaven

- **See:** to perceive by the eye (p. 291)
- **Open(ed):** to cause (something) to no longer be covered, sealed, or blocked (p. 290)
- **Ascending:** to move upward (p. 288)
- **Descended(ing):** to go or move from a higher to a lower place or level (p. 289)
- **Upon:** on (p. 291)
- **On/Upon:** used to indicate the location of something (p. 290)
- **From:** used to indicate the starting point of a physical movement or action (p. 289)

John 3:12-15

[12] If I have told you earthly things, and ye believe not, how shall ye believe, if I tell you of heavenly things? [13] **And no man hath <u>ascended</u> <u>up</u> <u>to</u> heaven, but he that <u>came</u> <u>down</u> <u>from</u> heaven, even the Son of man which is in heaven.** [14] And as Moses lifted up the serpent in the wilderness, even so must the Son of man be lifted up: [15] **That <u>whosoever</u> believeth in him should not perish, but have <u>eternal</u> life.** John 3:12-15 (KJV)

[12] I have spoken to you of earthly things and you do not believe; how then will you believe if I speak of heavenly things? [13] No one has ever gone into heaven except the one who came from heaven—the Son of Man. [14] Just as Moses lifted up the snake in the wilderness, so the Son of Man must be lifted up, [15] that everyone who believes may have eternal life in him." John 3:12-15 (NIV)

[12] If I have told you earthly things and you do not believe, how can you believe if I tell you heavenly things? [13] **No one has <u>ascended</u> into heaven except he who <u>descended</u> <u>from</u> heaven, the Son of Man.** [14] And as Moses lifted up the serpent in the wilderness, so must the Son of Man be lifted up, [15] **that <u>whoever</u> believes in him may have <u>eternal</u> life.** John 3:12-15 (ESV)

[12] If I have told you about earthly things and you do not believe, how can you believe if I tell you about heavenly things? [13] **No one has <u>ascended</u> into heaven except the one who <u>descended</u> <u>from</u> heaven, the Son of Man.** [14] And just as Moses lifted up the serpent in the wilderness, so must the Son of Man be lifted up, [15] **that <u>whoever</u> believes in him may have <u>eternal</u> life.** John 3:12-15 (NRSV)

- **Ascended:** to move upward (p. 288)

- **Up:** from a lower to a higher place or position (p. 291)

- **To:** in the direction of (p. 291)

- **Came:** to move toward something (p. 288)

- **Down:** from a higher to a lower place or position (p. 289)

- **Descended:** to go or move from a higher to a lower place or level (p. 289)

- **From:** used to indicate the starting point of a physical movement or action (p. 289)

- **Everyone:** every person (p. 289)

- **Whosoever:** Whoever (p. 291)

- **Whoever:** whatever person / no matter who (p. 291)

- **Eternal:** lasting forever (p. 289)

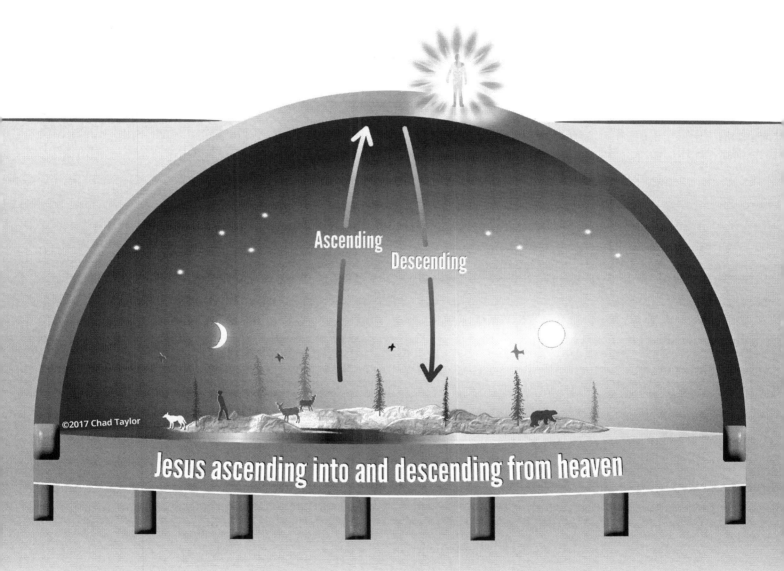

Ascending

Descending

©2017 Chad Taylor

Jesus ascending into and descending from heaven

John 6:47-51

[47] Verily, verily, I say unto you, **He that believeth on me hath everlasting life.** [48] I am that bread of life. [49] Your fathers did eat manna in the wilderness, and are dead. [50] This is the bread which <u>cometh</u> <u>down</u> <u>from</u> heaven, that a man may eat thereof, and not die. [51] I am the living bread which came <u>down</u> <u>from</u> heaven: if <u>any</u> man eat of this bread, he shall live <u>for ever</u>: and the bread that I will give is my flesh, which I will give for the life of the world. John 6:47-51 (KJV)

[47] Very truly I tell you, the one who believes has eternal life. [48] I am the bread of life. [49] Your ancestors ate the manna in the wilderness, yet they died. [50] But here is the bread that comes down from heaven, which anyone may eat and not die. [51] I am the living bread that came down from heaven. Whoever eats this bread will live forever. This bread is my flesh, which I will give for the life of the world." John 6:47-51 (NIV)

[47] Truly, truly, I say to you, <u>whoever</u> believes has <u>eternal</u> life. [48] I am the bread of life. [49] Your fathers ate the manna in the wilderness, and they died. [50] This is the bread that <u>comes</u> <u>down</u> <u>from</u> heaven, so that one may eat of it and not die. [51] I am the living bread that came <u>down</u> <u>from</u> heaven. If <u>anyone</u> eats of this bread, he will live <u>forever</u>. And the bread that I will give for the life of the world is my flesh." John 6:47-51 (ESV)

[47] Very truly, I tell you, <u>whoever</u> believes has eternal life. [48] I am the bread of life. [49] Your ancestors ate the manna in the wilderness, and they died. [50] This is the bread that <u>comes</u> <u>down</u> <u>from</u> heaven, so that one may eat of it and not die. [51] I am the living bread that came <u>down</u> <u>from</u> heaven. <u>Whoever</u> eats of this bread will live <u>forever</u>; and the bread that I will give for the life of the world is my flesh." John 6:47-51 (NRSV)

- **Comes(eth):** to move toward (p. 288)
- **Down:** from a higher to a lower place or position (p. 289)
- **From:** used to indicate the place that something comes out of (p. 289)
- **Any:** any person or persons / anyone (p. 288)
- **Anyone:** any person (p. 288)
- **Whoever:** whatever person / no matter who (p. 291)
- **Eternal:** lasting forever (p. 289)
- **Forever:** for a limitless time (p. 289)

©2017 Chad Taylor

Down

Jesus came down from heaven

Acts 1:6-11

⁶ When they therefore were come together, they asked of him, saying, Lord, wilt thou at this time restore again the kingdom to Israel? ⁷ And he said unto them, It is not for you to know the times or the seasons, which the Father hath put in his own power. ⁸ But ye shall receive power, after that the Holy Ghost is come upon you: and ye shall be witnesses unto me both in Jerusalem, and in all Judaea, and in Samaria, and **unto the <u>uttermost</u> part of the earth. ⁹ And when he had spoken these things, while they beheld, he was taken <u>up</u>; and a cloud received him out of their sight. ¹⁰ And while they looked stedfastly <u>toward</u> heaven as he <u>went up</u>, behold, two men stood by them in white apparel; ¹¹ Which also said, Ye men of Galilee, why stand ye gazing <u>up into</u> heaven? this same Jesus, which is taken <u>up</u> from you <u>into</u> heaven, shall so come in like manner as ye have seen him go <u>into</u> heaven.** Acts 1:6-11 (KJV)

⁶ Then they gathered around him and asked him, "Lord, are you at this time going to restore the kingdom to Israel?" ⁷ He said to them: "It is not for you to know the times or dates the Father has set by his own authority. ⁸ But you will receive power when the Holy Spirit comes on you; and you will be my witnesses in Jerusalem, and in all Judea and Samaria, and to the ends of the earth." ⁹ After he said this, he was taken up before their very eyes, and a cloud hid him from their sight. ¹⁰ They were looking intently up into the sky as he was going, when suddenly two men dressed in white stood beside them. ¹¹ "Men of Galilee," they said, "why do you stand here looking into the sky? This same Jesus, who has been taken from you into heaven, will come back in the same way you have seen him go into heaven." Acts 1:6-11 (NIV)

⁶ So when they had come together, they asked him, "Lord, will you at this time restore the kingdom to Israel?" ⁷ He said to them, "It is not for you to know times or seasons that the Father has fixed by his own authority. ⁸ But you will receive power when the Holy Spirit has come upon you, and you will be my witnesses in Jerusalem and in all Judea and Samaria, and **to the <u>end</u> of the earth." ⁹ And when he had said these things, as they were looking on, he was <u>lifted up</u>, and a cloud took him out of their sight. ¹⁰ And while they were gazing <u>into</u> heaven as he went, behold, two men stood by them in white robes, ¹¹ and said, "Men of Galilee, why do you stand looking <u>into</u> heaven? This Jesus, who was taken <u>up</u> from you <u>into</u> heaven, will come in the <u>same</u> way as you saw him go <u>into</u> heaven."** Acts 1:6-11 (ESV)

⁶ So when they had come together, they asked him, "Lord, is this the time when you will restore the kingdom to Israel?" ⁷ He replied, "It is not for you to know the times or periods that the Father has set by his own authority. ⁸ But you will receive power when the Holy Spirit has come upon you; and you will be my witnesses in Jerusalem, in all Judea and Samaria, and **to the <u>ends</u> of the earth." ⁹ When he had said this, as they were watching, he was <u>lifted up</u>, and a cloud took him out of their sight. ¹⁰ While he was going and they were gazing <u>up toward</u> heaven, suddenly two men in white robes stood by them. ¹¹ They said, "Men of Galilee, why do you stand looking <u>up toward</u> heaven? This Jesus, who has been taken <u>up</u> from you <u>into</u> heaven, will come in the <u>same</u> way as you saw him go <u>into</u> heaven."** Acts 1:6-11 (NRSV)

Up toward / into heaven

Up

End of the earth

Uttermost part of the earth

Jesus taken up in a cloud

©2017 Chad Taylor

Uttermost: outermost (p. 291)

End(s): the part at the edge or limit of an area (p. 289)

Lifted: to raise from a lower to a higher position (p. 290)

Went: to move on a course (p. 291)

Up: toward the sky or ceiling (p. 291)

Toward: in the direction of (p. 291)

Into: to the inside of (p. 290)

Same: in a way that is alike or very similar (p. 290)

Acts 7:55-56

⁵⁵ But he, being full of the Holy Ghost, **looked <u>up</u> stedfastly <u>into</u> heaven, and saw the <u>glory</u> of God, and Jesus <u>standing</u> on the right hand of God,** ⁵⁶ And said, Behold, **I see the heavens <u>opened</u>, and the Son of man <u>standing</u> on the right hand of God.** Acts 7:55-56 (KJV)

⁵⁵ But Stephen, full of the Holy Spirit, looked up to heaven and saw the glory of God, and Jesus standing at the right hand of God. ⁵⁶ "Look," he said, "I see heaven open and the Son of Man standing at the right hand of God." Acts 7:55-56 (NIV)

⁵⁵ But he, full of the Holy Spirit, **gazed <u>into</u> heaven and saw the <u>glory</u> of God, and Jesus <u>standing</u> at the right hand of God.** ⁵⁶ And he said, **"Behold, I see the heavens <u>opened</u>, and the Son of Man <u>standing</u> at the right hand of God."** Acts 7:55-56 (ESV)

⁵⁵ But filled with the Holy Spirit, **he gazed <u>into</u> heaven and saw the <u>glory</u> of God and Jesus <u>standing</u> at the right hand of God.** ⁵⁶ "Look," he said, **"I see the heavens <u>opened</u> and the Son of Man <u>standing</u> at the right hand of God!"** Acts 7:55-56 (NRSV)

⊏⊐ **Up:** toward the sky or ceiling (p. 291)

⊏⊐ **To:** in the direction of (p. 291)

⊏⊐ **Into:** to the inside of (p. 290)

⊏⊐ **Glory:** brilliance, splendor (p. 289)

⊏⊐ **Standing:** to be in an upright position with all of your weight on your feet (p. 291)

⊏⊐ **Open(ed):** to cause (something) to no longer be covered, sealed, or blocked (p. 290)

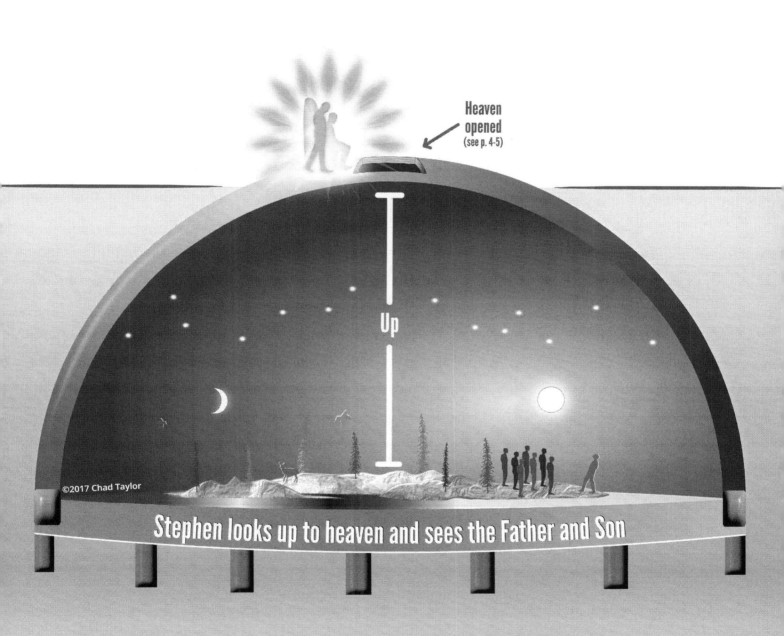

Heaven
opened
(see p. 4-5)

Up

©2017 Chad Taylor

Stephen looks up to heaven and sees the Father and Son

Acts 10:11-12

[11] And saw heaven <u>opened</u>, and a certain vessel <u>descending</u> <u>upon</u> him, as it had been a great sheet knit at the four corners, and <u>let down</u> <u>to</u> the earth: [12] Wherein were all manner of fourfooted beasts of the earth, and wild beasts, and creeping things, and fowls of the air. Acts 10:11-12 (KJV)

[11] He saw heaven opened and something like a large sheet being let down to earth by its four corners. [12] It contained all kinds of four-footed animals, as well as reptiles and birds. Acts 10:11-12 (NIV)

[11] and saw the heavens <u>opened</u> and something like a great sheet <u>descending</u>, being <u>let down</u> by its four corners <u>upon</u> the earth. [12] In it were all kinds of animals and reptiles and birds of the air. Acts 10:11-12 (ESV)

[11] He saw the heaven <u>opened</u> and something like a large sheet coming <u>down</u>, being <u>lowered</u> <u>to</u> the ground by its four corners. [12] In it were all kinds of four-footed creatures and reptiles and birds of the air. Acts 10:11-12 (NRSV)

- **Opened:** to cause (something) to no longer be covered, sealed, or blocked (p. 290)
- **Descending:** to go or move from a higher to a lower place or level (p. 289)
- **Let Down:** to allow to descend gradually (p. 290)
- **Lowered:** to let descend (p. 290)
- **Down:** from a higher to a lower place or position (p. 289)
- **Upon:** On (p. 291)
- **To:** in the direction of (p. 291)

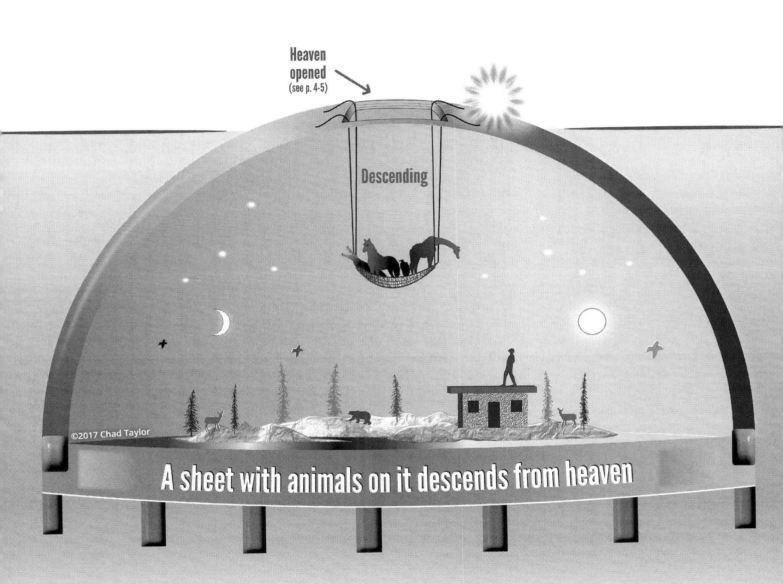

Heaven opened (see p. 4-5)

Descending

©2017 Chad Taylor

A sheet with animals on it descends from heaven

Romans 10:6-7

⁶ But the righteousness which is of faith speaketh on this wise, Say not in thine heart, **Who shall <u>ascend</u> <u>into</u>** heaven? **(that is, to bring Christ <u>down</u> <u>from</u> <u>above</u>:)** ⁷ **Or, Who shall <u>descend</u> <u>into</u> the deep? (that is, to bring <u>up</u> Christ again from the dead.)** Romans 10:6-7 (KJV)

⁶ But the righteousness that is by faith says: "Do not say in your heart, 'Who will ascend into heaven?'" (that is, to bring Christ down) ⁷ "or 'Who will descend into the deep?'" (that is, to bring Christ up from the dead). Romans 10:6-7 (NIV)

⁶ But the righteousness based on faith says, "Do not say in your heart, **'Who will <u>ascend</u> <u>into</u> heaven?'"** **(that is, to bring Christ <u>down</u>)** ⁷ **"or 'Who will <u>descend</u> <u>into</u> the abyss?'" (that is, to bring Christ <u>up</u> from the dead).** Romans 10:6-7 (ESV)

⁶ But the righteousness that comes from faith says, "Do not say in your heart, **'Who will <u>ascend</u> <u>into</u>** heaven?'" **(that is, to bring Christ <u>down</u>)** ⁷ **"or 'Who will <u>descend</u> <u>into</u> the abyss?'" (that is, to bring Christ <u>up</u>** from the dead). Romans 10:6-7 (NRSV)

- **Ascend:** to move upward   (p. 288)
- **Into:** used as a function word to indicate entry, introduction, insertion, superposition, or inclusion   (p. 290)
- **Down:** from a higher to a lower place or position   (p. 289)
- **From:** used to indicate the starting point of a physical movement or action   (p. 289)
- **Above:** in the sky / overhead   (p. 288)
- **Descend:** to go or move from a higher to a lower place or level   (p. 289)
- **Up:** from a lower to a higher place or position   (p. 291)

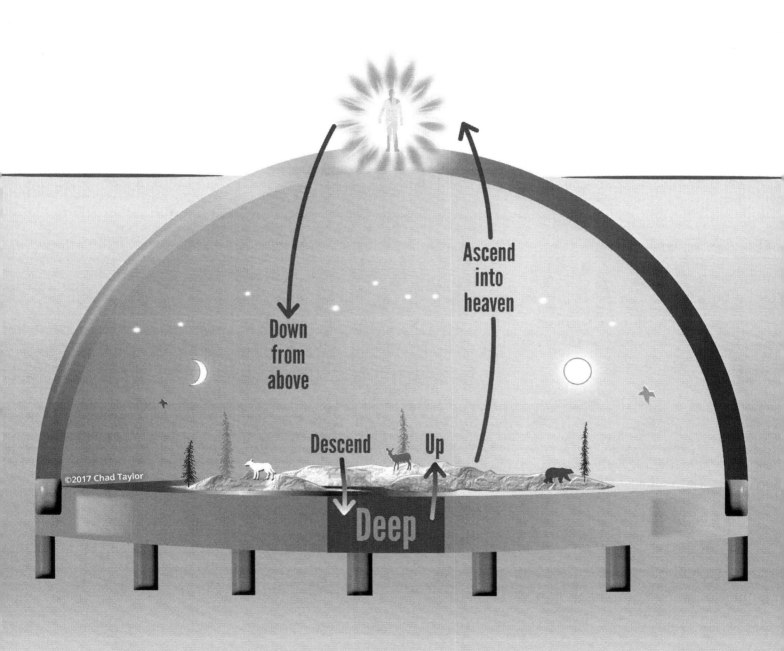

2 Corinthians 12:2-4

^{2} I knew a man in Christ above fourteen years ago, (whether in the body, I cannot tell; or whether out of the body, I cannot tell: God knoweth;) **such an one <u>caught up</u> <u>to</u> the <u>third</u> heaven.** ^{3} And I knew such a man, (whether in the body, or out of the body, I cannot tell: God knoweth;) ^{4} **How that he was <u>caught up into</u> paradise,** and heard unspeakable words, which it is not lawful for a man to utter. 2 Corinthians 12:2-4 (KJV)

^{2} I know a man in Christ who fourteen years ago was caught up to the third heaven. Whether it was in the body or out of the body I do not know—God knows. ^{3} And I know that this man—whether in the body or apart from the body I do not know, but God knows— ^{4} was caught up to paradise and heard inexpressible things, things that no one is permitted to tell. 2 Corinthians 12:2-4 (NIV)

^{2} I know a man in Christ who fourteen years ago **was <u>caught up</u> <u>to</u> the <u>third</u>** heaven—whether in the body or out of the body I do not know, God knows. ^{3} And I know that **this man was <u>caught up into</u> paradise**— whether in the body or out of the body I do not know, God knows— ^{4} and he heard things that cannot be told, which man may not utter. 2 Corinthians 12:2-4 (ESV)

^{2} I know a person in Christ who fourteen years ago **was <u>caught up</u> <u>to</u> the <u>third</u> heaven**—whether in the body or out of the body I do not know; God knows. ^{3} And I know that such a person—whether in the body or out of the body I do not know; God knows— ^{4} **was <u>caught up into</u> Paradise** and heard things that are not to be told, that no mortal is permitted to repeat. 2 Corinthians 12:2-4 (NRSV)

⊏⊐   **Caught up:** to pick up often abruptly (p. 288)

⊏⊐   **To:** used as a function word to indicate contact or proximity (p. 291)

⊏⊐   **Into:** to the inside of (p. 290)

⊏⊐   **Third:** occupying the number three position in a series (p. 291)

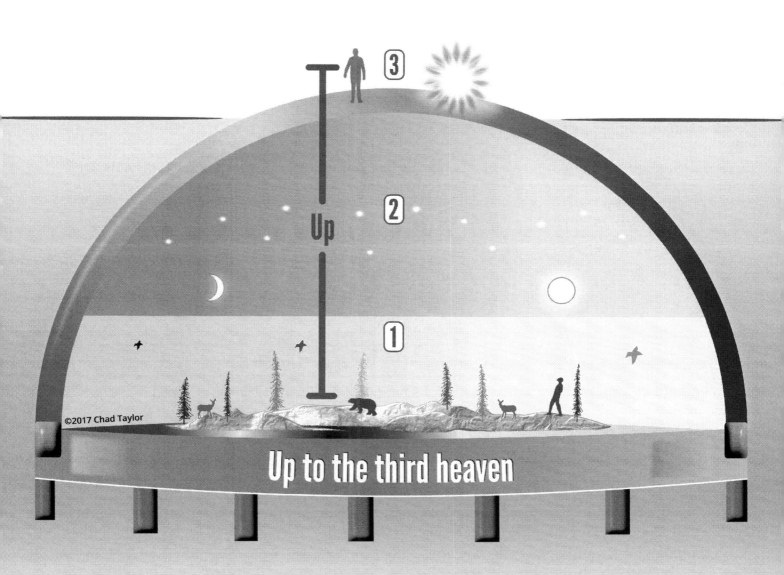

©2017 Chad Taylor

Up to the third heaven

1 Thessalonians 4:13-17

¹³ But I would not have you to be ignorant, brethren, concerning them which are asleep, that ye sorrow not, even as others which have no hope. ¹⁴ **For if we believe that Jesus died and rose again, even so them also which sleep in Jesus will God bring with him.** ¹⁵ For this we say unto you by the word of the Lord, that we which are alive and remain unto the coming of the Lord shall not prevent them which are asleep. ¹⁶ For the Lord himself shall <u>descend</u> <u>from</u> heaven with a shout, with the voice of the archangel, and with the trump of God: and the dead in Christ shall <u>rise</u> first: ¹⁷ <u>Then</u> we which are alive and remain shall be <u>caught up</u> <u>together</u> with them <u>in</u> the clouds, to <u>meet</u> the Lord <u>in</u> the air: and so shall we ever be with the Lord.
1 Thessalonians 4:13-17 (KJV)

¹³ Brothers and sisters, we do not want you to be uninformed about those who sleep in death, so that you do not grieve like the rest of mankind, who have no hope. ¹⁴ For we believe that Jesus died and rose again, and so we believe that God will bring with Jesus those who have fallen asleep in him. ¹⁵ According to the Lord's word, we tell you that we who are still alive, who are left until the coming of the Lord, will certainly not precede those who have fallen asleep. ¹⁶ For the Lord himself will come down from heaven, with a loud command, with the voice of the archangel and with the trumpet call of God, and the dead in Christ will rise first. ¹⁷ After that, we who are still alive and are left will be caught up together with them in the clouds to meet the Lord in the air. And so we will be with the Lord forever. 1 Thessalonians 4:13-17 (NIV)

¹³ But we do not want you to be uninformed, brothers, about those who are asleep, that you may not grieve as others do who have no hope. ¹⁴ **For since we believe that Jesus died and rose again, even so, through Jesus, God will bring with him those who have fallen asleep.** ¹⁵ For this we declare to you by a word from the Lord, that we who are alive, who are left until the coming of the Lord, will not precede those who have fallen asleep. ¹⁶ For the Lord himself will <u>descend</u> <u>from</u> heaven with a cry of command, with the voice of an archangel, and with the sound of the trumpet of God. And the dead in Christ will <u>rise</u> <u>first</u>. ¹⁷ <u>Then</u> we who are alive, who are left, will be <u>caught up</u> <u>together</u> with them <u>in</u> the clouds to <u>meet</u> the Lord <u>in</u> the air, and so we will <u>always</u> be with the Lord. 1 Thessalonians 4:13-17 (ESV)

¹³ But we do not want you to be uninformed, brothers and sisters, about those who have died, so that you may not grieve as others do who have no hope. ¹⁴ **For since we believe that Jesus died and rose again, even so, through Jesus, God will bring with him those who have died.** ¹⁵ For this we declare to you by the word of the Lord, that we who are alive, who are left until the coming of the Lord, will by no means precede those who have died. ¹⁶ For the Lord himself, with a cry of command, with the archangel's call and with the sound of God's trumpet, will <u>descend</u> <u>from</u> heaven, and the dead in Christ will <u>rise</u> <u>first</u>. ¹⁷ <u>Then</u> we who are alive, who are left, will be <u>caught up</u> <u>in</u> the clouds <u>together</u> with them to <u>meet</u> the Lord <u>in</u> the air; and so we will be with the Lord <u>forever</u>. 1 Thessalonians 4:13-17 (NRSV)

©2017 Chad Taylor

Jesus descends from heaven

- ⌷ **Come:** to move toward (p. 288)
- ⌷ **Descend:** to go or move from a higher to a lower place or level (p. 289)
- ⌷ **Down:** from a higher to a lower place or position (p. 289)
- ⌷ **From:** used to indicate the starting point of a physical movement or action (p. 289)
- ⌷ **Rise:** to assume an upright position especially from lying, kneeling, or sitting (p. 290)
- ⌷ **First:** before any other (p. 289)
- ⌷ **Then:** next in order of time (p. 291)
- ⌷ **After:** later in time (p. 288)
- ⌷ **Caught up:** to pick up often abruptly (p. 288)
- ⌷ **Together:** with each other (p. 291)
- ⌷ **In:** within a particular place (p. 290)
- ⌷ **Meet:** to come into the presence of (p. 290)
- ⌷ **Forever:** for a limitless time (p. 289)
- ⌷ **Always:** Forever (p. 288)

Hebrews 4:14

^{14} Seeing then that we have a great high priest, that is <u>passed</u> <u>into</u> the heavens, Jesus the Son of God, let us hold fast our profession. Hebrews 4:14 (KJV)

^{14} Therefore, since we have a great high priest who has ascended into heaven, Jesus the Son of God, let us hold firmly to the faith we profess. Hebrews 4:14 (NIV)

^{14} Since then we have a great high priest who has <u>passed</u> <u>through</u> the heavens, Jesus, the Son of God, let us hold fast our confession. Hebrews 4:14 (ESV)

^{14} Since, then, we have a great high priest who has <u>passed</u> <u>through</u> the heavens, Jesus, the Son of God, let us hold fast to our confession. Hebrews 4:14 (NRSV)

Passed: to move or go into or through a particular place (p. 290)

Into: used as a function word to indicate entry, introduction, insertion, superposition, or inclusion (p. 290)

Through: into one side and out the other side of (something) (p. 291)

Ascended: to move upward (p. 288)

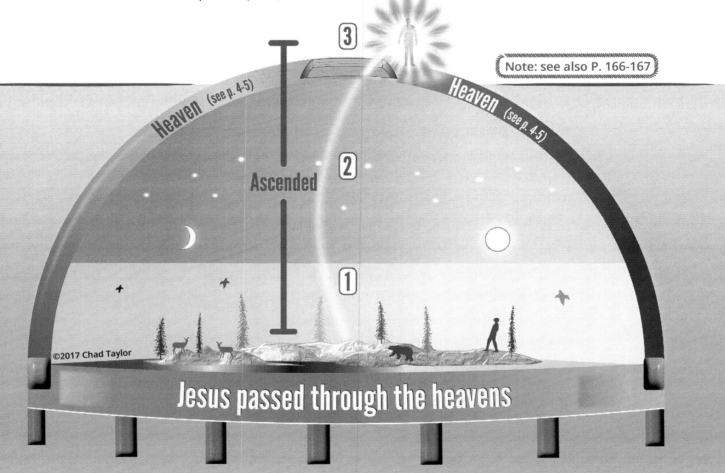

©2017 Chad Taylor

Jesus passed through the heavens

Note: see also P. 166-167

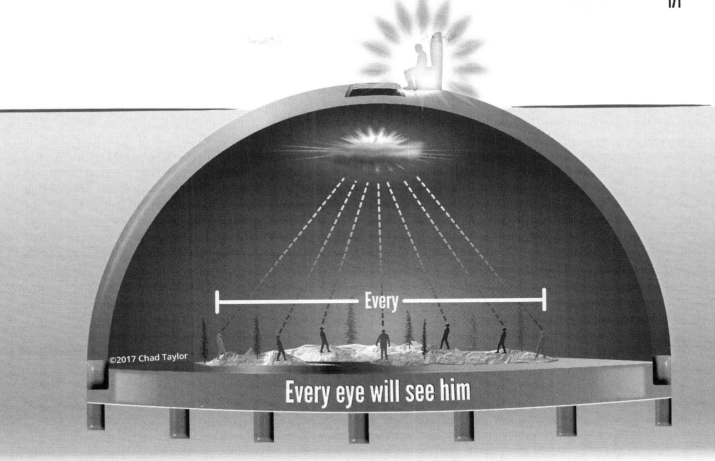

Every

Every eye will see him

©2017 Chad Taylor

Revelation 1:7

⁷ Behold, he cometh with clouds; and <u>every</u> eye shall <u>see</u> him, and they also which pierced him: and <u>all</u> kindreds of the earth shall wail because of him. Even so, Amen. Revelation 1:7 (KJV)

⁷ "Look, he is coming with the clouds," and "every eye will see him, even those who pierced him"; and all peoples on earth "will mourn because of him." So shall it be! Amen. Revelation 1:7 (NIV)

⁷ Behold, he is coming with the clouds, and <u>every</u> eye will <u>see</u> him, even those who pierced him, and <u>all</u> tribes of the earth will wail on account of him. Even so. Amen. Revelation 1:7 (ESV)

⁷ Look! He is coming with the clouds; <u>every</u> eye will <u>see</u> him, even those who pierced him; and on his account <u>all</u> the tribes of the earth will wail. So it is to be. Amen. Revelation 1:7 (NRSV)

- **Every:** including each of a group or series without leaving out any (p. 289)
- **All:** the whole, entire, total amount, quantity, or extent of (p. 288)
- **See:** to perceive by the eye (p. 291)

Revelation 6:12-17

¹² And I beheld when he had opened the sixth seal, and, lo, **there was a great earthquake; and the sun became black as sackcloth of hair, and the moon became as blood;** ¹³ **And the stars of heaven <u>fell</u> <u>unto</u> the earth,** even as a fig tree casteth her untimely figs, when she is shaken of a mighty wind. ¹⁴ **And the heaven <u>departed</u> <u>as</u> a <u>scroll</u> when it is <u>rolled</u> together; and <u>every</u> mountain and island were <u>moved</u> out of their places.** ¹⁵ And the kings of the earth, and the great men, and the rich men, and the chief captains, and the mighty men, **and <u>every</u> bondman, and <u>every</u> free man,** hid themselves in the dens and in the rocks of the mountains; ¹⁶ And said to the mountains and rocks, **Fall on us, and hide us from the <u>face</u> of him that sitteth <u>on</u> the <u>throne</u>, <u>and</u> from the <u>wrath</u> of the Lamb:** ¹⁷ **For the great day of his <u>wrath</u> is come; and who shall be able to stand?**
Revelation 6:12-17 (KJV)

---

¹² I watched as he opened the sixth seal. There was a great earthquake. The sun turned black like sackcloth made of goat hair, the whole moon turned blood red, ¹³ and the stars in the sky fell to earth, as figs drop from a fig tree when shaken by a strong wind. ¹⁴ The heavens receded like a scroll being rolled up, and every mountain and island was removed from its place. ¹⁵ Then the kings of the earth, the princes, the generals, the rich, the mighty, and everyone else, both slave and free, hid in caves and among the rocks of the mountains. ¹⁶ They called to the mountains and the rocks, "Fall on us and hide us from the face of him who sits on the throne and from the wrath of the Lamb! ¹⁷ For the great day of their wrath has come, and who can withstand it?" Revelation 6:12-17 (NIV)

---

¹² When he opened the sixth seal, I looked, and behold, **there was a great earthquake, and the sun became black as sackcloth, the full moon became like blood,** ¹³ **and the stars of the sky <u>fell</u> <u>to</u> the earth** as the fig tree sheds its winter fruit when shaken by a gale. ¹⁴ **The sky vanished <u>like</u> a <u>scroll</u> that is being <u>rolled</u> up, and <u>every</u> mountain and island was <u>removed</u> from its place.** ¹⁵ <u>Then</u> the kings of the earth and the great ones and the generals and the rich and the powerful, **and <u>everyone</u>,** slave and free, hid themselves in the caves and among the rocks of the mountains, ¹⁶ calling to the mountains and rocks, **"Fall on us and hide us from the <u>face</u> of him who is seated <u>on</u> the <u>throne</u>, <u>and</u> from the <u>wrath</u> of the Lamb,** ¹⁷ for the great day of <u>their</u> <u>wrath</u> has come, and who can stand?" Revelation 6:12-17 (ESV)

---

¹² When he opened the sixth seal, I looked, and there came **a great earthquake; the sun became black as sackcloth, the full moon became like blood,** ¹³ **and the stars of the sky <u>fell</u> <u>to</u> the earth <u>as</u> the fig tree <u>drops</u> its winter fruit when shaken by a gale.** ¹⁴ **The sky <u>vanished</u> <u>like</u> a <u>scroll</u> <u>rolling</u> itself up, and <u>every</u> mountain and island was <u>removed</u> from its place.** ¹⁵ <u>Then</u> the kings of the earth and the magnates and the generals and the rich and the powerful, **and <u>everyone</u>,** slave and free, hid in the caves and among the rocks of the mountains, ¹⁶ calling to the mountains and rocks, **"Fall on us and hide us from the <u>face</u> of the one seated <u>on</u> the <u>throne</u> <u>and</u> from the <u>wrath</u> of the Lamb;** ¹⁷ for the great day of <u>their</u> <u>wrath</u> has come, and who is able to stand?"
Revelation 6:12-17 (NRSV)

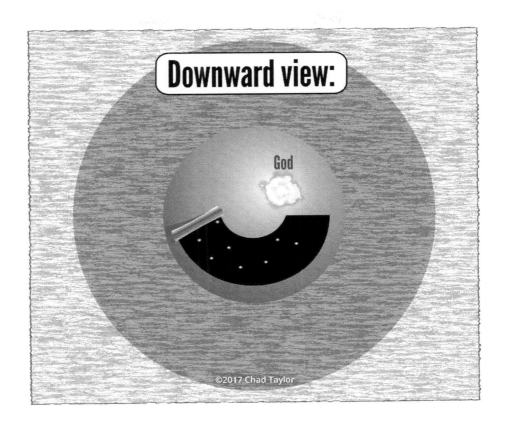

Downward view:

God

©2017 Chad Taylor

☐ **Fell:** to descend freely by the force of gravity (p. 289)

☐ **Unto:** To (p. 291)

☐ **To:** used to indicate the direction of something (p. 291)

☐ **Drop(s):** to fall (p. 289)

☐ **Departed:** to go away (p. 289)

☐ **Receded:** to move back or away (p. 290)

☐ **Rolled/rolling:** to wrap round on itself (p. 290)

☐ **Vanished:** to pass quickly from sight (p. 291)

☐ **As:** in the way that (p. 288)

☐ **Like:** similar to (p. 290)

☐ **Scroll:** a long piece of paper that rolls around one or two cylinders and that usually has something written or drawn on it (p. 290)

☐ **Every:** including each of a group or series without leaving out any (p. 289)

☐ **Moved:** to go from one place or position to another (p. 290)

☐ **Removed:** away from something (p. 290)

☐ **Then:** next in order of time (p. 291)

☐ **Everyone:** every person (p. 289)

☐ **Face:** the front part of the head (p. 289)

☐ **On:** touching and being supported by the top surface of (something) (p. 290)

☐ **Throne:** the special chair for a king, queen, or other powerful person (p. 291)

☐ **And:** plus (p. 288)

☐ **Their:** of or relating to them or themselves especially as owners or as agents or objects of an action (p. 291)

☐ **Wrath:** violent anger / rage (p. 291)

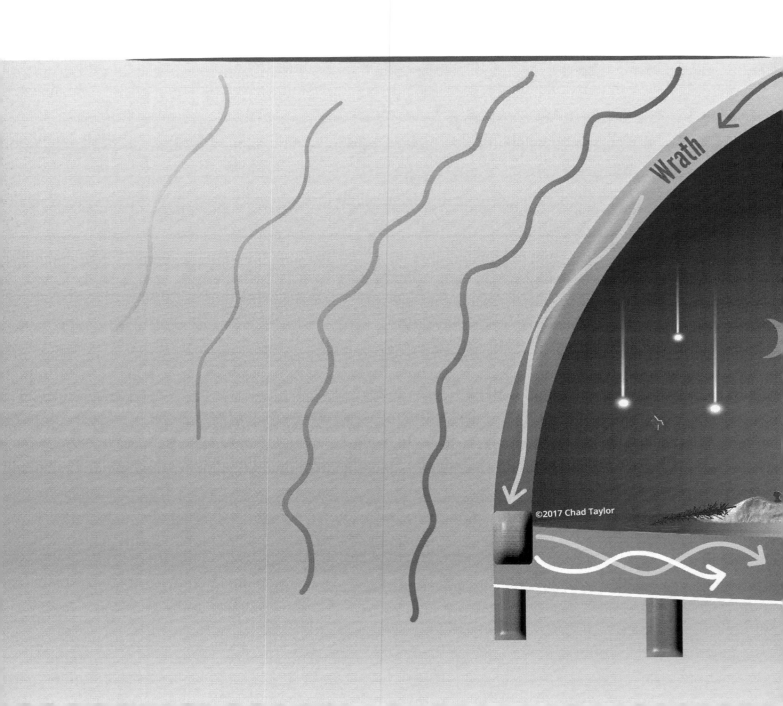

©2017 Chad Taylor

Rolled up like a scroll

Anger

©2017 Chad Taylor

Every mountain and island moves from it's place

Revelation 8:5

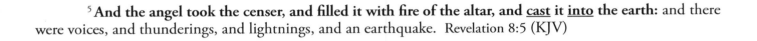

⁵ And the angel took the censer, and filled it with fire of the altar, and <u>cast</u> it <u>into</u> the earth: and there were voices, and thunderings, and lightnings, and an earthquake. Revelation 8:5 (KJV)

⁵ Then the angel took the censer, filled it with fire from the altar, and hurled it on the earth; and there came peals of thunder, rumblings, flashes of lightning and an earthquake. Revelation 8:5 (NIV)

⁵ Then the angel took the censer and filled it with fire from the altar and <u>threw</u> it <u>on</u> the earth, and there were peals of thunder, rumblings, flashes of lightning, and an earthquake. Revelation 8:5 (ESV)

⁵ Then the angel took the censer and filled it with fire from the altar and <u>threw</u> it <u>on</u> the earth; and there were peals of thunder, rumblings, flashes of lightning, and an earthquake. Revelation 8:5 (NRSV)

⁵ Then the angel filled the incense burner with fire from the altar and <u>threw</u> it <u>down</u> <u>upon</u> the earth; and thunder crashed, lightning flashed, and there was a terrible earthquake. Revelation 8:5 (NLT)

⊏⊐   **Cast:** throw (p. 288)

⊏⊐   **Threw:** to propel through the air by a forward motion of the hand and arm (p. 291)

⊏⊐   **Hurled:** to throw (something) with force (p. 289)

⊏⊐   **Into:** to a position of contact with (p. 290)

⊏⊐   **Down:** from a higher to a lower place or position (p. 289)

⊏⊐   **Upon:** on (p. 291)

⊏⊐   **On:** used to indicate the location of something (p. 290)

©2017 Chad Taylor

He threw it to the earth

Revelation 9:1-2

¹ And the fifth angel sounded, **and I saw a star <u>fall</u> <u>from</u> heaven <u>unto</u> the earth: and to <u>him</u> was <u>given</u> the key of the bottomless pit.** ² **And <u>he</u> opened the bottomless pit;** and there arose a smoke out of the pit, as the smoke of a great furnace; and the sun and the air were darkened by reason of the smoke of the pit. Revelation 9:1-2 (KJV)

¹ The fifth angel sounded his trumpet, and I saw a star that had fallen from the sky to the earth. The star was given the key to the shaft of the Abyss. ² When he opened the Abyss, smoke rose from it like the smoke from a gigantic furnace. The sun and sky were darkened by the smoke from the Abyss. Revelation 9:1-2 (NIV)

¹ And the fifth angel blew his trumpet, **and I saw a star <u>fallen</u> <u>from</u> heaven <u>to</u> earth, and <u>he</u> was <u>given</u> the key to the shaft of the bottomless pit.** ² <u>He</u> **opened the shaft of the bottomless pit,** and from the shaft rose smoke like the smoke of a great furnace, and the sun and the air were darkened with the smoke from the shaft. Revelation 9:1-2 (ESV)

¹ And the fifth angel blew his trumpet, and **I saw a star that had <u>fallen</u> <u>from</u> heaven <u>to</u> earth, and <u>he</u> was <u>given</u> the key to the shaft of the bottomless pit;** ² <u>he</u> **opened the shaft of the bottomless pit,** and from the shaft rose smoke like the smoke of a great furnace, and the sun and the air were darkened with the smoke from the shaft. Revelation 9:1-2 (NRSV)

- **Fall/fallen:** to descend freely by the force of gravity (p. 289)
- **From:** used to indicate the starting point of a physical movement or action (p. 289)
- **Unto:** To (p. 291)
- **To:** used to indicate the direction of something (p. 291)
- **Given:** presented as a gift (p. 289)
- **Him:** he (p. 289)
- **He:** that male one (p. 289)

©2017 Chad Taylor

A star falls to earth

Fall

Bottomless Pit

Revelation 10:5-6

[5] And the angel which I saw stand upon the sea and upon the earth **lifted** up his hand **to** heaven, [6] And sware by him that liveth for ever and ever, who created heaven, and the things that therein are, and the earth, and the things that therein are, and the sea, and the things which are therein, that there should be time no longer: Revelation 10:5-6 (KJV)

[5] Then the angel I had seen standing on the sea and on the land raised his right hand to heaven. [6] And he swore by him who lives for ever and ever, who created the heavens and all that is in them, the earth and all that is in it, and the sea and all that is in it, and said, "There will be no more delay! Revelation 10:5-6 (NIV)

[5] And the angel whom I saw standing on the sea and on the land **raised** his right hand **to** heaven [6] and swore by him who lives forever and ever, who created heaven and what is in it, the earth and what is in it, and the sea and what is in it, that there would be no more delay, Revelation 10:5-6 (ESV)

[5] Then the angel whom I saw standing on the sea and the land **raised** his right hand **to** heaven [6] and swore by him who lives forever and ever, who created heaven and what is in it, the earth and what is in it, and the sea and what is in it: "There will be no more delay, Revelation 10:5-6 (NRSV)

[5] Then the angel I saw standing on the sea and on the land **raised** his right hand **toward** heaven. [6] He swore an oath in the name of the one who lives forever and ever, who created the heavens and everything in them, the earth and everything in it, and the sea and everything in it. He said, "There will be no more delay. Revelation 10:5-6 (NLT)

⌐⌐   **Lifted:** to raise from a lower to a higher position   (p. 290)

⌐⌐   **Raised:** to lift up   (p. 290)

⌐⌐   **To:** in the direction of   (p. 291)

⌐⌐   **Toward:** in the direction of   (p. 291)

©2017 Chad Taylor

He raised his hand to heaven

Revelation 11:11-12

[11] And after three days and an half the spirit of life from God entered into them, and they stood upon their feet; and great fear fell upon them which saw them. [12] And **they heard a great voice <u>from</u> heaven saying unto them, Come <u>up</u> hither. And they <u>ascended</u> <u>up</u> <u>to</u> heaven <u>in</u> a cloud;** and their enemies beheld them. Revelation 11:11-12 (KJV)

[11] But after the three and a half days the breath of life from God entered them, and they stood on their feet, and terror struck those who saw them. [12] Then they heard a loud voice from heaven saying to them, "Come up here." And they went up to heaven in a cloud, while their enemies looked on. Revelation 11:11-12 (NIV)

[11] But after the three and a half days a breath of life from God entered them, and they stood up on their feet, and great fear fell on those who saw them. [12] **Then they heard a loud voice <u>from</u> heaven saying to them, "Come <u>up</u> here!" And they <u>went</u> <u>up</u> <u>to</u> heaven <u>in</u> a cloud,** and their enemies watched them. Revelation 11:11-12 (ESV)

[11] But after the three and a half days, the breath of life from God entered them, and they stood on their feet, and those who saw them were terrified. [12] **Then they heard a loud voice <u>from</u> heaven saying to them, "Come <u>up</u> here!" And they <u>went</u> <u>up</u> <u>to</u> heaven <u>in</u> a cloud** while their enemies watched them. Revelation 11:11-12 (NRSV)

- **From:** used to indicate the starting point of a physical movement or action (p. 289)

- **Ascended:** to move upward (p. 288)

- **Went:** to move on a course (p. 291)

- **Up:** toward the sky or ceiling (p. 291)

- **To:** in the direction of (p. 291)

- **In:** used to indicate location or position within something (p. 290)

"Come up here"

Up

©2017 Chad Taylor

They went up to heaven in a cloud

Revelation 12:3-8

³ And there appeared another wonder in heaven; and behold a great red dragon, having seven heads and ten horns, and seven crowns upon his heads. ⁴ **And his tail drew the third part of the stars of heaven, and did cast them to the earth:** and the dragon stood before the woman which was ready to be delivered, for to devour her child as soon as it was born. ⁵ **And she brought forth a man child, who was to rule all nations with a rod of iron: and her child was caught up unto God, and to his throne.** ⁶ And the woman fled into the wilderness, where she hath a place prepared of God, that they should feed her there a thousand two hundred and threescore days. ⁷ **And there was war in heaven: Michael and his angels fought against the dragon; and the dragon fought and his angels,** ⁸ **And prevailed not; neither was their place found any more in heaven.** ⁹ **And the great dragon was cast out, that old serpent, called the Devil, and Satan, which deceiveth the whole world: he was cast out into the earth, and his angels were cast out with him.** Revelation 12:3-8 (KJV)

³ Then another sign appeared in heaven: an enormous red dragon with seven heads and ten horns and seven crowns on its heads. ⁴ Its tail swept a third of the stars out of the sky and flung them to the earth. The dragon stood in front of the woman who was about to give birth, so that it might devour her child the moment he was born. ⁵ She gave birth to a son, a male child, who "will rule all the nations with an iron scepter." And her child was snatched up to God and to his throne. ⁶ The woman fled into the wilderness to a place prepared for her by God, where she might be taken care of for 1,260 days. ⁷ Then war broke out in heaven. Michael and his angels fought against the dragon, and the dragon and his angels fought back. ⁸ But he was not strong enough, and they lost their place in heaven. ⁹ The great dragon was hurled down—that ancient serpent called the devil, or Satan, who leads the whole world astray. He was hurled to the earth, and his angels with him.   Revelation 12:3-8 (NIV)

³ And another sign appeared in heaven: behold, a great red dragon, with seven heads and ten horns, and on his heads seven diadems. ⁴ **His tail swept down a third of the stars of heaven and cast them to the earth.** And the dragon stood before the woman who was about to give birth, so that when she bore her child he might devour it. ⁵ **She gave birth to a male child, one who is to rule all the nations with a rod of iron, but her child was caught up to God and to his throne,** ⁶ and the woman fled into the wilderness, where she has a place prepared by God, in which she is to be nourished for 1,260 days. ⁷ **Now war arose in heaven, Michael and his angels fighting against the dragon. And the dragon and his angels fought back,** ⁸ **but he was defeated, and there was no longer any place for them in heaven.** ⁹ **And the great dragon was thrown down, that ancient serpent, who is called the devil and Satan, the deceiver of the whole world—he was thrown down to the earth, and his angels were thrown down with him.** Revelation 12:3-8 (ESV)

³ Then another portent appeared in heaven: a great red dragon, with seven heads and ten horns, and seven diadems on his heads. ⁴ **His tail swept down a third of the stars of heaven and threw them to the earth.** Then the dragon stood before the woman who was about to bear a child, so that he might devour her child as soon as it was born. ⁵ **And she gave birth to a son, a male child, who is to rule all the nations with a rod of iron. But her child was snatched away and taken to God and to his throne;** ⁶ and the woman fled into the wilderness, where she has a place prepared by God, so that there she can be nourished for one thousand two hundred sixty days. ⁷ **And war broke out in heaven; Michael and his angels fought against the dragon. The dragon and his angels fought back,** ⁸ **but they were defeated, and there was no longer any place for them in heaven.** ⁹ **The great dragon was thrown down, that ancient serpent, who is called the Devil and Satan, the deceiver of the whole world—he was thrown down to the earth, and his angels were thrown down with him.**
Revelation 12:3-8 (NRSV)

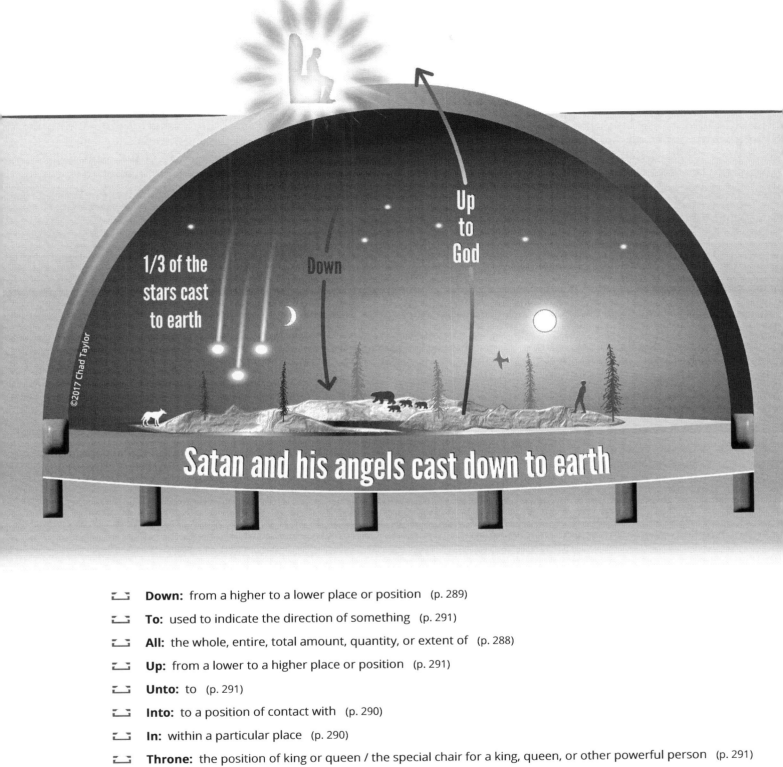

1/3 of the stars cast to earth

Down

Up to God

©2017 Chad Taylor

Satan and his angels cast down to earth

☐ **Down:** from a higher to a lower place or position (p. 289)

☐ **To:** used to indicate the direction of something (p. 291)

☐ **All:** the whole, entire, total amount, quantity, or extent of (p. 288)

☐ **Up:** from a lower to a higher place or position (p. 291)

☐ **Unto:** to (p. 291)

☐ **Into:** to a position of contact with (p. 290)

☐ **In:** within a particular place (p. 290)

☐ **Throne:** the position of king or queen / the special chair for a king, queen, or other powerful person (p. 291)

☐ **Cast Out:** to drive out / expel (p. 288)

☐ **Deceive(th/r):** to make (someone) believe something that is not true (p. 289)

☐ **Whole:** not lacking or leaving out any part (p. 291)

☐ **Astray:** away from what is right, good, or desirable (p. 288)

Revelation 17:7-8

⁷ And the angel said unto me, Wherefore didst thou marvel? **I will tell thee the mystery of the woman, and of the beast that carrieth her, which hath the seven heads and ten horns.** ⁸ The beast that thou sawest was, and is not; and shall <u>ascend</u> <u>out</u> of the bottomless pit, and go into perdition: and they that dwell on the earth shall wonder, whose names were not written in the book of life from the foundation of the world, when they behold the beast that was, and is not, and yet is. Revelation 17:7-8 (KJV)

⁷ Then the angel said to me: "Why are you astonished? I will explain to you the mystery of the woman and of the beast she rides, which has the seven heads and ten horns. ⁸ The beast, which you saw, once was, now is not, and yet will come up out of the Abyss and go to its destruction. The inhabitants of the earth whose names have not been written in the book of life from the creation of the world will be astonished when they see the beast, because it once was, now is not, and yet will come. Revelation 17:7-8 (NIV)

⁷ But the angel said to me, "Why do you marvel? **I will tell you the mystery of the woman, and of the beast with seven heads and ten horns that carries her.** ⁸ The beast that you saw was, and is not, and is about to <u>rise</u> <u>from</u> the bottomless pit and go to destruction. And the dwellers on earth whose names have not been written in the book of life from the foundation of the world will marvel to see the beast, because it was and is not and is to come. Revelation 17:7-8 (ESV)

⁷ But the angel said to me, "Why are you so amazed? **I will tell you the mystery of the woman, and of the beast with seven heads and ten horns that carries her.** ⁸ The beast that you saw was, and is not, and is about to <u>ascend</u> <u>from</u> the bottomless pit and go to destruction. And the inhabitants of the earth, whose names have not been written in the book of life from the foundation of the world, will be amazed when they see the beast, because it was and is not and is to come. Revelation 17:7-8 (NRSV)

⁷ "Why are you so amazed?" the angel asked. "**I will tell you the mystery of this woman and of the beast with seven heads and ten horns on which she sits.** ⁸ The beast you saw was once alive but isn't now. And yet he will soon <u>come</u> <u>up</u> <u>out</u> of the bottomless pit and go to eternal destruction. And the people who belong to this world, whose names were not written in the Book of Life before the world was made, will be amazed at the <u>reappearance</u> of this beast who had died. Revelation 17:7-8 (NLT)

The woman and the beast

Bottomless Pit

©2017 Chad Taylor

Up

☐ **Ascend:** to move upward   (p. 288)

☐ **Rise:** to move upward   (p. 290)

☐ **Come:** to move toward   (p. 288)

☐ **Up:** from a lower to a higher place or position   (p. 291)

☐ **Out:** in or to a place outside of something   (p. 290)

☐ **From:** used to indicate the place that something comes out of   (p. 289)

☐ **Reappearance:** to appear again   (p. 290)

Revelation 18:1

[1] And after these things I saw <u>Another</u> angel <u>come</u> <u>down</u> <u>from</u> heaven, having great power; and the earth was <u>lightened</u> with his <u>glory</u>. Revelation 18:1 (KJV)

[1] After this I saw another angel coming down from heaven. He had great authority, and the earth was illuminated by his splendor. Revelation 18:1 (NIV)

[1] After this I saw <u>another</u> angel <u>coming</u> <u>down</u> <u>from</u> heaven, having great authority, and the earth was made <u>bright</u> with his <u>glory</u>. Revelation 18:1 (ESV)

[1] After this I saw <u>another</u> angel <u>coming</u> <u>down</u> <u>from</u> heaven, having great authority; and the earth was made <u>bright</u> with his <u>splendor</u>. Revelation 18:1 (NRSV)

⌐⌐   **Another:** one that is different   (p. 288)

⌐⌐   **Come/Coming:** to move toward   (p. 288)

⌐⌐   **Down:** from a higher to a lower place or position   (p. 289)

⌐⌐   **From:** used to indicate the place that something comes out of   (p. 289)

⌐⌐   **Lightened:** to make light or clear / illuminate   (p. 290)

⌐⌐   **Illuminated:** brightened with light   (p. 289)

⌐⌐   **Bright:** filled with light   (p. 288)

⌐⌐   **Glory:** brilliance, splendor   (p. 289)

⌐⌐   **Splendor:** great brightness or luster   (p. 291)

Down

Another angel comes down, illuminating the earth

©2017 Chad Taylor

Revelation 20:1-3

¹ And I saw an angel <u>come</u> <u>down</u> <u>from</u> heaven, having the key of the bottomless pit and a great chain in his hand. ² And he laid hold on the dragon, that old serpent, which <u>is</u> the Devil, <u>and</u> Satan, and bound him a thousand years, ³ And cast him <u>into</u> the bottomless pit, and shut him up, and set a seal upon him, that he should <u>deceive</u> the nations no more, <u>till</u> the thousand years should be fulfilled: and <u>after</u> that he must be loosed a little season. Revelation 20:1-3 (KJV)

¹ And I saw an angel coming down out of heaven, having the key to the Abyss and holding in his hand a great chain. ² He seized the dragon, that ancient serpent, who is the devil, or Satan, and bound him for a thousand years. ³ He threw him into the Abyss, and locked and sealed it over him, to keep him from deceiving the nations anymore until the thousand years were ended. After that, he must be set free for a short time. Revelation 20:1-3 (NIV)

¹ Then I saw an angel <u>coming</u> <u>down</u> <u>from</u> heaven, holding in his hand the key to the bottomless pit and a great chain. ² And he seized the dragon, that ancient serpent, who <u>is</u> the devil <u>and</u> Satan, and bound him for a thousand years, ³ and threw him into the pit, and shut it and sealed it over him, so that he might not <u>deceive</u> the nations any longer, <u>until</u> the thousand years were ended. <u>After</u> that he must be released for a little while. Revelation 20:1-3 (ESV)

¹ Then I saw an angel <u>coming</u> <u>down</u> <u>from</u> heaven, holding in his hand the key to the bottomless pit and a great chain. ² He seized the dragon, that ancient serpent, who <u>is</u> the Devil <u>and</u> Satan, and bound him for a thousand years, ³ and threw him <u>into</u> the pit, and locked and sealed it over him, so that he would <u>deceive</u> the nations no more, <u>until</u> the thousand years were ended. <u>After</u> that he must be let out for a little while. Revelation 20:1-3 (NRSV)

Down

An angel comes down

Bottomless Pit

©2017 Chad Taylor

⌐⌐   **Come/Coming:** to move toward   (p. 288)

⌐⌐   **Down:** from a higher to a lower place or position   (p. 289)

⌐⌐   **From:** used to indicate the starting point of a physical movement or action   (p. 289)

⌐⌐   **Out:** away from a particular place   (p. 290)

⌐⌐   **Is:** to equal in meaning   (p. 290)

⌐⌐   **And:** plus   (p. 288)

⌐⌐   **Or:** either   (p. 290)

⌐⌐   **Into:** to the inside of   (p. 290)

⌐⌐   **Deceive/Deceiving:** to make (someone) believe something that is not true   (p. 289)

⌐⌐   **Until/Till:** up to (a particular time)   (p. 291)

⌐⌐   **After:** later in time   (p. 288)

Revelation 20:7-9

⁷ And when the thousand years are <u>expired</u>, Satan shall be loosed out of his prison, ⁸ And shall go out to <u>deceive</u> the nations which are in the four <u>quarters</u> of the earth, Gog, and Magog, to gather them together to battle: the number of whom is as the sand of the sea. ⁹ And they went up on the <u>breadth</u> of the earth, and <u>compassed</u> the camp of the saints about, and the beloved city: and fire came <u>down</u> <u>from</u> God <u>out</u> of heaven, and devoured them. Revelation 20:7-9 (KJV)

⁷ When the thousand years are over, Satan will be released from his prison ⁸ and will go out to deceive the nations in the four corners of the earth—Gog and Magog—and to gather them for battle. In number they are like the sand on the seashore. ⁹ They marched across the breadth of the earth and surrounded the camp of God's people, the city he loves. But fire came down from heaven and devoured them. Revelation 20:7-9 (NIV)

⁷ And when the thousand years are ended, Satan will be released from his prison ⁸ and will come out to <u>deceive</u> the nations that are at the four <u>corners</u> of the earth, Gog and Magog, to gather them for battle; their number is like the sand of the sea. ⁹ And they marched up over the <u>broad</u> <u>plain</u> of the earth and surrounded the camp of the saints and the beloved city, but fire came <u>down</u> <u>from</u> heaven and consumed them,
Revelation 20:7-9 (ESV)

⁷ When the thousand years are ended, Satan will be released from his prison ⁸ and will come out to <u>deceive</u> the nations at the four <u>corners</u> of the earth, Gog and Magog, in order to gather them for battle; they are as numerous as the sands of the sea. ⁹ They marched up over the <u>breadth</u> of the earth and surrounded the camp of the saints and the beloved city. And fire came <u>down</u> <u>from</u> heaven and consumed them.
Revelation 20:7-9 (NRSV)

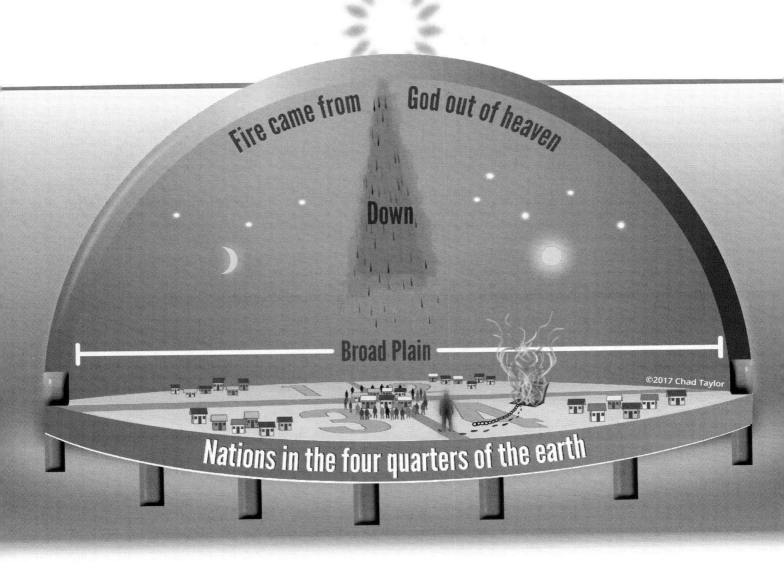

Fire came from God out of heaven

Down

Broad Plain

©2017 Chad Taylor

Nations in the four quarters of the earth

- ⌐⌐ **Quarters:** any of various units of length or area equal to one fourth of some larger unit (p. 290)
- ⌐⌐ **Expired:** to come to an end (p. 289)
- ⌐⌐ **Deceive:** to make (someone) believe something that is not true (p. 289)
- ⌐⌐ **Corners:** a private, secret, or remote place (p. 288)
- ⌐⌐ **Across:** from one side to the other (p. 288)
- ⌐⌐ **Breadth:** something of full width (p. 288)
- ⌐⌐ **Broad:** having ample extent from side to side or between limits (p. 288)
- ⌐⌐ **Plain:** a broad unbroken expanse (p. 290)
- ⌐⌐ **Compassed:** to extend or stretch around; hem in; surround; encircle (p. 288)
- ⌐⌐ **Down:** from a higher to a lower place or position (p. 289)
- ⌐⌐ **From:** used to indicate the starting point of a physical movement or action (p. 289)
- ⌐⌐ **Out:** away from a particular place (p. 290)

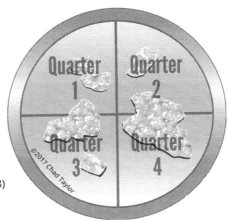

Downward View

Revelation 21:1-4

¹ And I saw a <u>new</u> heaven and a <u>new</u> earth: for the <u>first</u> heaven and the <u>first</u> earth were <u>passed away</u>; and there was no more sea. ² And I John saw the holy city, <u>new</u> Jerusalem, <u>coming</u> <u>down</u> <u>from</u> God <u>out</u> of heaven, prepared as a bride adorned for her husband. ³ And I heard a great voice out of heaven saying, Behold, the <u>tabernacle</u> of God is <u>with</u> men, and he will <u>dwell</u> <u>with</u> them, and they shall be his people, and God himself shall be <u>with</u> them, and be their God. ⁴ And God shall wipe away <u>all</u> tears from their eyes; and there shall be no more death, neither sorrow, nor crying, neither shall there be any more pain: for the former things are <u>passed</u> <u>away</u>. Revelation 21:1-4 (KJV)

¹ Then I saw "a new heaven and a new earth," for the first heaven and the first earth had passed away, and there was no longer any sea. ² I saw the Holy City, the new Jerusalem, coming down out of heaven from God, prepared as a bride beautifully dressed for her husband. ³ And I heard a loud voice from the throne saying, "Look! God's dwelling place is now among the people, and he will dwell with them. They will be his people, and God himself will be with them and be their God. ⁴ 'He will wipe every tear from their eyes. There will be no more death' or mourning or crying or pain, for the old order of things has passed away."   Revelation 21:1-4 (NIV)

¹ Then I saw a <u>new</u> heaven and a <u>new</u> earth, for the <u>first</u> heaven and the <u>first</u> earth had <u>passed away</u>, and the sea was no more. ² And I saw the holy city, <u>new</u> Jerusalem, <u>coming</u> <u>down</u> <u>out</u> of heaven <u>from</u> God, prepared as a bride adorned for her husband. ³ And I heard a loud voice <u>from</u> the <u>throne</u> saying, "Behold, the <u>dwelling</u> place of God is <u>with</u> man. He will <u>dwell</u> with them, and they will be his people, and God himself will be <u>with</u> them as their God. ⁴ He will wipe away <u>every</u> tear from their eyes, and death shall be no more, neither shall there be mourning, nor crying, nor pain anymore, for the former things have <u>passed away</u>." Revelation 21:1-4 (ESV)

¹ Then I saw a <u>new</u> heaven and a <u>new</u> earth; for the <u>first</u> heaven and the <u>first</u> earth had <u>passed away</u>, and the sea was no more. ² And I saw the holy city, the <u>new</u> Jerusalem, <u>coming</u> <u>down</u> <u>out</u> of heaven <u>from</u> God, prepared as a bride adorned for her husband. ³ And I heard a loud voice <u>from</u> the <u>throne</u> saying, "See, the <u>home</u> of God is <u>among</u> mortals. He will <u>dwell</u> <u>with</u> them; they will be his peoples, and God himself will be <u>with</u> them; ⁴ he will wipe <u>every</u> tear from their eyes. Death will be no more; mourning and crying and pain will be no more, for the first things have <u>passed away</u>." Revelation 21:1-4 (NRSV)

Note: see also P. 222-223

Coming down from God out of heaven

A new heaven, new earth and new Jerusalem

©2017 Chad Taylor

- **New:** having recently come into existence / being other than the former or old (p. 290)
- **First:** before any other (p. 289)
- **Passed Away:** to go out of existence (p. 290)
- **Coming:** an act or instance of arriving (p. 288)
- **Down:** from a higher to a lower place or position (p. 289)
- **From:** used to indicate the starting point of a physical movement or action (p. 289)
- **Out:** in or to a place outside of something (p. 290)
- **Throne:** the position of king or queen / the special chair for a king, queen, or other powerful person (p. 291)
- **Tabernacle:** a dwelling place (p. 291)
- **Home:** one's place of residence (p. 289)
- **Dwell(ing):** to live in a particular place (p. 289)
- **With:** in the company of (p. 291)
- **Among:** in the presence of (p. 288)
- **All:** the whole, entire, total amount, quantity, or extent of (p. 288)
- **Every:** including each of a group or series without leaving out any (p. 289)

Revelation 21:22-27

²² And I saw no temple therein: for the Lord God Almighty <u>and</u> the Lamb <u>are</u> the temple of it. ²³ And the city had no need of the sun, neither of the moon, to shine in it: for the <u>glory</u> of God did lighten it, and the Lamb <u>is</u> the light thereof. ²⁴ **And the nations of them which are saved shall walk in the light of it**: and the kings of the earth do bring **their <u>glory</u> and honour into it.** ²⁵ And the gates of it shall not be shut at all by day: **for there shall be no night there.** ²⁶ And they shall bring the glory and honour of the nations into it. ²⁷ And there shall in no wise enter into it any thing that defileth, neither whatsoever worketh abomination, or maketh a lie: **but they which are written in the Lamb's book of life.** Revelation 21:22-27 (KJV)

²² I did not see a temple in the city, because the Lord God Almighty and the Lamb are its temple. ²³ The city does not need the sun or the moon to shine on it, for the glory of God gives it light, and the Lamb is its lamp. ²⁴ The nations will walk by its light, and the kings of the earth will bring their splendor into it. ²⁵ On no day will its gates ever be shut, for there will be no night there. ²⁶ The glory and honor of the nations will be brought into it. ²⁷ Nothing impure will ever enter it, nor will anyone who does what is shameful or deceitful, but only those whose names are written in the Lamb's book of life. Revelation 21:22-27 (NIV)

²² And I saw no temple in the city, for its temple <u>is</u> the Lord God the Almighty <u>and</u> the Lamb. ²³ And the city has no need of sun or moon to shine on it, for the <u>glory</u> of God gives it light, and its lamp <u>is</u> the Lamb. ²⁴ **By its light will the nations walk, and the kings of the earth will bring their <u>glory</u> into it,** ²⁵ and its gates will never be shut by day—**and there will be no night there.** ²⁶ They will bring into it the glory and the honor of the nations. ²⁷ But nothing unclean will ever enter it, nor anyone who does what is detestable or false, **but <u>only</u> those who are written in the Lamb's book of life.** Revelation 21:22-27 (ESV)

²² I saw no temple in the city, for its temple <u>is</u> the Lord God the Almighty <u>and</u> the Lamb. ²³ And the city has no need of sun or moon to shine on it, for the <u>glory</u> of God is its light, and its lamp <u>is</u> the Lamb. ²⁴ **The nations will walk by its light, and the kings of the earth will bring their <u>glory</u> into it.** ²⁵ Its gates will never be shut by day—**and there will be no night there.** ²⁶ People will bring into it the glory and the honor of the nations. ²⁷ But nothing unclean will enter it, nor anyone who practices abomination or falsehood, **but <u>only</u> those who are written in the Lamb's book of life.** Revelation 21:22-27 (NRSV)

©2017 Chad Taylor

Note: see also P. 222-223

- ☐ **Are:** to have a specified qualification or characterization   (p. 288)
- ☐ **Is:** to equal in meaning   (p. 290)
- ☐ **And:** plus   (p. 288)
- ☐ **Glory:** brilliance, splendor   (p. 289)
- ☐ **Illuminates:** brightened with light   (p. 289)
- ☐ **Is:** to have a specified qualification or characterization   (p. 290)
- ☐ **Only:** excluding all others / nobody or nothing except   (p. 290)

Revelation 22:1-5

[1] And he shewed me a pure river of water of life, clear as crystal, proceeding out of the throne of God and of the Lamb. [2] In the midst of the street of it, and on either side of the river, was there the tree of life, which bare twelve manner of fruits, and yielded her fruit every month: and the leaves of the tree were for the healing of the nations. [3] And there shall be no more curse: but the throne of God and of the Lamb shall be in it; and his servants shall serve him: [4] And they shall see his face; and his name shall be in their foreheads. [5] And there shall be no night there; and they need no candle, neither light of the sun; for the Lord God giveth them light: and they shall reign for ever and ever. Revelation 22:1-5 (KJV)

[1] Then the angel showed me the river of the water of life, as clear as crystal, flowing from the throne of God and of the Lamb [2] down the middle of the great street of the city. On each side of the river stood the tree of life, bearing twelve crops of fruit, yielding its fruit every month. And the leaves of the tree are for the healing of the nations. [3] No longer will there be any curse. The throne of God and of the Lamb will be in the city, and his servants will serve him. [4] They will see his face, and his name will be on their foreheads. [5] There will be no more night. They will not need the light of a lamp or the light of the sun, for the Lord God will give them light. And they will reign for ever and ever. Revelation 22:1-5 (NIV)

[1] Then the angel showed me the river of the water of life, bright as crystal, flowing from the throne of God and of the Lamb [2] through the middle of the street of the city; also, on either side of the river, the tree of life with its twelve kinds of fruit, yielding its fruit each month. The leaves of the tree were for the healing of the nations. [3] No longer will there be anything accursed, but the throne of God and of the Lamb will be in it, and his servants will worship him. [4] They will see his face, and his name will be on their foreheads. [5] And night will be no more. They will need no light of lamp or sun, for the Lord God will be their light, and they will reign forever and ever. Revelation 22:1-5 (ESV)

[1] Then the angel showed me the river of the water of life, bright as crystal, flowing from the throne of God and of the Lamb [2] through the middle of the street of the city. On either side of the river is the tree of life with its twelve kinds of fruit, producing its fruit each month; and the leaves of the tree are for the healing of the nations. [3] Nothing accursed will be found there any more. But the throne of God and of the Lamb will be in it, and his servants will worship him; [4] they will see his face, and his name will be on their foreheads. [5] And there will be no more night; they need no light of lamp or sun, for the Lord God will be their light, and they will reign forever and ever. Revelation 22:1-5 (NRSV)

©2017 Chad Taylor

200

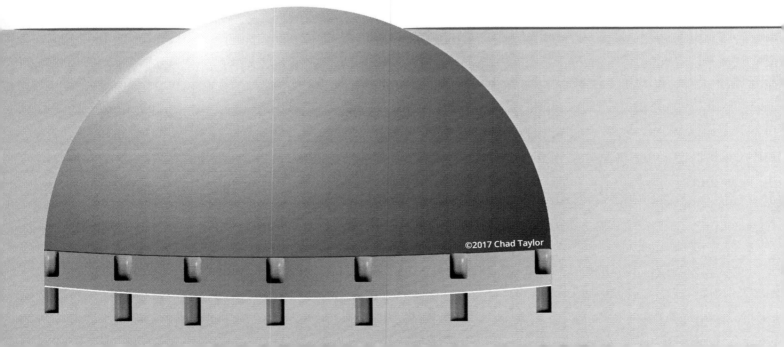

PART FOUR

Common Themes and Review

For ever since the world was created, people have seen the earth and sky. Through everything God made, they can clearly see his invisible qualities—his eternal power and divine nature. So they have no excuse for not knowing God.

- Romans 1:20 (NLT)

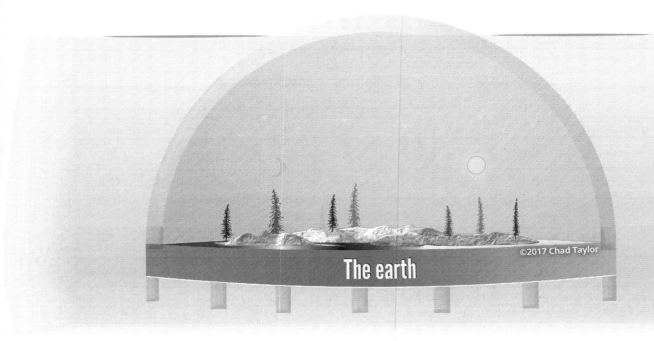

The earth

- The earth can not be moved. See pages: 22, 37, 40

- The earth is circle shaped, (when viewed from above). See pages: 26, 46, 50, 108

- The earth is spread out / abroad. See pages: 52, 55

- The earth is a broad plain / face. See pages: 12, 59, 70, 74, 102, 136, 144, 146, 171, 192

- The earth has ends / outermost parts. See pages: 32, 56, 100, 102, 108, 136, 158

- The earth is set on foundations / pillars. See pages: 20, 30, 38, 40, 46, 54, 58, 96, 99

- The earth is not hanging. See page: 26

- The earth has borders / boundaries. See pages: 26, 34, 46

- The earth is underneath the firmament.
  See pages: 6, 10, 32, 50, 54, 56, 58, 70, 74, 92, 100, 114, 116, 128, 132, 136, 146, 160, 162, 172, 176, 184, 194

- The earth has four quarters / corners. See pages: 101, 108, 192

- The earth trembles / quakes. See pages: 26, 36, 56, 96, 110, 114, 124, 138, 172

- The earth has edges / skirts. See page: 102

- The earth has a place it sits. See page: 110

- The earth is God's footstool. See page 55

Foundations of the earth

©2017 Chad Taylor

Foundations of the earth

- ▭ The earth is set on foundations. See pages: 20, 30, 38, 40, 46, 54, 58, 96, 114

- ▭ The foundations of the earth are also called pillars: See pages: 20, 36, 99

- ▭ The foundations can not be searched out. See page: 58

- ▭ God holds earth's foundations steady. See page: 36

- ▭ God laid the foundations of the earth. See pages: 30, 38, 40, 54

- ▭ Man can not measure earth's foundations, but God did. See page: 30

- ▭ The foundation of the earth has a cornerstone. See page: 30

- ▭ The foundations of the earth were exposed. See page: 96

- ▭ The foundations of the earth were marked out. See page: 46

- ▭ The foundations of the earth can shake. See pages: 99, 114

- ▭ The foundations of the earth are attached to something else. See page: 30

- ▭ The foundation of the earth is on a level plain, God measured across it. See page: 30

The firmament

- The firmament is also referred to as a dome, vault, expanse, sky, heaven, curtain, and a tent/tabernacle for the sun. See pages: 4, 6, 8, 10, 24, 40, 50, 59, 114, 128

- The firmament and the heavens are above us, over the earth.
  See pages: 6, 10, 32, 50, 54, 56, 58, 70, 74, 92, 100, 114, 116, 128, 132, 136, 146, 160, 162, 172, 176, 184, 194

- The firmament is set in place. See page: 46

- The firmament sits on foundations which are on the earth. See pages: 29, 59, 96

- The firmament is firm / strong. See pages: 28, 46

- The firmament can shake / tremble. See pages: 110, 138

- There are ends to the firmament. See pages: 32, 146

- The firmament contains the sun, moon and stars. See pages: 8, 32, 48, 64, 94, 116

- The firmament can not be measured. See pages: 58, 104

- The firmament proclaims God's handiwork. See page: 32

- The firmament has four quarters. See page: 126

- The firmament is like crystal / glass. See page: 28, 128

- The firmament has windows and other openings.
  See pages: 68, 70, 80, 96, 114, 116, 124, 152 (x2), 160, 162, 172, 176

- The firmament separates the waters above from the waters below, down here.
  See pages: 4, 24, 40, 44, 68, 70

- The firmament is stretched out. See pages: 28, 32, 40, 50, 52, 56, 58, 59, 99, 128

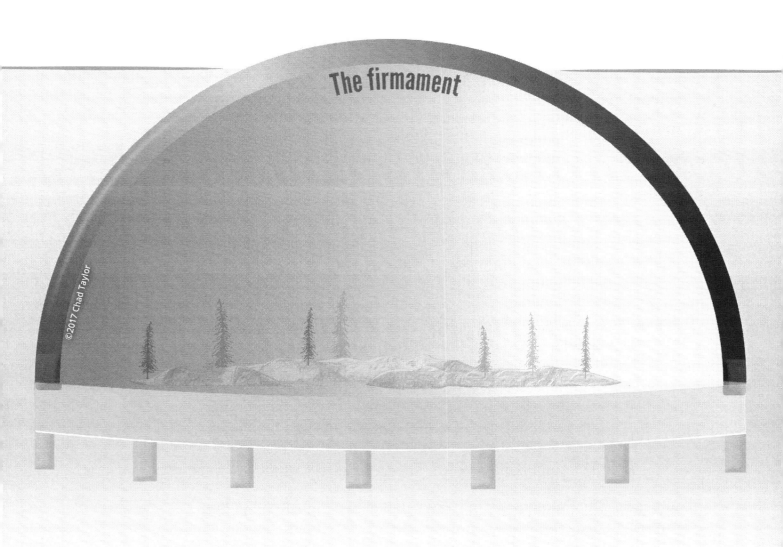

Foundations of heaven

- The foundations of heaven are on the earth. See pages: 59, 96

- The foundations of heaven are also called pillars: See page: 26

- The foundations of heaven can shake / tremble. See pages: 26, 96

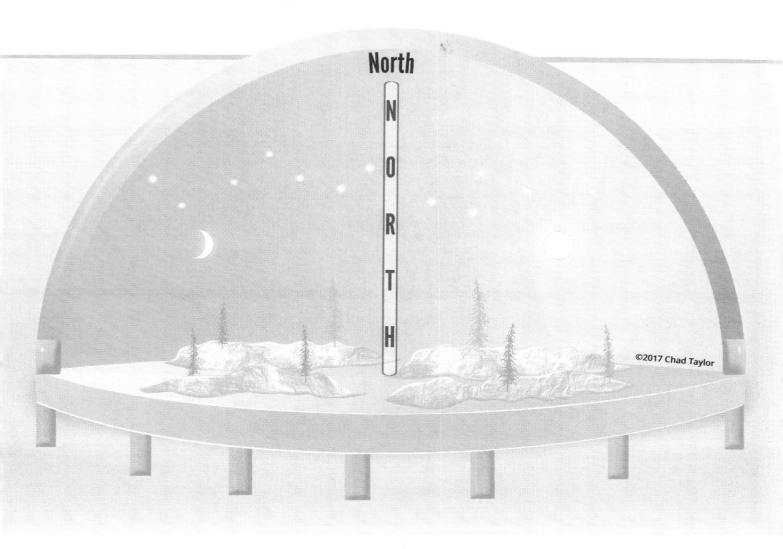

North

©2017 Chad Taylor

The North

▢ **The north is over empty space.** See page: 26

▢ **God comes out of the north.** See page: 28

▢ **North is the location of "The" heaven and the mount of the congregation.** See page: 112

▢ **Ezekiel's vision in Ezekiel chapter one came out of the north.** See page: 128

▢ **God's golden splendor comes out of the north.** See pages: 28, 252

Lights in the firmament

☐ **The sun, moon and stars are inside the firmament.** See pages: 8, 32, 48, 64, 94, 116, 140, 146

☐ **The sun has a course that it runs.** See pages: 32, 48, 94, 99

☐ **The sun, moon and stars are above the earth.** See pages: 8, 92, 94, 106, 116, 134, 172, 178, 184

☐ **The moon gives off it's own light.** See pages: 8, 110, 122, 134, 138, 146, 172, 196

☐ **God can stop the sun on it's course. He can also have it go backwards.** See also: 94, 118, 140

☐ **There can be life without the sun.** See pages: 6, 26, 110, 122, 138, 172, 196, 198

☐ **God can stop the sun, moon and stars from shining.** See pages: 99, 110, 134, 138, 146, 172

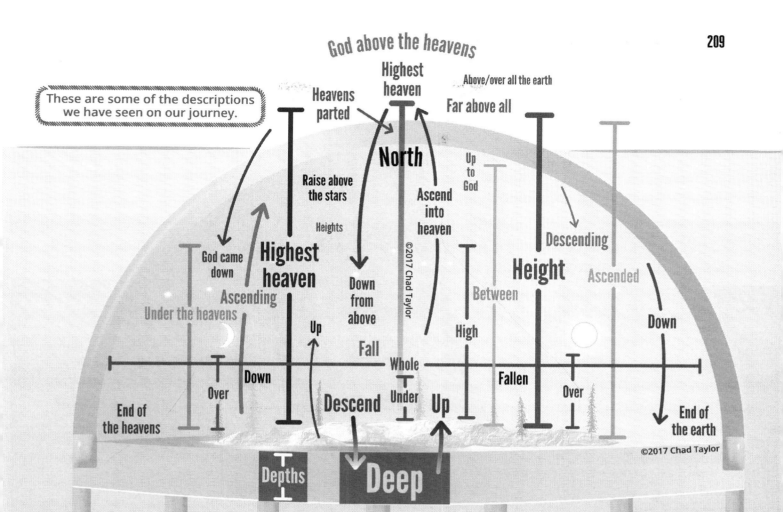

These are some of the descriptions we have seen on our journey.

God above the heavens

Highest heaven

Above/over all the earth

Heavens parted

Far above all

North

Raise above the stars

Up to God

Ascend into heaven

Heights

God came down

Highest heaven

Descending

Ascended

Height

Ascending

Between

Under the heavens

Down from above

High

Down

Up

Fall

Whole

End of the heavens

Down

Fallen

Over

Over

Under

Up

End of the earth

Descend

©2017 Chad Taylor

Depths

Deep

©2017 Chad Taylor

Common descriptions

(For even more detail, see the **definition** reference section, pages 288-291)

- **High, height, highest.** See pages: 24, 38, 42, 44, 62, 98, 104, 112, 114, 121, 129, 136, 144, 150

- **Ends of heaven and earth.** See pages: 32, 56, 100, 102, 108, 136, 146, 158

- **Circuit / course.** See pages: 24, 32, 48

- **Borders / boundaries of the earth.** See pages: 26, 34, 46

- **Tent / tabernacle.** See pages: 32, 40, 50, 90, 115, 194

- **Over / under / above / below, etc.**
  See pages: 4, 6, 26, 42, 44, 46, 50, 54, 56, 58, 60, 64, 70, 92, 95, 100, 102, 104, 106, 112, 114, 128, 134, 142

- **Ascend / descend / up / down, etc.**
  See pages: 38, 56, 64, 74, 76, 80, 82, 84, 86, 88, 90, 94, 96, 112, 116, 120, 121, 124, 132, 136, 144, 146, 152 (x2), 154, 156, 158, 160, 162, 164, 166, 168, 170, 176, 178, 182, 184, 186, 188, 190, 192, 194

Where is God?

He said to them, "You are from below; I am from above. You are of this world; I am not of this world.

- John 8:23 (ESV)

☐ **God is above the heavens and above all the earth.** See pages: 42, 60

☐ **God is above and looks down at us.** See pages: 38, 84

☐ **God is enthroned above the circle of the earth.** See page: 50

☐ **God is above the firmament.** See page: 128

☐ **God walks on the dome / vault.** See page: 24

☐ **God is in the (far reaches) of the north.** See pages: 28, 112

☐ **God is in the heavens.** See pages: 59, 60

☐ **God is in the height of heaven.** See pages: 24, 38, 152

☐ **God is above.** See pages: 64, 74, 78, 80, 86, 88, 90, 94, 96, 154, 156, 164, 168, 170, 172, 192, 194

☐ **God is up.** See pages: 76, 82, 84, 120, 124, 158, 160, 166, 180, 182, 184

☐ **God is in the highest heaven.** See pages: 98, 112, 150

☐ **God is above the stars.** See page: 112

☐ **God is the most high.** See page: 112

☐ **God ascends to heaven and descends to earth.**
See pages: 74, 76, 82, 86, 88, 90, 96, 110, 124, 132, 138, 146, 152, 154, 156, 158, 168, 170, 171, 172, 184, 194

☐ **God moves his home from heaven above to earth below to be with his people.**
See pages: 98, 194, 196, 198

⁴The Lord is exalted over all the nations, his glory above the heavens. ⁵Who is like the Lord our God, the One who sits enthroned on high, ⁶who stoops down to look on the heavens and the earth?

- Psalm 113:4-6 (NIV)

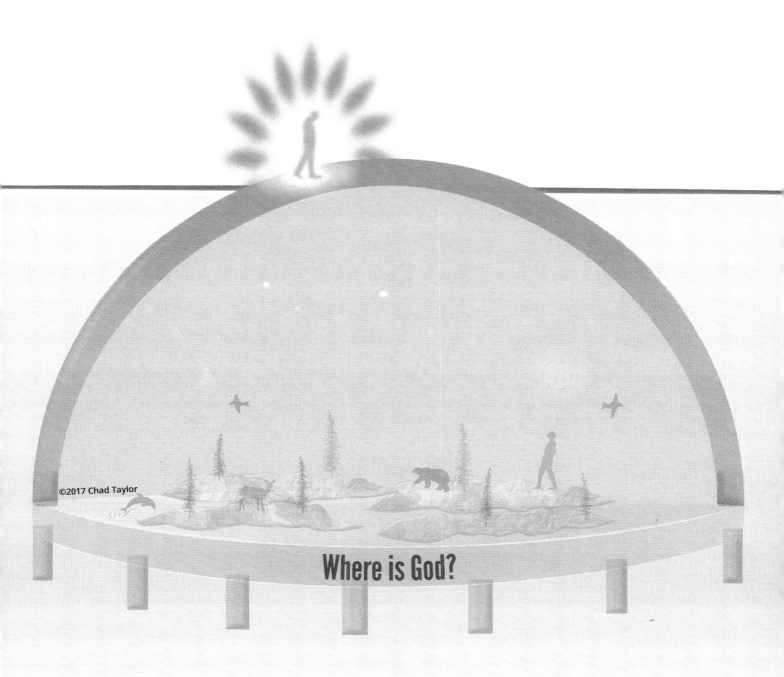

©2017 Chad Taylor

Where is God?

Stars, Angels and Heavenly Host

Stars

The **stars** were set in the firmament. *P. 8*

The **stars** sang as the angels shouted for joy. *P. 30*

When God calls out to them, they appear in order/stand at attention. *P. 54*

The **star** went ahead of the wise men and stopped over where Jesus was. *P. 142*

All the stars of heaven fall to earth. *P. 172*

A **star** falls to earth and TO HIM was given the key of the bottomless pit. *P. 178*

Satan draws 1/3 of the **stars** of heaven down to earth. *P. 184*

Lucifer is called a shining / morning / day **star**, thrown down to earth. *Isaiah 14:12 (compare various versions)*

Angels

An **angel** comes down from heaven and the earth is made bright by his splendor. *P. 188*

An **angel** comes down from heaven with the key of the bottomless pit. *P. 190*

And no marvel; for Satan himself is transformed into an **angel of light**. *2 Corinthians 11:14 (KJV)*

Heavenly Host

Praise him heavenly **host**. *P. 44*

All the **host of heaven** / **starry host** shall fall down. *P. 116*

The Lord at the head of his **army/host**. *P. 138*

The sun, moon and all the **host of heaven**... *Jeremiah 8:2 (some versions say stars)*

An angel appears to shepherds, his glory shines around them and they are terrified. Then a great **company of the heavenly host** appear. Upon their departure they are all referred to as angels. *P. 150*

©2017 Chad Taylor

Men's hearts failing them for fear, and for looking after those things which are coming on the earth: for the powers of heaven shall be shaken.

- Luke 21:26 (KJV)

Stars

Angels

Central Theme

The gods in the heavens. *P. 56, 114*

Spiritual wickedness in high places/heavenly realms. *P. 62*

Punish the gods in the heavens / host of the high ones on high. *P. 114*

All the host of heaven / starry host shall fall down. *P. 116*

Host / Stars (like an army) are named. *P. 121*

Like the sound of an army / host. *P. 128 & 129*

Powers in the heavens shaken. *P. 146*

Heavenly Host

Do you notice any similarities between Stars, Angels and the Heavenly Host?

If you were to forget what "the world" says about the stars above and only look at what the Bible says, what would your conclusion be? Are millions of huge balls of flaming gas going to impact our tiny (by comparison), earth in the future? Or are the shining lights above something entirely different than what we have come to believe. What if those brilliant lights in the sky are much smaller and much closer than we think they are? What if they are not flaming balls of gas at all?

Does this make you think of the 'Twinkle, twinkle, little star' lullaby?

"Twinkle, twinkle, little star,
How I wonder what you are!
Up above the world so high,
Like a diamond in the sky."

©2017 Chad Taylor

PART FIVE

Questions and Conclusions

For the time will come when people will not put up with sound doctrine. Instead, to suit their own desires, they will gather around them a great number of teachers to say what their itching ears want to hear. They will turn their ears away from the truth and turn aside to myths.

- 2 Timothy 4:3-4 (NIV)

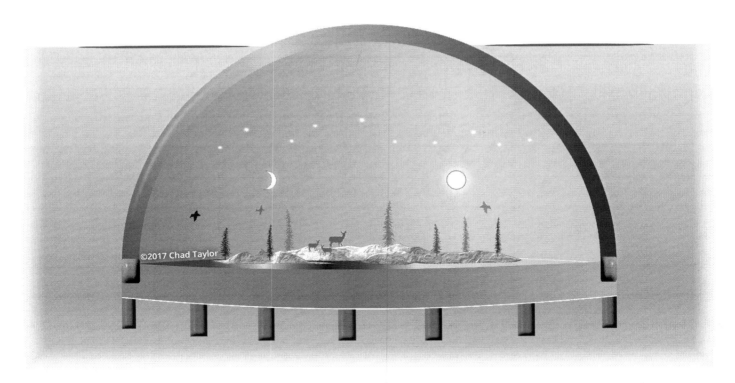

©2017 Chad Taylor

What has excited you the most on our journey through the pages of the Bible? Did new insights hit you like a ton of bricks? Are you stirred up and full of new questions? It's time to bring this journey into our daily lives.

Years ago a friend of mine asked me what the Bible said about earth, he wanted to know *where we are*. I was fairly new to reading the Bible at the time and like many who are asked this question, I shared two 'examples' with him. They were the second half of Job 26:7, (p. 26) and Isaiah 40:22, (P. 50). These were the verses that I thought, (at the time) described earth as a spinning ball in space. I remember hoping that he wouldn't ask a follow up question, those two examples were all that I had.

Doesn't it seem funny that we gingerly skip over the first half of Job 26:7 and go right to something that *we think* describes a ball earth? Why do we skip over; *"He stretches out the north over the void..."* Job 26:7 (ESV)? Is it because we have no clue what that actually means? Do we skip over it because it does not fit into our understanding? I know back then it was just my ignorance. I didn't know what that part meant, so I skipped it. Isn't it interesting though, that when we take these two verses in their entirety, how accurate they really are....... to the rest of the Bible?

It's almost comical really. I use to share a verse-and-a-half to 'show' how the Bible described earth one way. Now, years later I share over a hundred examples, with a seemingly endless supply more to choose from. All of which consistently describe *where we are* entirely different than the go-to, verse-and-a-half.

What can we conclude from our journey so far? Does the Bible say what you thought it did about *where we are*? Have you noticed any consistent themes throughout all of the examples?

It has been a long journey for me since that day on the mountain in Montana. There was a process I needed to go through to be able to understand Genesis Chapter One. During this process there were many questions I had, most of which I often get asked today.

Starting on the next page are some examples of questions I have either personally been asked, or have heard others asked. After each question I will give my response.

Question and Answer

Q: So what! What if the verse-and-a-half most people use to show earth as a ball in space, doesn't really describe that. What's the point?

A: The point is there are no verses in the Bible that describe earth as a spinning ball. Let alone a spinning ball flying through an endless space. The Bible makes it very clear that earth does not move and is sitting on foundations.

> I wanted to start with this 'question.' Believe it or not, this is the most common type of response I see, emotional.

Q: Doesn't the Bible describe planets?

A: The King James is the only Bible version I have found that uses the word "planets." It is only used one time in the entire King James version, in 2 Kings 23:5. Where the King James uses "planets," every other Bible version I have found uses "constellations." Are constellations the same thing as what we know as planets? I have found zero examples in the Bible to support what we currently believe, regarding planets.

Q: Where did all of the water come from for Noah's flood?

A: In Genesis, (p. 68-73) we read that the flood waters came from three places; the fountains of the deep, the windows of heaven and rainfall. I think most of us can imagine underwater springs gushing water up and we can certainly imagine alot of rainfall, but what about the windows of heaven? Well, if we look back through all of the examples, it is clear that the Bible describes a very large amount of water being above us. On the upper side of the firmament. When the windows opened in the story of Noah's flood, they let down a huge amount of water. This water, along with the spring water and rain water is what led to all of the earth being covered.

Q: What things may have changed with the flood?

A: If we were to take a plastic bowl, turn it upside down and push it straight down into a tub of water there would still be air inside of the plastic bowl. Now, imagine we poke some holes in the bowl......what would happen? Three simple and obvious things would happen; water would go into the upside-down bowl, air bubbles would come out of the bowl and the water level above the bowl would drop as water goes into the bowl.

With that being said, when the windows of heaven opened up, a large amount of water came in, but how much air in the process went out? Obviously there is no way for us to know the answer to this. However, what is one significant change we start to notice after the flood? The age that mankind is able to reach starts to decline from roughly nine hundred years to a little over one hundred years. What impact does a lower air pressure have to this world? Is there a reason people dig up old fossils and don't understand how certain things could be possible? Would a higher air pressure be the answer to their question? Also, what possible changes to the PH or salinity of earth's waters could have occurred from the new water being added?

These are just a few things to ponder. I would imagine there are many more possible changes that could have occurred during the flooding process that we are unaware of.

Q: What about the rainbow God shows to Noah, why does it sound like it wasn't around before the flood?

A: An interesting thought to consider about the flood is when we look at Genesis Chapter Two, we see a description from before man was created.

> *And every plant of the field before it was in the earth, and every herb of the field before it grew: for the Lord God had not caused it to rain upon the earth, and there was not a man to till the ground. But there went up a mist from the earth, and watered the whole face of the ground.*
>
> - Genesis 2:5-6 (KJV)

If the earth had a higher air pressure and was watered by a mist, perhaps the visibility in Noah's time may not have been what it is today. What if the conditions on earth back then didn't allow for rainbows to be visible? After the flood however, the conditions were different than they were before. What if the air pressure was lower and the mist stopped watering the earth? Now, rainclouds water the land. God knows what other changes occurred, but it certainly seems like there were not rainbows visible before the flood. When God showed Noah the rainbow and told him it was a sign, it makes sense that it was literally the first time Noah had ever seen one.

Or would this make more sense; "Oh yeah, and Noah, you know that rainbow you have seen for the last hmm, hundreds and hundreds of years of your life, well it means this now." This idea seems pretty silly to me. The conditions that could have changed to allow this to happen are certainly up for discussion, I only listed a few things that may have contributed to it.

Fun thought: Ever wonder why rainbows are shaped the way they are? (See p. 73)

Q: If the windows of heaven opened at the flood to let water in, why do we see the windows of heaven open again after the flood and not flood the earth again?

A: First, it is important to understand that it is impossible for us to know the scale of the firmament or the scale of the things outside of it, (p. 104-105). Who knows what volume of water is above the firmament. People in general don't like the idea of not knowing something and accepting it. However, the Bible makes it very clear, there are some things about the earth and it's surroundings that mankind cannot measure and does not understand. We must be willing to accept that there are some things we are not capable of knowing, at least in this lifetime.

Going back to the example on the previous page; Imagine you took a plastic bowl and set it upside down in a small bucket. Next, you put enough water in the bucket to almost cover the bowl, then punch holes in the bowl halfway down the side. What would happen? There would be a significant drop in the water level of the bucket as water entered the upside-down plastic bowl. Simple right?

Now, imagine we took that same plastic bowl and set it upside down in a parking lot, flooded by a few inches of water. Next, we do the same experiment and poke holes in the upside-down plastic bowl. What would happen? Obviously the bowl would fill up with water, but in this example, would the drop in the water level of the parking lot even be detectable? With all of mankind's gadgets, I doubt we could measure that small of a drop in water level.

Here's the point: I know it is hard to imagine, but theoretically, if there were enough water outside of the firmament, the entire earth could be flooded and the drop in water level above the firmament could be undetectable. So, there could have been a large drop, small drop or maybe even an undetectable drop, (by man's ability) in the water level outside of the firmament.

With all of that being said; here are two simple, possible answers to the original question.

Scenario 1. When the windows of heaven opened up again after the flood, they didn't open as far as they did for the flood. There could still be a huge amount of water the windows/floodgates are holding back, but they don't go down far enough to let any water in.

Scenario 2. Do you think God knew he was going to have to flood the earth before he created it? Does he really know the end from the beginning? Well, with that in mind, imagine in this example the windows of heaven were left open until water stopped running in. At what point would the water stop flowing in? When the water level reached the bottom of the windows of course.

There could still be an incredible amount of water above us, it is just not able to get in through the windows again. This means the windows can be opened all the way countless times and still never flood the earth again. The water level is at or below the bottom of the windows. Meaning, there was only enough water to flood the earth once. It's kind of like God knew it would only be flooded once, (p. 72-73).

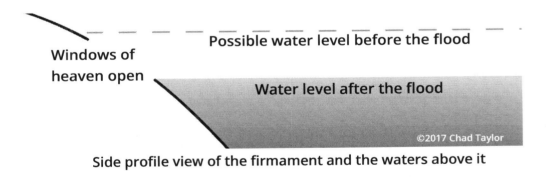

Windows of heaven open

Possible water level before the flood

Water level after the flood

©2017 Chad Taylor

Side profile view of the firmament and the waters above it

Q: **What was the point of the tower of Babel?** (p. 74-75)

A: Well, the simplified story is a group of people were working very well together and were building a tower to reach heaven. Maybe they knew roughly where one of the windows of heaven was, (perhaps from stories passed down). Or maybe they figured they could get through the firmament once they got there. Bottom line, what if they thought they could get into the highest heaven?

Can we assume it was theoretically possible to get that high due to God's reaction to their attempt? What was their motive to do this? Or was the tower just a representation of something? God only knows the answers to this, but it is interesting to think about.

> **Fun fact:** There is an extremely popular children's / family entertainment company whose logo is a kingdom under a 'dome,' with a single tower poking through the dome, coincidence? (It is probably the first company you think of).

Q: The Bible seems to talk about more than one heaven, is that right?

A: It is very important that when we see the word "heaven" in the Bible, to stop and think about which heaven it is referring to. The firmament is called heaven on day two and many places elsewhere. There are also examples of birds flying in heaven, as well as the sun, moon and stars being in heaven. Also, where God's home currently is, is called the highest heaven. This is the heaven we usually think of when we hear the word heaven. Just keep in mind that in the Bible, "heaven" is used for different geographical locations besides the highest heaven. As an example, review pages 4, 166 and 170.

Q: Is the sun a star?

A: We have all grown up being told that the sun is a star. It may come as a surprise to learn that the Bible never calls the sun a star. The sun, moon and stars are always described as being separate.

Q: Is the moon really giving off it's own light?

A: Nowhere in the Bible does it even suggest that the moon is reflecting the sun's light. As an example, let's review day four of creation. How many great lights did God *set inside* the firmament to give light onto the earth?

> *And God made two great lights; the greater light to rule the day, and the lesser light to rule the night: he made the stars also. And God set them in the firmament of the heaven to give light upon the earth,*

> - Genesis 1:16-17 (KJV)

Two. Not a big rock reflecting a great light, two lights.
(See page 208 for more examples).

A fun experiment: Purchase a $30 infrared thermometer. On a bright moonlit night, (preferably a full moon overhead), take the temperature of things in the direct moonlight. Then, compare the same thing in the shadows. For instance, asphalt in the direct moonlight verses asphalt right beside it in a shadow. Or maybe a steel bar that is half in the moonlight and half in a shadow, etc. You will find that *the temperature in the shadows is WARMER* than in the direct moonlight. This means the moonlight has a cooling effect. How can this be if it is reflecting sunlight?

Q: How can every eye on earth see Jesus when he descends in the future if not every eye on earth can see the north star?

A: This is another one of those questions that may seem hard to answer at first, but there is actually a very simple explanation. If we look at Job 26:7 (P. 26-27), this 'phenomenon' is pretty easy to explain.

He stretcheth out the north over the empty place, and hangeth the earth upon nothing.

- Job 26:7 (KJV)

The most likely reason people on the outer parts of the earth cannot see the stars towards the inner parts of the earth is they are much lower and smaller than we think they are. Just like an airplane going out of sight, we can only watch it for so long due to its shallow angle and relatively small size. Even if there were no mountains to block the view, you still have thousands of miles of clouds, weather, haze, etc. to try to look through.

As the verse above says, there is an empty place below the north. Since we cannot see the distance between the highest star and the bottom of the firmament, this gives us an illusion of infinite height. We will see the real height of heaven after the sun and moon stop shining, the stars fall, the firmament opens and we see Jesus begin his descent.

Q: What is with the New Jerusalem coming down from heaven to earth?
I thought we spend eternity with God in heaven?

A:

New Jerusalem

*The city lies foursquare, its length the same as its width; and he measured the city
with his rod, fifteen hundred miles; its length and width and height are equal.*

- Revelation 21:16 (NRSV)

Personally, I find the subject of the New Jerusalem fascinating. I do not know what your experience has been, but from my experience it is very rarely discussed. Why is that? From the verse above, it appears to describe a structure that would cover an area of 2.25 million square miles! Allow me to put this into perspective. The United States is approximately 3.8 million square miles. We are talking about a single city, made of pure gold as well as all sorts of precious stones and metals. It is going to descend from heaven to earth and cover an area roughly half the size of the United States of America! And.......why don't we talk about it?

I may have a simple answer, but first I have a simple question. Where do most people, most Christians even, say we spend eternity? Heaven, right? That is certainly what I heard growing up and still hear repeated like a mantra, over and over again. I am willing to bet you have heard the same thing as well. I know spending eternity with God in heaven sounds amazing, but there is one big problem with that thought....that's not what the Bible says.

When we look at the end of the book of Revelation, it is very clear that the New Jerusalem descends out of heaven and that God our Father and Jesus spend eternity with us here, *on earth.* (See pages 194-199).

I know, I know. This is likely as controversial as the rest of this book has been. Statistically speaking I am sure some of you are getting upset again right about now. This subject can be another wrench in the gears we have all grown up turning, but please bear with me and let me explain;

*In my Father's house are many mansions: if it were not so, I would have told you.
I go to prepare a place for you. And if I go and prepare a place for you, I will come again,
and receive you unto myself; that where I am, there ye may be also. And whither I go ye
know, and the way ye know.*

- John 14:2-4 (KJV)

Most people, (including myself not that long ago), use this verse to show how Jesus is preparing a place for each of us in heaven for when we spend eternity there. Please forgive my simpleness, but let me ask another question. If someone were to go and build a car for you, how would you receive it? Well, you can either go there and receive it yourself, or it could be delivered to you. In the second example, a person went and prepared a car for you, then at some point delivered it and you received it. Jesus in the New Jerusalem, *down here on earth.*

This sounds extremely simple, but comparing a car to a city, really? Well, I could use a house in my example, but we don't have the same mindset of being able to move a house like we do a car. I would imagine God can move a 2+ million square mile city with less effort than we would in moving a car. *Side note; how many mansions do you suppose fit in 2.25 million square miles?*

*Lay not up for yourselves treasures upon earth, where moth and rust doth corrupt,
and where thieves break through and steal: But lay up for yourselves treasures in heaven,
where neither moth nor rust doth corrupt, and where thieves do not break through nor
steal: For where your treasure is, there will your heart be also.*

- Matthew 6:19-21 (KJV)

Again, this seems simple to me. If something is stored somewhere for you, you can either go to it and receive it, or it can come to you and then you receive it. This doesn't say we spend eternity in heaven with our treasures that are stored there. It says our treasures are stored in heaven....I totally agree. But, just maybe, those same treasures being stored for you, descend to earth at some point, where we spend eternity with God. (See pages 194-199).

To me, the question isn't where do we spend eternity? The feel-good idea of spending eternity in heaven is not Biblical, (no matter how much I would have argued the contrary not long ago). Jesus and the Father come down here in the future to spend eternity with us. I think the real question is what happens to us in the span of time between our death and the New Jerusalem descending to earth? Do we go to heaven during any of that time? Do we sleep (in Jesus) for part of that time, then spend 1000 years with Jesus? I have my opinions on this subject, but it is a topic for another day. I only mention this to put the New Jerusalem into context.

The top right image (below), shows what the New Jerusalem would look like on the spinning ball we are told we live on. It is to scale and shows what a 1500 mile wide and tall structure would look like on a 7,926 mile diameter ball. The square in the center of the ball shows what area the city would cover.

Special note; after reading Revelation 21:16, (previous page, top) most people come to the conclusion that the New Jerusalem is a cube shape. However, many other people believe a tall pyramid could fit the same descriptions. This is why both possibilities are represented together.

From a practicality standpoint, which of these two images seems more logical for a city this size?

Can you imagine how much a city like this would weigh? Made of pure gold, etc.

How out of balance would a spinning ball become with this much weight added to one place while it (supposedly) spins at roughly 1000 mph?

1500 miles / 1500 miles

This is 2.25 Million square miles on the earth we believe we live on.

1500 miles

1500 miles

©2017 Chad Taylor

Have you ever noticed the size of a wheel weight on a car's wheel? Such a small amount of weight moved here or there can make a wheel wobble or spin freely. Imagine a car wheel compared to the image above.

Will all the nations really walk by it's light in the future? (p. 196) In the image above, wouldn't at least half the earth always be completely without it's light?

Q: Where are we? How did we get here?

A: <u>What "the world" tells us:</u>

The Bible is foolish.

In the beginning, there was nothing and then it exploded in a "big bang."

Earth is not significant at all. It is a mathematical probability that we just happened to have the right circumstances for us to evolve into what we are after millions of years.

Earth is a planet, spinning around at roughly 1000 miles per hour at the equator, while flying around a star once a year at mind boggling speeds.

The moon reflects the sun's light.

"Space" is constantly expanding.

Stars are massive and very far away. If even a single one got too close to earth we would all be doomed.

Stars died to give you life.

You are not special, you are here by chance and in the end your life is meaningless.

<u>What is the significance if we accept what "the world" tells us, as truth?</u>

If we accept the countless so called 'indisputable facts' we receive from "the world" as truth, we have a very serious problem on our hands. Hundreds and hundreds, if not thousands of Bible verses make no sense when compared to *where we are,* according to "the world." While spinning around on a ball at 1000 mph, flying around the sun, not to mention what we are told about the 'galaxy' and 'universe,' where is *above*? *Above* does not exist. On a round ball, your above is different than mine, and so on. So, in the end, we are forced to blindly twist and distort massive pieces of the Bible to fit our understanding of what we have been told to believe.

Can we really read such a common word like *above*, and say; "I know it says above, but above could mean something else." Really? For the countless instances the Bible says God and heaven are *above* us, the Bible is...well, wrong? If we can do that for *above*, what other words can we choose to ignore? *Answer:* any word that does not conform to what we have chosen to believe! *(See page XVII).* We are then left with a Bible that says and means whatever we want it to say.

Q: Where are we? How did we get here?

©2017 Chad Taylor

A: What God's Word tells us:

The wisdom of this world is foolish to God.

God created the earth, plants, animals and man over six days and then rested on the seventh.

There is a very large, hard, domed structure above us. God is above it and walks on the upper surface of it. He looks down at us and in the future he will descend down here to earth.

The sun, moon and stars are all above the circular shaped earth and move on a course above the earth designated by God.

The earth sits on foundations and does not move.

The moon gives off it's own light.

Stars are much smaller, much closer and are intelligent. All of them are going to fall to earth.

God put himself into his own creation to bring it back to the way he originally intended.

You are special and God loves you.

Jesus died to give you everlasting life so you can live with Him forever.

What is the significance if we accept what the Bible tells us, as truth?

If we accept the consistent examples of what the Bible has to say about *where we are,* are we in turn making a decision? Are we making a decision to believe God more than "the world?" Are we making a decision to question our foundational beliefs? Beliefs that we began to form before we could walk or talk? Do we start taking our own observations more seriously and form our own conclusions? Is earth in fact not moving as the Bible says? Are the sun, moon and stars really just running their course above a motionless earth? Is the idea of us spinning around on a ball flying through an endless space as far opposite as you can get to what the Bible actually says? Are we going to open our eyes and question the validity of the images we are shown daily of earth and space?

The unfolding of your words gives light; it imparts understanding to the simple.
                                                    - Psalm 119:130 (ESV)

"<u>The world</u>" vs. <u>The Word</u>

Now is a good time to ask this question....are both views compatible? Could both be correct? Can we trust and believe what "the world" tells us about *where we are* and also trust and believe what the Bible tells us about *where we are?*

In the past I would have said yes to these questions. I would have used a couple partial verses from the Bible to support my understanding and I would have believed what I heard from "the world." In my blissful ignorance, I thought both "the world" and the Bible supported each other incredibly well. Oh, how naive I was. Back then I had put in as much time studying what the Bible said about *where we are* as I did studying the violin, none. I'm sure it's something we have all done, but back then I was just repeating what someone else with more 'credibility' had told me about the subject.

Ask me now if both of these views of earth and it's surroundings are compatible.........I think you already know my answer. How can they be? If we look back at all of the examples in this book and how consistent they are, do they even kind-of resemble the image above? Also, think of this; between every example in this book there are many more similar examples that could have also been used. Totaling hundreds and hundreds more. Personally I do not see how "the world" and the Bible could be more apart from each other. When we look at this from a Christian point of view this really should not be a surprise. We should actually expect things like this. How many examples in the Bible are there of "the world" and God being opposed to each other? Can we believe what "the world" tells us as truth and also accept what the Bible tells us as truth?

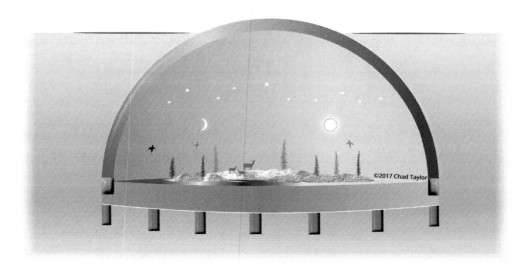

Below are some examples that demonstrate the relationship between "the world" and God.

[18] "If the world hates you, know that it has hated me before it hated you. [19]If you were of the world, the world would love you as its own; but because you are not of the world, but I chose you out of the world, therefore the world hates you.
- John 15:18-19 (ESV)

[33]I have said these things to you, that in me you may have peace. In the world you will have tribulation. But take heart; I have overcome the world."
- John 16:33 (ESV)

[2]Do not be conformed to this world, but be transformed by the renewal of your mind, that by testing you may discern what is the will of God, what is good and acceptable and perfect.
- Romans 12:2 (ESV)

[4]You adulterers! Don't you realize that friendship with the world makes you an enemy of God? I say it again: If you want to be a friend of the world, you make yourself an enemy of God.
- James 4:4 (NLT)

[15]Do not love the world or the things in the world. If anyone loves the world, the love of the Father is not in him. [16]For all that is in the world—the desires of the flesh and the desires of the eyes and pride of life—is not from the Father but is from the world. [17]And the world is passing away along with its desires, but whoever does the will of God abides forever.
- 1 John 2:15-17 (ESV)

[1]Beloved, do not believe every spirit, but test the spirits to see whether they are from God, for many false prophets have gone out into the world. [2]By this you know the Spirit of God: every spirit that confesses that Jesus Christ has come in the flesh is from God, [3]and every spirit that does not confess Jesus is not from God. This is the spirit of the antichrist, which you heard was coming and now is in the world already. [4]Little children, you are from God and have overcome them, for he who is in you is greater than he who is in the world. [5]They are from the world; therefore they speak from the world, and the world listens to them. [6]We are from God. Whoever knows God listens to us; whoever is not from God does not listen to us. By this we know the Spirit of truth and the spirit of error.
- 1 John 4:1-6 (ESV)

[19]We know that we are from God, and the whole world lies in the power of the evil one.
- 1 John 5:19 (ESV)

©2017 Chad Taylor

December 24th

Have you ever heard a four year old question if Santa Claus is real? I certainly have not. Why? Is it because flying reindeer and an overweight bearded man sliding down their chimney seems possible? Or is it because that is all they have ever known? Since before they can talk, most kids are told about Santa. They hear about him from their parents, friends and relatives. They see him on TV, on movies and billboards, not to mention they can sit on his lap at the mall! Santa even comes to their house and leaves presents while they sleep. He was obviously there, who else would have done that and ate the cookies left out for him? Oh, the special feeling kids get in anticipation for their visit from Santa. They think about him all year long as they try to be nice and make their list for him. Do you remember this when you were a child? I sure do.

Do you also remember the first time you heard that Santa may not be real? Do you remember how that made you feel? I remember that also. Decades later I am pretty sure I still remember where I was when I heard someone mention the absurdity. I am pretty sure I was in the bathroom at my grade school one wintry Montana day when I heard the ultimate blasphemy against Santa. "What!" He may as well have suggested my Dad was not real. What a dumb thing for someone to even think, let alone say out loud.

But the seed had been planted and the thought was not going away........*"How could Santa not be real? How could all of our parents, relatives and friends be lying about something like that? What about all of the shows I have seen on TV about Santa......and who do you think leaves all of those presents on Christmas Eve?!"* I scoffed at the notion that Santa was not real.

Like most kids I didn't want to believe Santa was not real, it was too much to accept. No matter how far fetched the idea of Santa and his reindeer started to become, I plugged my ears and didn't want to hear any more. Why? Is it because I would have to admit I had been lied to by people I trusted? Is it because there is a certain mystery and awe to the whole idea of Santa that would vanish if I accepted he wasn't real? Is it because that's all I have ever known and I wanted it to be real? Is it because I would have to admit I was wrong in what I believed?

Over time a few things about Santa started to wear on me; *"How could he really visit that many people in one night? How could reindeer fly, not to mention our fireplace isn't even hooked up anymore....how has he been getting into the house?"*

"You're telling me that I've been lied to my whole life?" All the cards fell, reality came crashing in. Santa was not real and never had been real. Christmas will never be the same again. It was traditions all along and I bought it; hook, line and sinker. Now that I knew the truth, could I go along like I did before? Could I pretend I didn't know?

Why do I tell you this story? Every year on December 24th news outlets everywhere give 'Santa tracking' reports about where Santa is on his journey around the earth. I'm sure you have seen them, they are very popular. What is interesting about them you ask? In all of my years watching for it, I have never seen a single one of those news stories end with them saying it was made-up. They have always sounded as real as could be and unless you were 'in the know,' it is as real as the news that was on before or after it.

My question to you....my fellow grade schooler....is this; what if all of the news stories you have seen and will see about earth, space, etc. are as real as the news stories on December 24th about Santa? What if reindeer flying around earth and space ships flying around earth have more in common than you think? What if a sleigh on your roof and a rover on mars are equally as believable? What if a bearded man in a red suit at the north pole is as real as an astronaut in a space suit on a space walk? Could you handle it? Could you handle knowing that you have been deceived since before you could talk? Could you acknowledge that your world view may be wrong? Can you humble yourself enough to examine your foundational beliefs for weak spots?

But why? Why would we be lied to? Do you remember my story from the mountaintop in the introduction? I was so frustrated on that mountain years ago with not being able to understand even the first chapter of the Bible. What I read that day did not conform to my understanding whatsoever. After all, by that point in time I had around 27 years experience building a faith that I didn't even realize was there. It was a foundational belief that my entire life sat on. I saw the world through lenses formed by those beliefs. I read my Bible that day on the mountain through the same lenses.

I remember coming back from that hike and unpacking everything. I didn't pick up my Bible for a while after that. I was so excited to get closer to God on that trip, but I felt like a total failure. How many other people have sat down to read their Bible and get closer to God, only to stop at the first chapter in unexpected frustration? The big question is, how many of those people never picked it up again? They decide to live the rest of their lives in a faith to "the world" because Genesis Chapter One was gibberish. It made no sense through the lenses "the world" gave them.

Do you suppose this is by design? It took me almost exactly six years from that day on the mountain to realize my life was built on a crumbling foundation. The most beautiful and amazing thing though was right beside the shaky foundation I had built my life on, was a foundation built on Truth. This sturdy foundation had always been there. I just never treated it the way I should have and I certainly didn't realize how badly I needed it. If you find the foundational beliefs your life is built on becoming shaky and crumbling, don't worry. The foundation built on Truth is right there for you to step onto and it is solid!

Deceptions in the end?

Many people from all over the world believe we are in, or near the 'end times.' The majority of Christians I know believe we are nearing the end of this chapter in our existence on earth. One of the basic traits that most Christians seem to hold about the end times is that there are going to be great deceptions. On page 227 we read some examples about "the world" compared to God. I think it's safe to say that until Jesus returns, we can expect deceptions daily. Anything that "the world" embraces is most likely against God's desires for us. If we look at some of the things becoming popular today, I don't think this is very hard to imagine.

In regards to the 'end times,' the Bible seems to elude to particular, larger deceptions than the average ones we encounter day to day. If I were to ask various Christians what these deceptions could be, I am sure we would get many different responses. I am certainly not going to say which ones may or may not be right, it would be foolish for me to do so.

If you have already made up your mind regarding what the biggest deceptions are, or could be, you may already be deceiving yourself. You may or may not be right, but always keep in mind that it is dangerous to think you have it all figured out. In doing so, you close yourself off to the possibility that there could be things you are missing.

As an example, look at the Jews who persecuted Jesus, even to death. These were his own people. They were the top religious men of the day and had already made up their minds about the Messiah they had been waiting for. The Savior they longed for was right in front of them and they couldn't see Him for who He was.......and is.

My point is this, remain light on your feet. Constantly compare things to scripture and please do not become dogmatic about this subject. If one of your thoughts doesn't pan out, oh well. Remain vigilant, we don't need to have all the answers, we have Jesus, the one who does.

<u>A few verses about deception:</u>

We know that we are children of God and that the world around us is under the control of the evil one.   - 1 John 5:19 (NLT)

And the great dragon was cast out, that old serpent, called the Devil, and Satan, which deceiveth the whole world: he was cast out into the earth, and his angels were cast out with him.   - Revelation 12:9 (KJV)

And cast him into the bottomless pit, and shut him up, and set a seal upon him, that he should deceive the nations no more, till the thousand years should be fulfilled: and after that he must be loosed a little season.   - Revelation 20:3 (KJV)

One good place to start for an overview of future events is Matthew chapter 24. Here is part of what Jesus had to say in that chapter;

[23]"Then if anyone tells you, 'Look, here is the Messiah,' or 'There he is,' don't believe it. [24]For false messiahs and false prophets will rise up and perform great signs and wonders so as to deceive, if possible, even God's chosen ones. [25]See, I have warned you about this ahead of time.

- Matthew 24:23-25 (NLT)

There is a whole lot to take away from these three verses, (as well as the rest of the chapter it comes from). I want to focus on three particular words that Jesus used in the verses above; "false, messiah and prophet."

- **False:** not real or genuine (p. 289)

- **Messiah:** a professed or accepted leader of some hope or cause / a person who is expected to save people from a very bad situation (p. 290)

- **Prophet:** a person who predicts the future / an effective or leading spokesman for a cause, doctrine, or group
(p. 290)

As Christians when we hear the terms "False Messiah" and "False Prophet," we tend to picture a wolf-in-sheep's-clothing type of person. Charming, well liked and well respected. Someone who wears a clean flowing robe while preaching to a congregation. At least this is what I usually tended to think of.

I am sure this imagery is very applicable in some instances, however let me share another *POSSIBILITY.* I am NOT saying the following is what Jesus was referring to in the verses above, but maybe to some degree it could be. With that disclaimer, turn the page:

On a recent trip to the gym, I found myself glancing at one of the TVs in the locker room. I was about to go jump in the pool when something caught my attention. There was a sports program on, but that wasn't what interested me. What interested me was *who* they had on as their guest. Along with the sports announcers, there happened to be one of the most well known atheist scientists on earth. In the middle of what sounded like a normal sports discussion, this famous 'expert' started sharing how earth is going to end. Not maybe end, not possibly end, how *it is* going to end.

He described how the sun is going to grow so large that it will be bigger than the orbit the earth takes around it. According to him, the earth will become a burnt spinning ball before it is eventually engulfed by the sun. Of course the 'expert' went on to reassure the audience that this horrible event will not happen for a very long time.

Let's slow down and think about this for a minute.

> *1. None of us are going to be around to verify that he is correct.....or not.*
>
> *2. This is a person foretelling a future event, (prophet).*

Well, if we look back through this book, what he is saying is obviously not true, making him false. Therefore, would it be a stretch to call this person a *false.......prophet?* Or would he need to be standing at a pulpit, wearing a robe to qualify?

How about another famous atheist scientist, who I actually ran into in Seattle years ago. Now, this person makes many television appearances, but one series he is on strikes me the most. The title of the program claims that he *saves the world.* So, let me get this straight, we have a person who, through logic and understanding can save the world. I have yet to see him in a flowing robe, but using the definition on the previous page, could he be called a type of messiah? If he is not in fact saving the world and is not the true messiah, that would make him false. Therefore, by God's standards, could the title of *false messiah* be applied to him?

I only mention these two examples of a possible *false prophet* and *false messiah*. However, if you pay attention there are people just like them in our lives every day. It is incredible how often these 'experts' appear in our lives, preaching their beliefs. Often at the strangest moments. They pop in just long enough to share what is 'going to happen' in the future and what they are doing to save us.

Do you find it interesting that whenever one of these 'experts' shares something, it almost always reinforces the belief that we are on a spinning ball flying through space?

Let's look again at verse 24 of Matthew 24, *(From page 231)*:

For false messiahs and false prophets will rise up and perform great signs and wonders so as to deceive, if possible, even God's chosen ones.
- Matthew 24:24 (NLT)

Perform great signs and wonders?

How many high definition videos have you seen showing the *many wonders of space?* Such amazing views of other planets, galaxies, distant moons, black holes, etc. Some of these videos are even hosted or narrated by the same 'experts' I mentioned earlier.

Years ago I remember finding these types of videos incredible. I said things like; *"Wow! Look at the amazing image of Jupiter and that distant galaxy."* Would it make you upset if you were to learn that much of these 'incredible' images are made on a computer? What if the image of that distant, newly discovered planet is as real as an image of Santa flying over the Pacific? Have you seen Hollywood movies with as good of footage as we get from any science channel?

Deceive God's chosen ones if possible?

How many Jesus followers believe they are on a spinning ball flying through space? Why would they ever question it? They have 'seen the images' and heard from 'experts' since childhood.

Don't let anyone capture you with empty philosophies and high-sounding nonsense that come from human thinking and from the spiritual powers of this world, rather than from Christ.
- Colossians 2:8 (NLT)

I briefly started to keep track of movies and TV programs that either mention or show something promoting earth as a spinning ball. I quickly discovered that it is almost impossible to watch a movie or TV show that does not contain reinforcement of that belief. When you really pay attention and watch for it, you will see it almost everywhere.

Sometimes it is comical just how obviously forced the brief moment is. *A dramatic scene in a movie suddenly cuts to an actor talking about distant planets.* What? Where did that come from? Why does it feel like a product placement ad? Something most people don't notice, yet is so obvious to those paying attention. Not seeing it for what it really is, most of us eat it up. We tune into our *daily programming* and gobble down whatever "the world" puts in front of us. Num, Num, Num.

The insertions use phrases and ideas like; planet, space, other planets, life out there, mission to mars, humans moving to another planet, a discovery of a new moon or planet, a planet like earth light years away, etc. Yes, I said planet five times in the last sentence on purpose. All of us need to realize that the words *planet* and *globe* are woven into the fabric of our daily vocabulary. It seems like not a single day goes by where I don't hear someone use the word *planet* or *globe*.

The last 500(ish) years

The idea of earth and the other 'planets' revolving around the sun seems to have been made popular by Nicolaus Copernicus. It started in 1543 with his *heliocentric theory.* People credit Copernicus with starting the 'Scientific Revolution.' Many other 'experts' have come along since him, like Kepler and Galileo who built off of his work and helped change people's understanding of *where we are.*

Some people say the idea of earth revolving around the sun wasn't widely accepted until the last 200-300 years. Regardless, let's keep things simple for this example. It seems that at least prior to the mid-1500's the consensus of where we live was that earth was at the center and the sun, moon and stars moved around the earth, or moved above a still motionless earth, (sound familiar)? Since we are not able to take a poll to find out what the majority of people believed hundreds of years ago, these are the most accurate dates I could find for this example.

The Bible does a great job with keeping track of genealogy, going back through family trees. The consensus is that the fall of Adam and Eve was approximately 6000 years ago. *Below* is a simple time line, showing what the last 474 years, (since Copernicus in 1543) looks like compared to 6000 years of mankind's history.

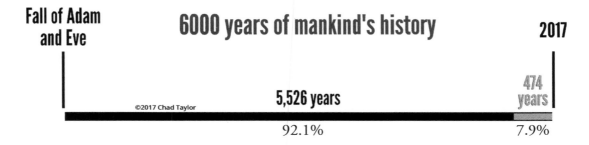

This would mean that for 92.1% of man's history, we did not believe what we believe today about *where we are.* Keep in mind that the 474 years is taken from the starting point of the *heliocentric theory.* Therefore, the 92.1% would only be larger if we knew how long it took to reach the majority accepting the belief. This would mean the 7.9% is a high estimate.

7.9% of time is like:

⌂   7.1 minutes of a 90 minute movie.

⌂   2.4 minutes of a 30 minute TV program,
(with no commercials).

Imagine, it's Friday night. You and your family are finished with dinner and you decide it would be nice to watch a movie together. You choose a movie that is about an hour and a half long and after everyone has their popcorn, you push play. Everything is going great, your entire family is enjoying the video. Over an hour later, the popcorn is gone and everyone is on the edge of their seats......at seven minutes left, the phone rings. What do you do?

Do you hit pause and interrupt the nice family moment? Or would you say something like; *"It's at the end of the movie, I'll call them back when it's over."* If you are like me, you would wait and call the person back. In simple terms, do you know what this could mean? It could mean that millions and millions of people are looking for big deceptions in 'the end times,' yet don't realize that events from hundreds of years ago could still be in 'the end times.'

What makes for a good suspenseful movie? Really think about this. What makes for a really good suspenseful movie? All of the good ones I can think of have one basic thing in common. They all get you interested and keep you guessing at what the twist is going to be. *"Is it this?....is it that?.....something is going to happen........what's it going to be?.........WHOA, I didn't see that coming!"*

The whole time you were trying to figure things out, the big twist came at the beginning and you didn't even see it. You kept looking for a big twist towards the end, but the big twist already happened. Usually when you sit down and watch it again, the same movie seems totally different. This time you catch the twist at the beginning, followed by the little hints you missed the first time around.

What if this is exactly how many of us live our lives? We try to figure out how Biblical prophesy lines up with current events. We sit and watch for the twist. *"Is it this?....is it that?.....something is going to happen........ what's it going to be?"*

What if a big twist has already come and gone? It's understandable that we missed it the first time around, it happened before all of us were born. However, we have a beautiful thing called The Word of God and it gives us the gift of hindsight. With the Bible and history books, we can look back and find the twist. The events we think are happening mean something totally different when you understand the difference the twist makes. What if we are born into a grand deception and we don't even know it? Most of us spend our lives being careful not to be deceived. But what if the whole time, the one thing we have *known* as absolute, the one thing no one seems to question is.......false?

Think about it, even if 'the end' (i.e. Jesus' return), happens a hundred years from now, 574 out of 6100 years is still only the last 9.4% of time. This is even using conservative numbers as mentioned earlier. We just need to recognize that God's definition of *end times* is probably much different than what we usually think of.

The Religion of 'Science'

Is much of what we call 'science' nothing more than another religion? I don't mean the chemistry class you took in high school. I'm talking about the larger segment of 'science' that is purely theoretical, yet masquerades as *indisputable fact*. Is it interesting to think about how many scientific *theories* we are taught as cold hard facts?

The "big bang" is a theory, taught to our children as fact.   Evolution is a theory, taught to our children as fact. The layers of the earth deep below us, yep theory. The deepest man has gone into the earth is around 7.7 miles.[1] Yet our children are taught the various layers down to the supposed center of the earth, 3963 miles down. Really? Even *the cause* of gravity is a theory. What 'experts' say *causes* gravity cannot be replicated or duplicated. Yet, is taught as fact to our children.

Another thing taught to our children is that their lives literally revolve around the sun. Our children are taught the sun is a star. They are also told that stars died and gave their lives for us. They say that without stars dying we would not have life, we are made of stardust. This reminds me of a verse:

> *They will be exposed to the sun and the moon and all the stars of the heavens, which they have loved and served and which they have followed and consulted and worshiped. They will not be gathered up or buried, but will be like dung lying on the ground.*
>
> - Jeremiah 8:2 (NIV)

I think there is a huge irony to all of this. We allow ourselves and our children to be taught by so-called 'experts' *what to believe.* We are taught what to have faith in. What is religion if it does not require faith?

Religion: a cause, principle, or system of beliefs held to with ardor and faith   (p. 290)

When you step back and think about it, it's kind of funny just how much theory, faith and belief is required in much of 'science.' Yet we allow their Elders to preach their faith to our children. We allow their doctrine to tarnish our understanding of scripture. We pay dearly to send our children to expensive schools. We set their impressionable, growing minds in front of Pastors of a religion we don't even recognize.

It's just with their religion it isn't faith in God, but faith in man's understanding. Faith in men that have expensive papers adorning their walls. Like most religions or denominations, do these so-called 'experts' choose to ignore evidence that contradicts the religion they preach?

If you think traditional religions have turned our children away from God, look at the religion preached every day to our children, *in public schools.* Our children are told that *life just happened. There is no God. They evolved from muck to monkeys to man and their life is meaningless. You live, you die, that's it. In the mean time, listen to this sermon about how birds evolved from dinosaurs.*

[1] *(See page 293)*

Not only are the most precious people in our lives taught this religion at schools that supposedly forbid teaching of religion, they are bombarded everywhere else as well. It's on their cereal boxes. On the clothes they wear and on the lunch boxes they take to school. They are especially taught this religion in almost every movie and TV show they watch. They learn it from the toys they play with and the video games we buy for them.

This religion has been passed down from generation to generation and we feed it to our kids without a second thought. It's in our daily vocabulary. It's in our foundational beliefs. It may even be sitting on your desk or as a picture on your wall. The religion of 'science' is taught and seen almost everywhere, *especially* as the spinning ball *we think* we are on. This religion is seemingly everywhere except one place......reality.

From the moment we enter this world, we live our lives through religious seminary. Just not the traditional kind. It's fiction, taught to our children as fact, all to discredit God's Word and promote the enlightened man as superior authority.

> [43] *Why do you not understand what I say? It is because you cannot bear to hear my word.* [44] *You are of your father the devil, and your will is to do your father's desires. He was a murderer from the beginning, and does not stand in the truth, because there is no truth in him. When he lies, he speaks out of his own character, for he is a liar and the father of lies.*
>
> - John 8:43-44 (ESV)

I remember being in grade school. It seemed like every year a crew of people would set up a dome inside of the gymnasium. Classrooms would take turns inside of it to be preached to. Oh, the gospel of this planet, the doctrine of that solar system. (By the way, do you find it funny that planetariums are dome shaped)?

It is a religion I vividly remember preaching to my wife. Not long ago, she and I were standing outside on a beautiful summer night. There was not a cloud in the sky and the stars were shining bright. I pointed up and started preaching from the gospel I had learned since my youth.

"Honey, do you see how those stars are twinkling? They twinkle because when their light hits earth's atmosphere it causes it to flicker like that. You know what else, those stars are so far away and light can only travel so fast that the light we see is much older than what we think it is. Who knows, maybe some of the stars we see don't even exist anymore. We are just seeing their light before they burned out."

Oh yes, how I loved to quote from the book of 1 Atheist 7:9-12*. I knew that scripture well and how proud it made me feel to share that wisdom with my wife. Even die hard atheists will preach this religion.

We are all hard-wired to worship and have faith. Many people worship their feelings and have faith in their abilities and understanding. Others worship their understanding and have faith in those with more understanding than them. Don't let yourself be fooled. The religion that much of 'science' has become still requires a huge amount of faith, ignorance, and/or willing blindness to believe it.

I use to be a follower of Jesus that was blissfully ignorant to the fact that I had atheist 'scientific' dogmas clouding my mind. Now I am a follower of Jesus, growing even closer to Him, after dumping the secondary religion I discovered I had. For me, the divide between The Truth and lies becomes wider and more obvious every day.

* Doesn't exist.

The construction site

24 "Anyone who listens to my teaching and follows it is wise, like a person who builds a house on solid rock. 25 Though the rain comes in torrents and the floodwaters rise and the winds beat against that house, it won't collapse because it is built on bedrock. 26 But anyone who hears my teaching and doesn't obey it is foolish, like a person who builds a house on sand. 27 When the rains and floods come and the winds beat against that house, it will collapse with a mighty crash." 28 When Jesus had finished saying these things, the crowds were amazed at his teaching, 29 for he taught with real authority—quite unlike their teachers of religious law.

- Matthew 7:24-29 (NLT)

A simple description of the building process for a house:

1. The ground is first confirmed to work for the size of the house to be built. Any prep work for the foundation is then completed. This would include any grade work to make sure the foundation is going to sit level with the proper dimensions.

2. Next, the foundation is poured. In this part of the building process the foundation is made to the correct dimensions; height, width and depth. Most foundations are not a simple rectangle. They tend to have many angles or offshoots that line up with the structure that is to be built on top of it. The foundation will hold the entire weight of everything built on it.

3. Once the foundation is complete, the framing begins. The more square and true the foundation is, the easier and better the building that goes on top of it will be. If the foundation is accurate, the walls should easily go up, the doorways and window frames should easily be square. The roof should line up perfectly with the walls and so on.

4. After the framing is complete, everything else goes in; plumbing, electrical, drywall, roofing, etc.

A common term in construction is to "True it up." To true something up, means to make it accurate or correct. For instance, in staking out a foundation for a house, if it is found to be out of square, it needs *trued up.* If you look at the synonyms of both *accurate* and *correct* you will find the word *true* and vice versa.

An accurate and correct foundation is a true foundation. Every measurement of a true foundation is what it should be. A true foundation is solid and strong, easily supporting everything that is built upon it, because it was designed that way. Every angle is precise and accurate in a true foundation. The framing of a house built on a true foundation will line up perfectly with the edges of the foundation. The house will be level and completely square, because it was built on a true foundation. Nothing will need to be tweaked or forced into place. With a house built on a true foundation there is no fear of it toppling over. It is built correct with longevity in mind and will stand the test of time.

However, a house built on an un-true foundation has many critical issues.   For example, a foundation could be too thin or weak in places, causing large cracks to appear before the framing even begins. Also, an un-true foundation may not be level or square, therefore the framers that build the walls would have to make odd calculations to keep the building process moving ahead.   Plumbers could find their job extra difficult from the odd calculations the framers had to make, because of the un-true foundation. After the plumbing, electrical and insulation have somehow been forced into place, the real fun begins, drywall.

With this type of house on an un-true foundation the drywall could turn into a nightmare. The floor may not be level and the wall may not be square, so every angle in every room could be different.   Countless pieces of drywall would need re-shaped in order to fit. After the painful task of drywall, every door and window could require extra shimming to sit close to level.   Eventually, roofers may be heard yelling from two stories up that they are having a hard time dealing with the roof leaking.

Now, imagine a news crew shows up to do a story about this *unique* house and it's construction. As hammers bang and tempers fly the various 'experts' from the job site gladly line up for their time in the spotlight.   Their proud smiles gleam from ear to ear as they are interviewed and proclaim their success and vision of the project.   It is now 'expert' #4's turn to be interviewed and he couldn't be more confident and proud. *Revolutionary......magnificent......breathtaking......*oh, the words he uses for their masterpiece.

Meanwhile, in the background a very different scene is taking place. The un-true foundation is slowly settling into the muck it was founded on. The walls that took so long to prop up are beginning to creek and pop from all of the added stress. Window panes begin to crack from the slowly drooping walls and if you look close, the painters may be seen packing up their tools, early.

⌐⌐

Q: "So you think you are smarter than Einstein and......"

A: Oh, if I had a dollar for every time someone has said something like this to me.   Why no, I do not consider myself to have a higher IQ than Einstein.   Intelligence has nothing to do with the subject at hand.   I view Einstein as a skilled framer building on an un-true foundation people like Copernicus, Kepler and Galileo poured.   Think about the other 'experts' we see on TV almost every day of our lives.   Are they smarter than me? Who cares!   That is not the point.   I view them all as skilled tradesmen, trimming away at their drywall to make it fit the clustered framework of a house, built on a slowly sinking un-true foundation.

Nearly every day, these 'expert' pawns are paraded on TV.   They speak about their grand vision, all the while holding utter contempt for anyone who dares to question their religion.   They cut away at their 'drywall,' trying to make the pieces fit.   Shhh, do you hear that?   Do you hear the sound of a house creeking and windows beginning to crack?   The foundation of someone's life is sinking.   The question is, which foundation?   The true foundation as solid rock, or the un-true foundation as sinking sand?

See previous page, top.

WHERE ARE WE?

Conclusions

26 "But don't be afraid of those who threaten you. For the time is coming when everything that is covered will be revealed, and all that is secret will be made known to all. 27 What I tell you now in the darkness, shout abroad when daybreak comes. What I whisper in your ear, shout from the housetops for all to hear!

- Matthew 10:26-27 (NLT)

Conclusions

Q: Well then, if we are not spinning around on a ball flying through space, how do you explain the movement of the sun? The changing seasons? Navigation? If I head West, wouldn't I just keep going outwards? Then what, do I bump into something? Is there an edge? Is there a drop off? *Where are we?*

A: In this final section, we will cover nine basic characteristics of earth. If the 101 examples in parts 1-3 were not enough, this should help clear up most remaining questions. We will use the Biblical examples we have seen in this book as the basis and then apply our observations to fine tune some of the details.

1. The course of the sun: Time Zones

2. The course of the sun: The Seasons

3. The North and the South

4. The East and the West

5. Navigation

6. The Icy Boundary

7. The cycles of earth

8. The future of earth

9. Who made it all?

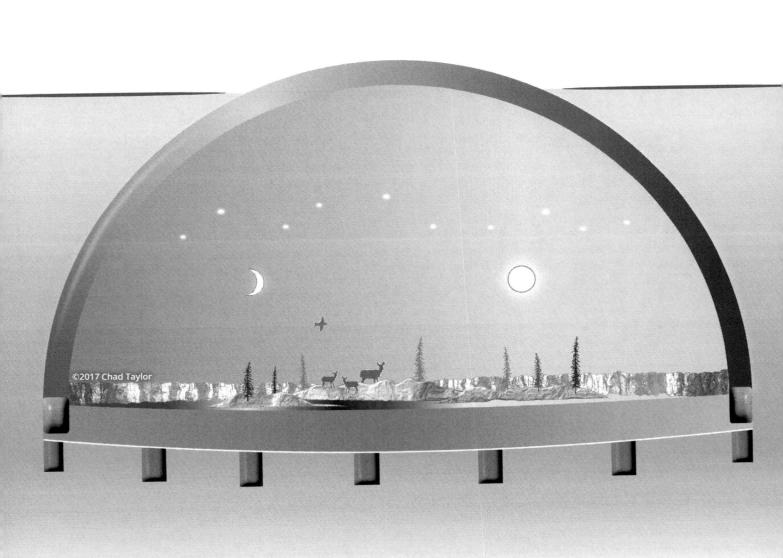

1. The course of the sun: Time Zones

[14] And God said, "Let there be lights in the dome of the sky to separate the day from the night; and let them be **for signs and for seasons and for days and years**, [15] and let them be lights in the dome of the sky to give light upon the earth." And it was so. [16] God made the two great lights—the greater light to rule the day and the lesser light to rule the night—and the stars. [17] God set them in the dome of the sky to give light upon the earth, [18] to rule over the day and over the night, and to separate the light from the darkness. And God saw that it was good. [19] And there was evening and there was morning, the fourth day.

- Genesis 1:14-19 (NRSV)

These verses were covered on pages 8-9 in part One. While they discuss the sun, moon and stars inside the firmament above us, the main focus here is *time*. There are various calenders that use the sun, moon and/or stars to keep track of time. Our traditional calender uses the 24 hour day from the sun taking 24 hours to run it's course above us.

Imagine the face of a watch. There is an hour hand, minute hand and second hand. Let's focus on the hour hand for this discussion.

When it is noon, the sun should be above you, or directly north or south of you. This all depends where you are on the face of the earth, as well as what season you are in. The Bible says in many places that the sun has a course it takes above the earth. It is constantly making a *clockwise, (right-hand)* rotation above the face of the earth, as it sets our hours and gives light onto the earth below.

When it is noon your time, 180° on the other side of the face of the earth it is midnight, and so on. For every 15° on the face of the earth, the time is one hour different. (360° / 24 hours = 15°).

The subject of the sun reminds me of one of my favorite Bible stories. It comes from Joshua 10:11-13, (p. 94-95). It describes Joshua commanding the sun and moon to stand still in the sky. It also gives the locations they stand still above. If we think of this story and similar ones with the belief that we are on a spinning ball, this account is laughable.

First of all, the earth would have to stop spinning at approximately 1000 mph for the sun and moon to stop. Then after about a day of battle, the earth would have to suddenly start spinning again. If we believe what "the world" tells us, Joshua is mistaken, the entire earth would have been wiped out. Imagine driving a car at 1000 mph and abruptly stopping. How far would you fly after going through the windshield? Then...splat.

Can you imagine the size of the tsunamis that would have occured, let alone all of the other catastrophic events that would have happened? However, in this story it seems like no big deal, the sun and moon stop, the battle goes on and then the sun and moon resume their course after the battle is won.

Who is mistaken, "the world" or Joshua?

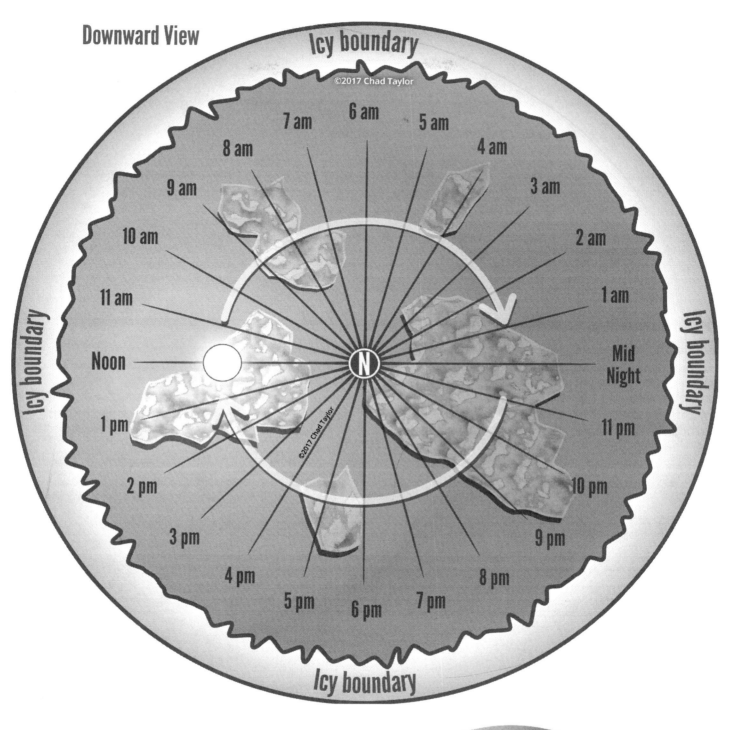

Downward View

Icy boundary

7 am
6 am
5 am
8 am
4 am
9 am
3 am
10 am
2 am
11 am
1 am
Noon
N
Mid Night
1 pm
11 pm
2 pm
10 pm
3 pm
9 pm
4 pm
8 pm
5 pm
6 pm
7 pm

Icy boundary

Icy boundary

Icy boundary

Side View

2. The course of the sun: The Seasons

What about the seasons? How do they work? While God knows the exact course the sun takes, I believe the basics of how the seasons work is relatively simple to understand.

If you are interested, please look up how "the world" defines the following terms. It is amazing just how well they describe what you are about to read.

Tropic of Cancer: The farthest north that the sun is directly overhead at noon, meaning this is the closest to the center of the earth that the sun gets on it's course. *The Northern solstice* is the day the sun reaches this point and starts it's winding journey outward again.

Tropic of Capricorn: The farthest south that the sun is directly overhead at noon, meaning this is the farthest outward the sun gets on it's course above the earth. *The southern solstice* is the day the sun reaches this point and begins it's winding journey towards the center again.

Equator: The center point between the tropic of Cancer and the tropic of Capricorn.

Imagine that every day, on it's *clockwise* course above the earth, the sun is either winding it's way inward or outward, (depending on the time of year). For six months of the year the sun slowly winds it's way outwards until it reaches the Tropic of Capricorn, *(the southern summer solstice)* and completes one of the two perfect circles it makes in the year. It spends the next six months slowly winding it's way inwards towards the north, until it reaches the tropic of cancer. The day it reaches it's most inward rotation is called the *northern summer solstice* and is the second day of the year it completes a perfect circle. Then, it begins it's winding journey outward again.

So, half of the year the sun has a slightly wider circular path, the other half a slightly narrower circular path. Half the year the sun is winding it's way outwards towards the south, the other half of the year the sun is winding it's way inwards towards the north.

While the sun is winding it's way inwards or outwards throughout the year, it would also need to be gradually speeding up or gradually slowing down. Due to having more ground to cover during it's outer course, the sun would need to travel faster than it does during it's course around the inner part of the earth. So, aside from the two solstice days of the year, the sun is either making a wider faster turn, or making a shallower slower turn, daily.

Downward View

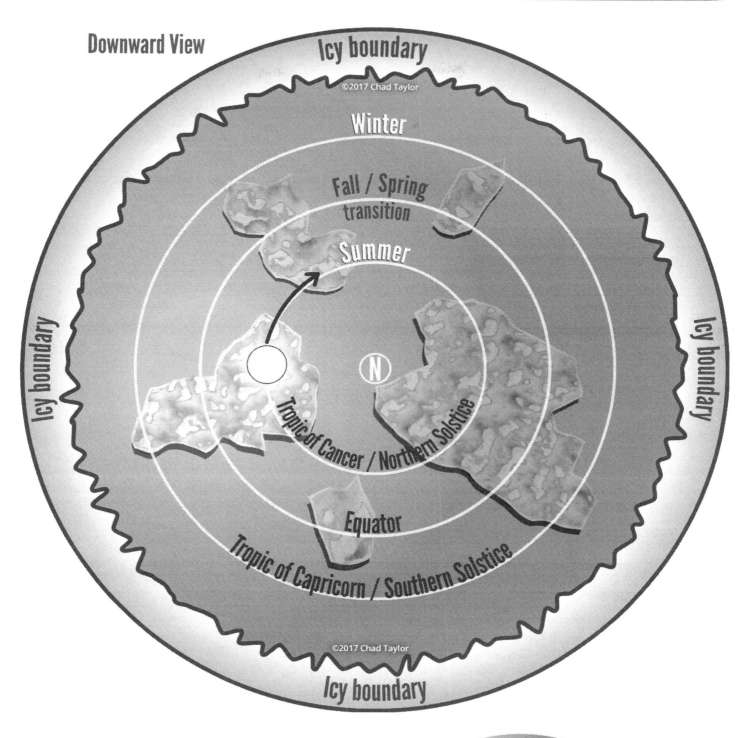

Icy boundary

Winter

Fall / Spring transition

Summer

Tropic of Cancer / Northern Solstice

Equator

Tropic of Capricorn / Southern Solstice

Icy boundary

©2017 Chad Taylor

Side View

3. The North and the South

⁵ Do not be afraid, for I am with you; I will bring your children from the east and gather you from the west. ⁶ I will say to the north, 'Give them up!' and to the south, 'Do not hold them back.' Bring my sons from afar and my daughters from the ends of the earth—⁷ everyone who is called by my name, whom I created for my glory, whom I formed and made."

- Isaiah 43:5-7 (NIV)

We are told by "the world" that the top half of the spinning ball *we think* we are on is called the *northern hemisphere* and the bottom half is called the *southern hemisphere.* In general terms we call them "the north" and "the south." The dividing line between the two is called the equator.

On the face of the earth, "the north" is the inner part closest to the center. "The south" is the outer part. The equator is the dividing line between *the north* and *the south.* It is mid-point between the two tropics discussed on the previous page.

Therefore, anything from the equator toward the center of earth is "the north" and anything from the equator outward is "the south."

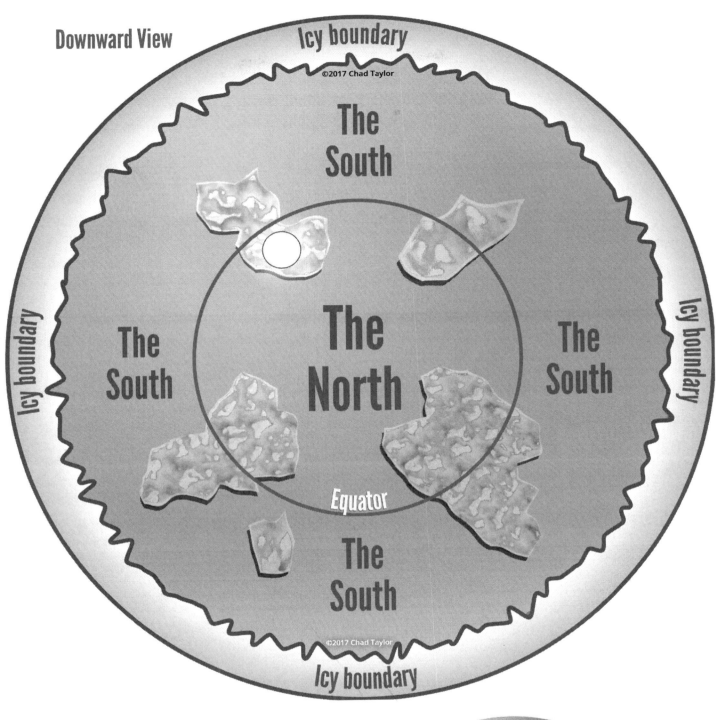

Downward View

Icy boundary

©2017 Chad Taylor

The South

Icy boundary

The South

The North

The South

Equator

The South

©2017 Chad Taylor

Icy boundary

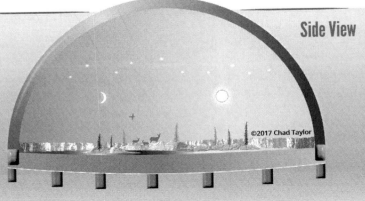

Side View

©2017 Chad Taylor

4. The East and the West

⁵Do not be afraid, for I am with you; I will bring your children from the east and gather you from the west. ⁶I will say to the north, 'Give them up!' and to the south, 'Do not hold them back.' Bring my sons from afar and my daughters from the ends of the earth—⁷everyone who is called by my name, whom I created for my glory, whom I formed and made."

- Isaiah 43:5-7 (NIV)

We are told by "the world" that the spinning ball we think we are on has a vertical dividing line called the prime meridian. 'They' say when carried all the way around the ball, it forms two halves of the earth. These two halves are referred to as *the east* and *the west*. "The world" has chosen what location as it's dividing line, (the prime meridian). I don't think it is a far stretch to say that what "the world" calls the east and west are probably not the same as what God calls the east and west. Basically, it is doubtful he uses the same dividing line that "the world" does.

Personally, I would be extremely surprised if the dividing point God uses is not Jerusalem. Imagine placing a ruler between Jerusalem and the center of the earth and drawing a line. "The west" would be on the left and "the east" would be on the right, (like the image to the right).

One thing is for sure, Jerusalem is extremely important to God and it seems likely this is where he would divide the earth from east and west. Whether Jerusalem is the dividing point or not, God certainly has an east and west for the earth. I like to refer to the dividing line between the east and west as the "Prime Partition." It divides the east and west into two "Hemi-Circles." (Yes, this is a spin-off of hemispheres)

On a side note, when referring to the east and west, another verse comes to mind;

For as the lightning cometh out of the east, and shineth even unto the west; so shall also the coming of the Son of man be. - Matthew 24:27 (KJV)

This verse makes me wonder about when Jesus descends from heaven in the future. Will heaven open from *the east* and roll up towards *the west?* If this is the case, then the light that shines down to us from heaven/God would begin in the east and extend to the west, (See pages 172-175).   Following this will be the greatest moment ever, Jesus descending on the clouds.

Whether this is what Matthew 24:27 is saying or not, it is going to be magnificent.

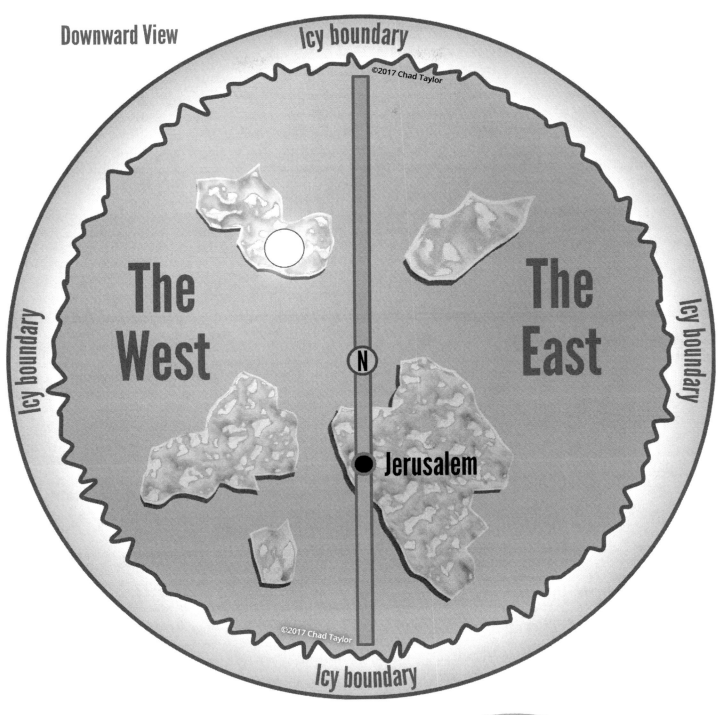

Downward View

Icy boundary

Icy boundary

Icy boundary

Icy boundary

The West

The East

N

Jerusalem

©2017 Chad Taylor

Side View

©2017 Chad Taylor

5. Navigation

Another thing I find particularly interesting is the subject of *north*. I have always thought the idea of there being multiple norths very strange. We are told about *true geodetic north, astronomical true north, grid north and magnetic north,* how confusing. If you want to fall asleep listening to people explain the differences, there are many videos on the internet to torture yourself with. I would like to share my simplified understanding about *north.*

In my opinion, the only two terms about north that are truly relevant are grid north and magnetic north. If you were to pick the point at the very center of the face of the earth, that is grid north. All of the longitudinal lines we see on our maps converge at that point. The lines for latitude are simply larger and larger circles whose center is grid north.

Now, regarding magnetic north. If you look up the term "north magnetic pole" online, you will notice something very interesting.......it moves! There is a particular point on the face of the earth where the magnetism for north comes *straight down*. Vertical to the face of the earth. This point is called the dip pole and it moves every year, currently at around 50 km per year.[2] Try your best to (at least temporarily) forget what tradition tells you about what is causing the magnetism. Those traditional beliefs only apply to a spinning ball.

So, in simplistic terms, there is something *ABOVE* the center of earth, (vertical to the face of the earth), that moves and all of our compasses point to it. Is it possible that there is an object above the firmament that is strongly magnetic that moves around every year? What if *IT* is a *WHO?* Who could be walking on the top side of the firmament, giving off a strong magnetic field? What if your compass literally points to God himself! Makes you think differently about a compass doesn't it?

> *Out of the north comes golden splendor; around God is awesome majesty.*
>
> - Job 37:22 (NRSV)   (From pages 28-29)

Does this verse sound like it could be talking about the northern lights? Aren't we told that the northern lights are caused by magnetism?

Whether it is an object or God himself, how hard is it to think that our compasses are pointing towards God? If we were to follow our compass to where north leads us, it would take us to a point where our compass would all of a sudden point backwards. How hard would it be to look straight up and imagine who is directly above you? Is this too unbelievable to comprehend? Or is a large spinning ball clouding your mind? What if, when viewed in high speed, the stars above form a bullseye, pointing to God in the farthest reaches of the north?

Regarding navigation, think of how we navigate now. If you were holding a compass with north pointing to your right, you are facing west. South is always away from north. If north is to your left, you are facing east. Whether you are on a spinning ball or on the face of the earth, a compass works the same.

This brings us to the subject of a south magnetic pole. On a spinning ball, it would be opposite the north magnetic pole. On the face of the earth, the south magnetic pole is not necessary and would not even need to exist, (in my opinion it probably doesn't, *see the image to the right*). North is attracted to south and vice versa. No matter where you are on the face of the earth, your compass always points north and south is 180° from north. It's how we've been navigating with compasses for a very long time. One thing is for sure, you don't need to have a "magnetic south pole" for a compass to work.

[2] *(See page 293)*

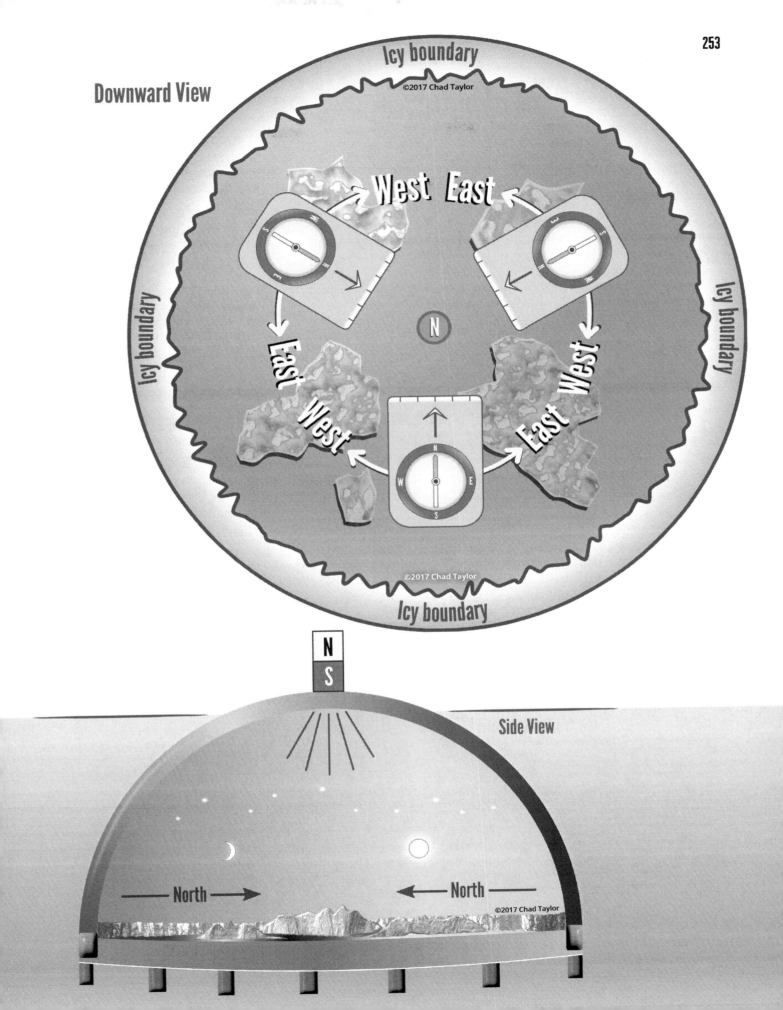

Downward View

Icy boundary

©2017 Chad Taylor

West East

East West

East West

N

Icy boundary

Icy boundary

Icy boundary

©2017 Chad Taylor

N
S

Side View

North →

← North

©2017 Chad Taylor

6. The Icy Boundary

He hath compassed the waters with bounds, until the day and night come to an end.

- Job 26:10 (KJV)   *From pages 26-27*

There are two important aspects to this verse, we will focus on the first half; the waters that are encompassed by a boundary. This is far from the only verse that describes a boundary around the waters. From our observations we know it's an inhospitable icy boundary we commonly refer to as 'antarctica.'

Have you ever noticed how much 'antarctica' is reinforced in our lives? For instance, not long ago I started a children's movie for my kiddo to watch before bed. I was amazed at what happened at the very beginning. This particular children's movie started off showing galaxies, solar systems and countless stars. Then zooming in past a massive sun and large moon, it focused in on the bottom part of a ball earth. At this bottom part of earth was a land we call 'antarctica.' That one short movie opening reaffirmed to millions of children the *belief* that not only is earth a spinning ball flying through space, but the sun and moon are massive and far away. Also, they learn there is a large continent at the bottom of the spinning ball *they think* they are on.

The movie then goes on to show the happy critters that live there. How does a spinning ball in space *and* 'antarctica' make kids feel? *Happy.* The reinforcement is far deeper than most people can begin to understand. What kind of child would question this? How many adults even question this? Is it like News:30 on December 24th?

"Of course the continent of 'antarctica' exists!" People say, it's been thoroughly reinforced since before any of us even entered the school system.

Thousands of tourists go to the icy boundary, I mean 'antarctica' every year. There are two main places they go, *the antarctic peninsula* or *eastern antarctica.* The point is, there are designated places you are allowed to go. The vast majority of the icy land is not accessible, inhospitable and/or off limits.[3] To me, unless you go on a tour, it sure seems very difficult to go wherever you want on the icy boundary. Is there good reason to not let people go wherever they would like? Is this accomplished under the guise of protecting the environment?

Something you may find interesting is the *Antarctic Treaty*[4] that was formed in the late 1950's after a series of strange events, (p. 256-257). Today that same treaty is comprised of over 50 countries. The gist of the treaty is that the icy boundary is off limits to most activities. No country can have an official claim to any part of it. It is a rainbow-fairytale land for tourists and scientists from various countries to come together, have a hug fest and sing kumbaya.

Apparently "the environment" was so important to the powers-that-be in the late 50's that they got together to set up a plan to protect the po-widdle-penguins. This idea seems absurd to me because during this same time they were also exploding nuclear missiles high in the sky, (along with the USSR).[5] This sounds very eco-friendly to me. Nuking the sky while getting control of the outer edge. This makes no sense on a spinning ball, however it makes complete sense when you turn the page.

Almost everyday on the news, we hear about fear and tension between U.S.A. and Russia. This is funny to me because they sure seem to get along great when it comes to things 'antarctica' and 'space' related. Do you find it interesting that these are the same two countries that got their advanced rocketry knowledge from the Nazis after WW2? (Who also happened to be very interested in the icy boundary). These are also the same two countries that were both nuking the sky for no apparent reason from 1958-62.[5] The same two countries (amongst others) that worked together to explore the icy boundary during the mid 1950's.[6] The same two countries that today work together to inspect what goes on in 'antarctica.'[7]

3, 4, 5, 6, 7 *(See page 293)*

Aside from 'antarctica,' can you think of any other example in history where dozens of countries all agreed to set aside an enormous chunk of land and leave it alone? Where countries agreed that military conflicts would never occur there. No fighting or disagreements of any kind. No military drills, no weapons testing, nothing. Millions of acres of land to be left alone. Really? Countries have fought for thousands of years to gain more land and yet everyone agrees not to expand there?

Lastly, imagine what could be found on the icy boundary if we were somehow allowed to freely explore there. Did you know there is not a single video of a rocket flying straight up into space and continuing in the same direction? They always appear to take a suspicious course. They go up, turn sideways and then fly parallel to the earth and out of sight. After this, an even more suspicious thing happens, they conveniently lose contact with their rocket as it flies over the Indian Ocean. Miraculously, they regain contact and 'fly' their contraption wherever their computer says they are flying it. What is the likelihood the people in the control room are actually controlling the rocket and not just a computer program after they 'regain contact' with it?

If you were to draw a line from Florida towards the Indian Ocean and continue it onward, what would you eventually find? Thousands of square miles of icy land, that's what. What if, on this cold desolate land, lies a secret, a rocket graveyard, covering countless square miles? What if this is one more reason you and I are not allowed to go wherever we feel like on the icy boundary?[3] Sooner or later would someone trip over a multi-billion dollar rocket that was suppose to be somewhere in 'space?'

Have billions of tax dollars worth of amazing technology turned into cold useless scrap metal after a brief flight? Did the destiny of those magnificent machines lay on a land of ice, tucked away on the edge of this world, never to be seen again? Does the pinnacle of man's tool to reach into 'space' only need to survive until it's plummet to a cold icy grave, out of view from prying eyes? Do the very people that build them remain oblivious to this possibility?

Why would "the world" collectively agree to treat this cold land the way it does? Why does it seem like we are shown the icy boundary a particular way? Do you get the sense that we are shown enough images to satisfy our curiosity, yet nothing big happens there to draw our attention to it? No disputes or friction of any kind. *We 'know' it's there, but it's cold and boring. What's on TV tonight?* However, imagine if conflicts arose there between countries. How much attention would be brought to the icy land if a war was going on there?

Why do you suppose all the countries of "the world" have agreed not to have disputes there? To not bring unwanted attention to it? Really think about it.....what would it take for over 50 countries to collectively work together for decades with no incidents? A large common goal, right? What could that common goal be? Scientific research? Um, no. What is big enough to get the string pullers of every country to agree on something? How about hiding proof of God! The day someone (uncontrolled) crosses the icy boundary and taps on the edge of the dome that is over us, everything changes. That would be the day all faith is lost in the governments that have been keeping it from us. That would be the day we lose faith in man and grow faith in God.

What would happen to the societies of the world if people took selfies while leaning against the firmament? Do you suppose "the world" would lose it's control over people? Do you suppose hundreds of millions of people would start to take their Bibles seriously? Would people want to know The One who created all of this? Would millions of people take to the streets demanding answers? The governments of "the world" most certainly have a common goal, *survival.*

Who would you need to go through to go way up high? Who would you need to go through to go way out wide? Are you starting to notice any consistencies?

[3] *(See page 293)*

A series of strange events:

Operation Paperclip: 1945

Following WWII, under 'operation paperclip' the USA acquires many Nazi scientists. Many of them are rocket scientists. Arguably the most famous of these is Wernher von Braun. *For interesting fun;* check out Wernher von Braun's gravestone and compare it to pages 32-33.

The UN flag is created: 1946

Now where have I seen this image before?

[A] Operation Highjump: 1946-47

Admiral Byrd explores 'antarctica.'[8]

[B] Operation Deep Freeze: 1955-56

Admiral Byrd explores further into 'antarctica.' This was a teamed mission with the USSR and other countries.[6/8]

[C] Sputnik launched: 1957

The USSR launches the first 'artificial satellite.' This (supposedly) triggers the 'space race' between the USA and USSR. This event also (supposedly) helped fuel the cold war between the two countries. So, the USA and USSR are buddies for years while searching out the icy boundary. Then, like a high school couple, both countries say they don't like each other and start acting weird. The following year, (for some reason), both of them start shooting huge bombs into the sky. They got the nukes up there with the knowledge they both had gained about rockets from the Nazis, who they both teamed up and defeated years prior.

[D] Van Allen 'Radiation belt' found: 1958*

In 1958 a huge obstacle is (supposedly) found over the earth. It is a big problem for anyone wanting to go that far or beyond. No kidding, there is a huge barrier for anyone wanting to go high enough.

> There is an interesting term in radio communication called *skywave.* It refers to radio waves reflected back to earth. They are able to travel much further than they should because they bounce off something above us, any guess what that could be?

[E] High altitude nuclear tests: 1958* - 62

For approximately four years, both the USA and USSR detonate nuclear missiles up in the sky.[5] This happens after both the USA and USSR were on a teamed mission to explore the icy boundary, *(B).*[6/8]

> In which are we able to think more clearly, while at peace or under constant fear? Imagine if the millions of people living during this time would have not been in fear, but living in peace. Do you suppose more questions would have been asked about why both countries started shooting nukes straight up into the sky? Was the 'cold war' nothing more than a tool to paralyze the public and keep them from asking questions?

Nasa Founded: 1958*

'Space' is now government controlled.

*Same year

[F] Antarctic Treaty: 1959-61

Created and implemented from 1959-61 This treaty set the stage for how the icy boundary would be treated. [3/4]

3, 4, 5, 6, 8 *(See page 293)*

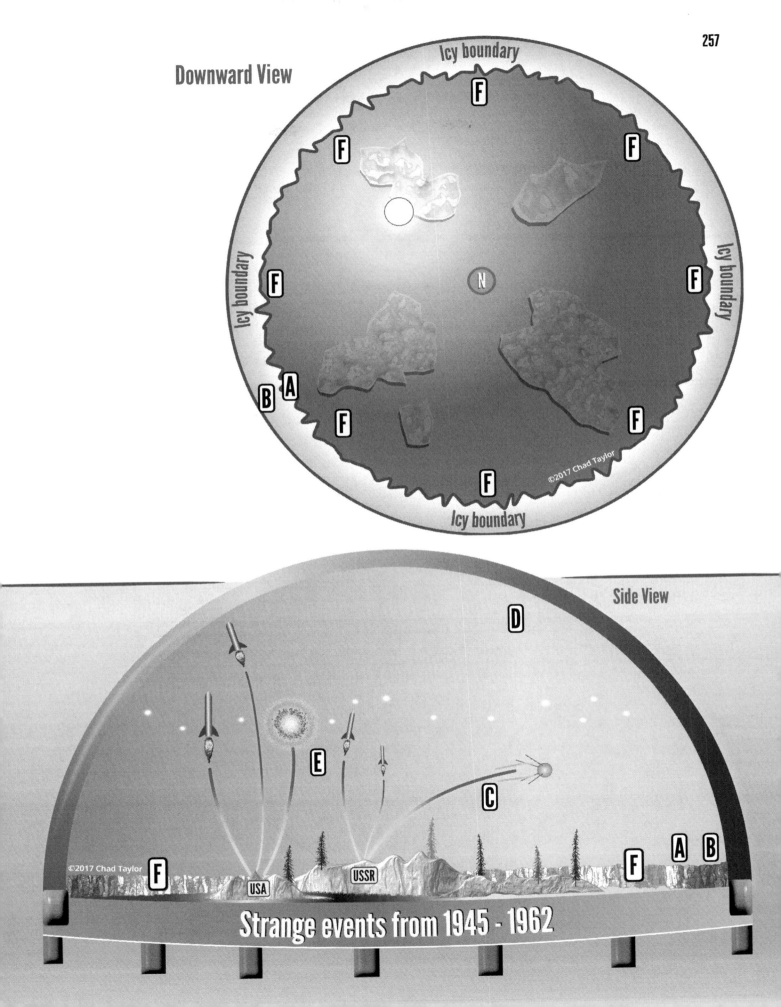

Downward View

Icy boundary

Icy boundary

Icy boundary

Icy boundary

N

Side View

Strange events from 1945 - 1962

USA

USSR

©2017 Chad Taylor

©2017 Chad Taylor

7. The cycles of earth

⁵ The sun rises and the sun sets, then hurries around to rise again. ⁶ The wind blows south, and then turns north. Around and around it goes, blowing in circles. ⁷ Rivers run into the sea, but the sea is never full. Then the water returns again to the rivers and flows out again to the sea.

- Ecclesiastes 1:5-7 (NLT)   *From pages 48-49*

There is a symbiotic order to the way God made the earth. With Him in the middle of everything, earth is self sustaining and an absolute marvel to behold. Do any of us question if the sunlight will greet us in the morning? Do we doubt if the moon and stars will shine at night? Can we plan our lives for the changing seasons, knowing they will be there? Do all of us, young and old take the cycles God put in place for granted? I know I do. Let me give you an example, let's look at the moon.

Every time I see the moon shining in the sky, it almost brings me to tears. We all see it there. Sometimes it may be hard to notice. Other times it is almost blinding in the night sky. *We have seen it our whole lives, so what?* We don't even know what we are really looking at. I have heard it is the most photographed object ever. Such magnificence, yet very few of us slow down to ponder what we are looking at. It is one of countless things God made that almost all of us pay little attention to. That is what almost brings me to tears.

We have been told to believe it is a rock in space, a quarter million miles away and reflecting the sun. What if none of that is true? What if it is much closer? What if it is much smaller? What if it is not a rock at all? What if it is not reflecting light but giving off light as the Bible says it is?

Will you now give it a second thought when you see it in the sky? Will you gaze upward at it's light in wonder? Why do we only see one side of the moon, ever? Why does it give off a cooling light? *(See page 220)* Why is it so incredibly bright on a full moon, like a huge L.E.D. light in the sky? Like an L.E.D. that gives off a cooling light that for some reason, we only see one side of.

None of us fully understand the true characteristics of the moon. We completely take it and it's cycles for granted. We dismiss even the 'simplest' things God made, due to repetition and the beliefs of "the world." *It's always been shining and always will be*..........No it won't.

Some of the many cycles of the earth, etc.:

- The water has cycles and natural filters for drinking it. Many lakes even have cycles called *lake turnover.*

- The seasons and temperatures have cycles.

- The sun, moon and stars have cycles, repeating their courses over and over.

- The wind has cycles and courses that it takes.

- The cycles of oxygen, used and then recreated.

- The cycles of living plants, animals and people coexisting and reproducing.

- The cycles on the face of the moon, called *phases.*

If you want to see something interesting, examine the image to the right. Then look up the term "north azimuthal equidistant wind map." You should find real-time wind currents of the earth from a downward perspective. Notice anything similar?

Downward View

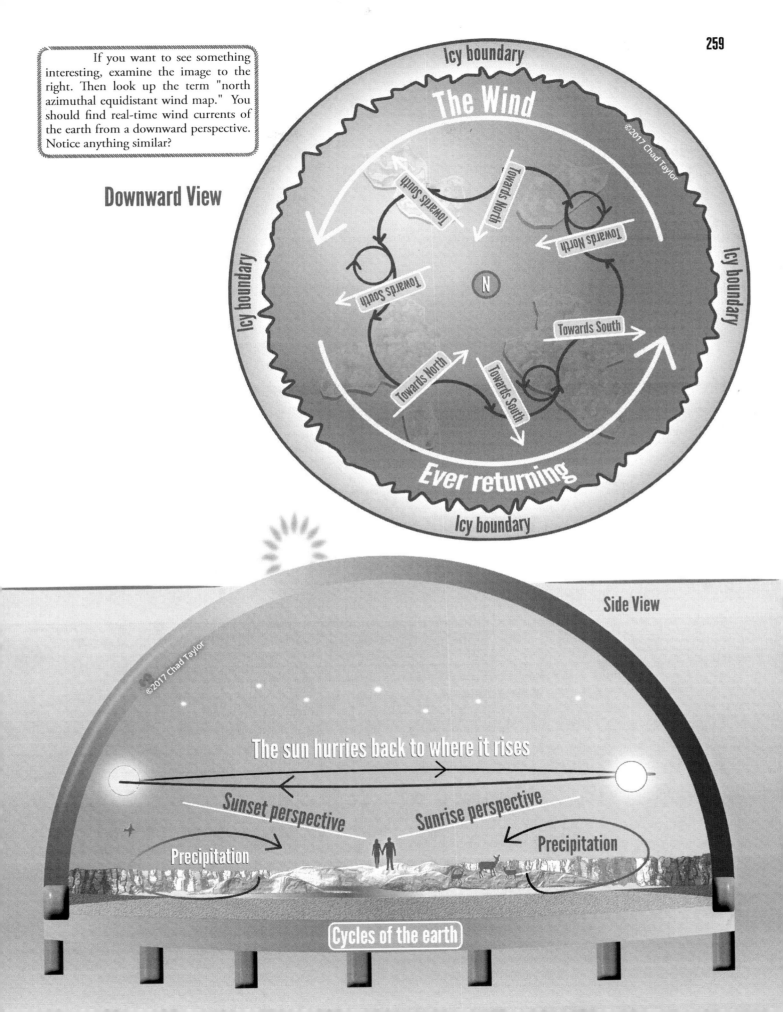

A god called 'the environment'

Over the years I have heard people use phrases like *mother earth, mother nature,* or *the environment* to describe earth and it's functions. I know many people believe earth came into existence in some sort of mathematical probability after *nothing exploded.*

To me, this belief is like saying 'if you shake a box full of old electrical parts long enough it will assemble into a top-of-the-line working HD flatscreen TV.' Anything harmful to the faith of evolution is simply hidden in millions or billions of years. *Just shake the box long enough.* Sure. Where did the electrical parts come from in the first place? The belief of order out of chaos has never sat right with me, especially now.

In many ways, God's creation has become the god to many. Countless die-hard atheists have a god they don't even realize and the God they ignore created it. The true Creator is disregarded and the creation is worshiped.

I believe in being respectful and taking care of what God has given us. To be a steward of His creation. Someone who manages it but understands that he doesn't own it. We are here for a short time and we should leave it nicer than when we found it. However, this discussion is regarding the people that take things way over the top. So much so that it becomes worship. What do you give yourself over to? That is what you worship. For some, it is God. For some, it is booze or drugs. For some, it is the earth.

Why would it matter if people take things over the top? They can believe whatever they want!

Of course they can. My question is, how are these kinds of people being used? Most of them are probably well meaning people that want to see good in the world. They probably have kind hearts but are completely controlled by fear and anger. We need to ask, are they being used like pawns? Are they fed with cherry-picked information to make them demand change? Change that was planned long before they got wound up from the 6:00 news. Are they being used to push an agenda under the guise of helping an 'endangered' earth?

Can you imagine millions of people being oppressed through unjust regulations in a ploy called *saving the environment?* Saving it from what? Who knows, but make sure you donate your hard earned money to help!

What if the term *global warming* is as real as *cubic warming?* Does earth's climate stay exactly the same year to year? Of course not, some years can be hotter or colder. Have you noticed that the term *global warming* is seldom used anymore? Now it's just *climate change.* Any change and it's your fault, man did it. No way to prove or disprove, just twist the numbers to suit the desired outcome.

Using fear and guilt, how much control would the powers-that-be gain over the masses in such a hoax? Did you know that cattle farts are starting to be regulated? Cattle farts aren't the only thing that smell like B.S.

How much control and money would certain people lose if we learned the real threats, or lack of threats 'the environment' faces? What if most threats to 'the environment' are no more real than certain news stories on December 24th? Ozone layer-schmozone layer, *REGULATE, REGULATE, REGULATE.* Greenhouse gas-schmeenhouse gas, *REGULATE, REGULATE, REGULATE.* What if *climate change* is just a ploy for creating money and power while reinforcing the belief in a spinning ball? As long as we pay our indulgence to "the world," our carbon footprint sin is forgiven. Has this charade gone far enough?

Have you heard the term *carbon footprint?* I'm willing to bet you have. When I use to hear people talk about *carbon footprint* and *carbon tax,* I would envision black charcoal particles filling the air. Is that the same with you?

Eventually I learned what 'they' are really talking about. *Carbon* is short for the invisible gas *carbon dioxide.* I'm sure you've had a *carbon*ated beverage before. That fizz in your soda, carbon dioxide. That foamy beer, carbon dioxide. Another funny thing is that carbon dioxide is vital for plants to live. We all exhale carbon dioxide, which plants use and then give off oxygen. Your breath literally helps plants live, so they can live and help you breath. Total harmony.

Why do 'they' say *carbon* instead of *carbon dioxide?* Is it because you don't get the same dirty picture 'they' want you to have? Is it because 'they' can keep you confused and scared over this evil six letter word? When was the last time you heard anyone use the actual term *carbon dioxide?*

Billions and trillions of dollars can be created through these extra taxes. While at the same time subjecting the masses to more and more unnecessary regulations. Should you have to pay a carbon tax for exhaling more than other people do?

There are certainly people, companies and countries that are not taking care of God's creation in the way they should. But do you see a larger picture of *artificial* scarcity? Are we put in fear of supposed diminishing resources? Should we believe there is a dwindling supply to go around and be happy with whatever crumbs we can get? Or can we live a life of abundance and prosperity? I have made my decision, how about you?

The thief comes only to steal and kill and destroy.
I came that they may have life and have it abundantly.

John 10:10 (ESV)

8. The future of earth

After Jesus returns in the future, things will be even more incredible on the earth. There seems to be two distinct time frames in the future:

- After Jesus returns, He will reign on earth for 1000 years.

- After the 1000 years, God makes a new heaven and new earth, *(see pages 194-199)*.
  Then the New Jerusalem descends from heaven to earth, *(see also pages 222-223)*.
  It is hard to call this part a time frame because this period goes on *forever*.

We can not imagine how incredible the future of earth and our time with God is going to be. I can only picture a state of peace and order on earth that is indescribable. Before the fall of Adam and Eve, the earth seemed to be an incredibly peaceful place. Where God was physically in the presence of man. Everything was at peace with everything. It sure seems like there are going to be massive amounts of peaceful time returning in our future. As if God is going to put things back to the way he originally planned, before satan and man messed it up. Where He will be with us on this earth in a state of peace and order we cannot currently fathom.

Of course there are other huge events that happen before the new heavens and new earth. Big events like everyone being resurrected at some point, (yes, that includes you), the bema seat judgment, the great white throne judgment, satan being bound and then released 1000 years later, followed by a short battle. Who knows what else is going to happen, but it sure seems fascinating.

What does a new heaven mean? I think all we have is educated guesses as to what this could mean. I think it is a safe bet that the heavens above will look different than they do now. Is this referring to the heaven as in the sun, moon and stars? Will they be different or not be there at all? Will the sun and moon no longer shine? Or is *heaven* referring to the firmament? Could it be different or gone altogether? If God removed the water outside the firmament, could he then remove the firmament itself? What would the view of the sky look like then?

What does a new earth mean? Just like the new heaven, all we know for sure is that earth is going to be different than it is now. There are many verses that make it seem like there are not going to be oceans in the future. If that is the case, that would be different. Could the entire earth be new, or just vastly different? Will we ... to communicate with plants and animals, literally? That would be new, to us. Will earth be like it ... fall of Adam and Eve? *(See Genesis 3).* Will it not take sweat from the brow to produce a harvest? ... to simply command fruit to be? Will there be no more weeds or thistles? If or when childbirth ... less painful as it seems prior to the fall of man? Will God's curse on the ground be gone, ... w ground altogether? Rest assured, there will be a day that we understand the meaning of ... e see it first hand.

Below are two examples that may give us an idea of the peace that will be in the future:

⁶In that day the wolf and the lamb will live together; the leopard will lie down with the baby goat. The calf and the yearling will be safe with the lion, and a little child will lead them all. ⁷The cow will graze near the bear. The cub and the calf will lie down together. The lion will eat hay like a cow. ⁸The baby will play safely near the hole of a cobra. Yes, a little child will put its hand in a nest of deadly snakes without harm. ⁹Nothing will hurt or destroy in all my holy mountain, for as the waters fill the sea, so the earth will be filled with people who know the Lord.

- Isaiah 11:6-9 (NLT)

¹⁶All who invoke a blessing or take an oath will do so by the God of truth. For I will put aside my anger and forget the evil of earlier days. ¹⁷"Look! I am creating new heavens and a new earth, and no one will even think about the old ones anymore. ¹⁸Be glad; rejoice forever in my creation! And look! I will create Jerusalem as a place of happiness. Her people will be a source of joy. ¹⁹I will rejoice over Jerusalem and delight in my people. And the sound of weeping and crying will be heard in it no more.

-Isaiah 65:16-19 (NLT)

"...the river of the water of life..." Revelation 22:1 (ESV) *See Page 199*

9. Who made it all?

Let's take a quick look back at the beginning of the Bible.

And God said, Let there be light: and there was light.

- Genesis 1:3 (KJV)   *(page 2)*

And God said, Let there be a firmament in the midst of the waters, and let it divide the waters from the waters.

- Genesis 1:6 (KJV)   *(Page 4)*

And God said, Let the waters under the heaven be gathered together unto one place, and let the dry land appear: and it was so.

- Genesis 1:9 (KJV)   *(page 6)*

And God said, Let there be lights in the firmament of the heaven to divide the day from the night; and let them be for signs, and for seasons, and for days, and years:

- Genesis 1:14 (KJV)   *(page 8)*

And God said, Let the waters bring forth abundantly the moving creature that hath life, and fowl that may fly above the earth in the open firmament of heaven.

- Genesis 1:20 (KJV)   *(page 10)*

And God said, Let the earth bring forth the living creature after his kind, cattle, and creeping thing, and beast of the earth after his kind: and it was so.

- Genesis 1:24 (KJV)   *(page 12)*

From what we have seen on our journey so far, it is obvious that God made everything. Now, before we shut the book and call it a day, I'd like to dig a little deeper into this subject. For instance, let's compare two examples regarding the creation of the heavens. Let's see if we notice something interesting.

⁶ By the word of the Lord the heavens were made, and by the breath of his mouth all their host. ⁷ He gathers the waters of the sea as a heap; he puts the deeps in storehouses. ⁸ Let all the earth fear the Lord; let all the inhabitants of the world stand in awe of him! ⁹ For he spoke, and it came to be; he commanded, and it stood firm.

- Psalm 33:6-9 (ESV)

Okay, there you have it, God's Word made the heavens. Wait a minute, what do we do with this?:

¹² "Listen to me, O Jacob, and Israel, whom I called! I am he; I am the first, and I am the last. ¹³ My hand laid the foundation of the earth, and my right hand spread out the heavens; when I call to them, they stand forth together.

- Isaiah 48:12-13 (ESV) (From page 54)

What! Which one is it? Did God's Word make the heavens or did His right hand do it? When I originally noticed these 'contradictions,' I knew there had to be something to learn. Some of you already know the answer and perhaps some of you are like I was, expecting to learn something.

Well, did God's Word create the heavens (and everything else) or did his right hand? Which one is true? *Both*. It may be obvious to some, but the connection I was missing in the past was *who*? *Who* is God's Word and *Who* is God's right hand?

¹In the beginning the Word already existed. The Word was with God, and the Word was God. ²He existed in the beginning with God. ³God created everything through him, and nothing was created except through him. ⁴The Word gave life to everything that was created, and his life brought light to everyone. ⁵The light shines in the darkness, and the darkness can never extinguish it.

⁶God sent a man, John the Baptist, ⁷to tell about the light so that everyone might believe because of his testimony. ⁸John himself was not the light; he was simply a witness to tell about the light. ⁹The one who is the true light, who gives light to everyone, was coming into the world.

¹⁰He came into the very world he created, but the world didn't recognize him. ¹¹He came to his own people, and even they rejected him. ¹²But to all who believed him and accepted him, he gave the right to become children of God. ¹³They are reborn—not with a physical birth resulting from human passion or plan, but a birth that comes from God.

¹⁴So the Word became human and made his home among us. He was full of unfailing love and faithfulness. And we have seen his glory, the glory of the Father's one and only Son.

- John 1:1-14 (NLT)

The Word:

- ☐ Existed in the beginning with God

- ☐ Was with God

- ☐ Is God

- ☐ God created <u>everything</u> through him

- ☐ Gave life to <u>everything</u> that was created

- ☐ He is the true light and gives light to everyone

- ☐ He came into the world *he* created

- ☐ He became human and lived among us

- ☐ He was rejected by his own people

- ☐ He gives the right to be children of God to those who believe and accept him

- ☐ He is full of love and faithfulness

- ☐ He is the one and only Son of God the Father

Who is God's one and only Son that created everything?

Jesus

©2017 Chad Taylor

¹³*For he has rescued us from the kingdom of darkness and transferred us into the Kingdom of his dear Son,* ¹⁴*who purchased our freedom and forgave our sins.* ¹⁵*Christ is the visible image of the invisible God. He existed before anything was created and is supreme over all creation,*

¹⁶*for through him God created everything in the heavenly realms and on earth. He made the things we can see and the things we can't see—such as thrones, kingdoms, rulers, and authorities in the unseen world. Everything was created through him and for him.* ¹⁷*He existed before anything else, and he holds all creation together.*

¹⁸*Christ is also the head of the church, which is his body. He is the beginning, supreme over all who rise from the dead. So he is first in everything.* ¹⁹*For God in all his fullness was pleased to live in Christ,* ²⁰*and through him God reconciled everything to himself. He made peace with everything in heaven and on earth by means of Christ's blood on the cross.*

- Colossians 1:13-20 (NLT)

Jesus Christ:

- ☐ Purchased our freedom and forgives our sins

- ☐ Is the visible image of the invisible God

- ☐ He created everything and holds all of creation together

- ☐ God made peace with everything through Jesus' blood on the cross

God's right hand:

Oh sing to the Lord a new song, for he has done marvelous things! His right hand and his holy arm have worked salvation for him.

- Psalm 98:1 (ESV)

This is an interesting statement. *God's right hand and arm worked salvation for Him.* I think there is much more depth to this example than any of us can understand, *(at least in this lifetime)*. But if we can bring this down to the very basics, who did God the Father have work salvation for Him? Who sweat blood knowing what he was going to endure for you, me and the rest of humanity? Who gave Himself as a sacrifice to take our place so that we could have His?

Jesus

What are some examples of salvation being through Jesus?

Jesus saith unto him, I am the way, the truth, and the life: no man cometh unto the Father, but by me.

- John 14:6 (KJV)

And this is the record, that God hath given to us eternal life, and this life is in his Son. He that hath the Son hath life; and he that hath not the Son of God hath not life.

- 1 John 5:11-12 (KJV)

[9] If you openly declare that Jesus is Lord and believe in your heart that God raised him from the dead, you will be saved. [10] For it is by believing in your heart that you are made right with God, and it is by openly declaring your faith that you are saved. [11] As the Scriptures tell us, "Anyone who trusts in him will never be disgraced." [12] Jew and Gentile are the same in this respect. They have the same Lord, who gives generously to all who call on him. [13] For "Everyone who calls on the name of the Lord will be saved."

- Romans 10:9-13 (NLT)

More examples of <u>**God's right hand:**</u>

[34] For David did not ascend into the heavens, but he himself says, "'The Lord said to my Lord, "Sit at my right hand, [35] until I make your enemies your footstool."' [36] Let all the house of Israel therefore know for certain that God has made him both Lord and Christ, this Jesus whom you crucified."

- Acts 2:34-36 (ESV)

(see also Psalm 110:1)

And Jesus said, "I am, and you will see the Son of Man seated at the right hand of Power, and coming with the clouds of heaven."

- Mark 14:62 (ESV)

Your right hand, O Lord, glorious in power, your right hand, O Lord, shatters the enemy.

- Exodus 15:6 (ESV)

His splendor was like the sunrise; rays flashed from his hand, where his power was hidden.

- Habakkuk 3:4 NIV)

Or how about this example. It is God the Father talking to Jesus. God the Father calls Jesus God and then refers back to Himself as His God. It feels like such an honorable statement of approval from a Father to a Son:

[8] But of the Son he says, "Your throne, O God, is forever and ever, the scepter of uprightness is the scepter of your kingdom. [9] You have loved righteousness and hated wickedness; therefore God, your God, has anointed you with the oil of gladness beyond your companions."

- Hebrews 1:8-9 (ESV)

(See also Psalm 45:6-7)

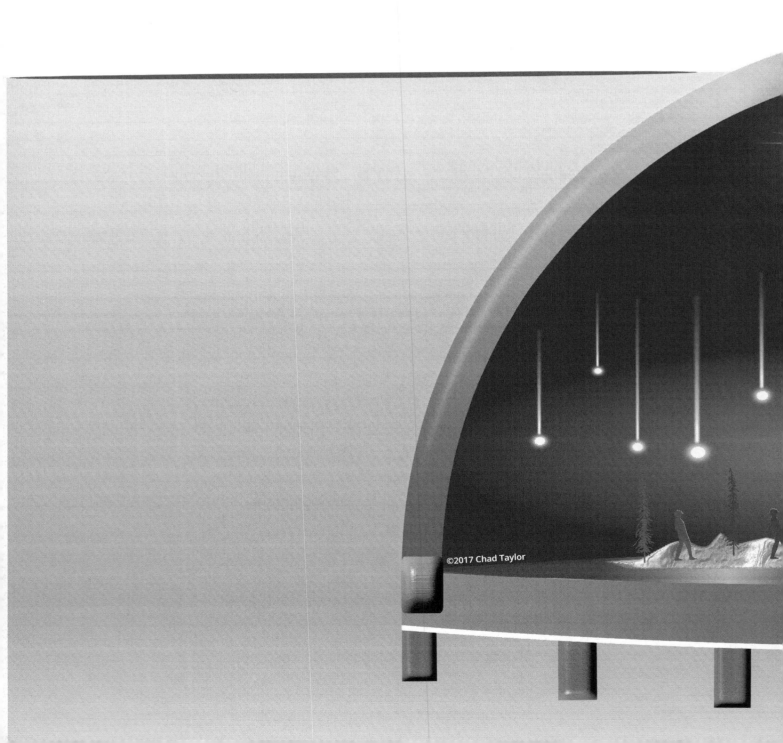

©2017 Chad Taylor

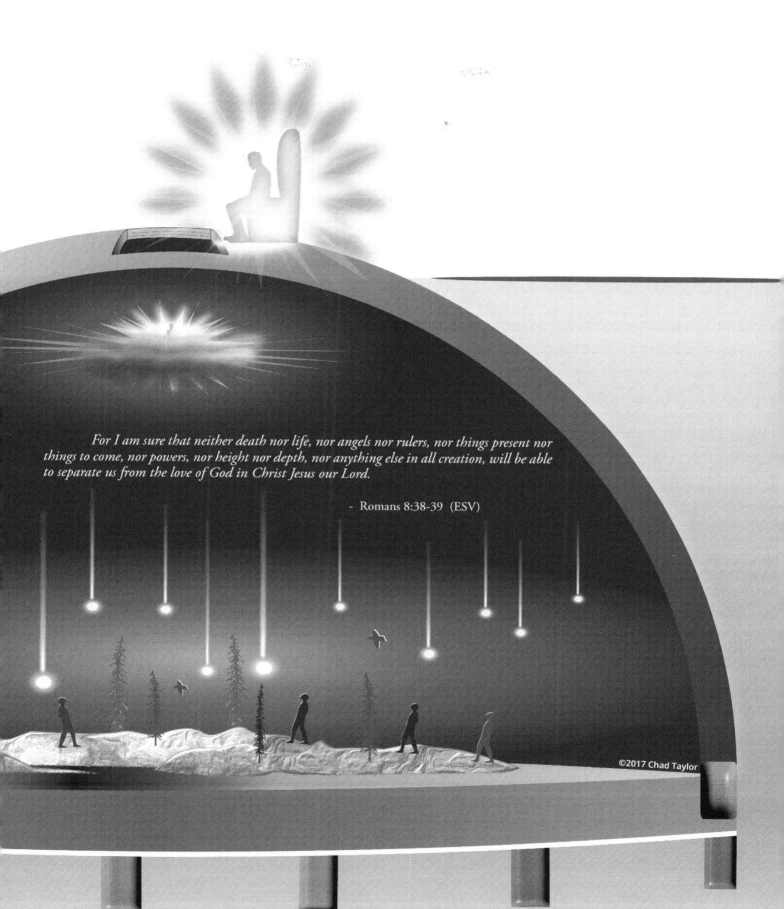

For I am sure that neither death nor life, nor angels nor rulers, nor things present nor things to come, nor powers, nor height nor depth, nor anything else in all creation, will be able to separate us from the love of God in Christ Jesus our Lord.

- Romans 8:38-39 (ESV)

©2017 Chad Taylor

The last question:

Q: What Difference does it make? What does it matter if we are not on a spinning ball? Who cares.

A: Believe it or not, this is the most common response I get and I wanted to save it for the end. If you have gone all the way through this book and have a similar response, it means the implications probably haven't sunk in yet. Maybe you are not ready for it or maybe you are blinded by pride. Perhaps you are caught up with the worries of this world and don't want to think about anything but your problems. Only God knows what you need to change.

One of the biggest fears of man is the fear of change. Change can be a big struggle for many of us. We naturally get stuck in the ruts of our life. Even though the rut holds us back, it's *our* rut. We are use to *our* rut, it has become comfortable. We have been in *our* rut for so long, we feel it may be harder to get out of it than to just stay in it.

I am here to tell you, it is liberating to look in the mirror and admit when you are wrong. It starts with you. It is a beautiful, humbling experience. This was difficult for me in the past. I didn't want to be wrong and I would defend my position, whether right or wrong. This was pride and eventually I recognized it for what it was. Change is not easy at first, but each time you do it, allowing yourself to be corrected by The Truth, the easier and better life gets.

The implications of this topic are the exact opposite of being able to simply brush off. It matters because *EVERYTHING in your life CHANGES.* God is very real and very close. Whether you believe it or not, whether you accept it or not, there is one Truth. The world you have lived your whole life in, is very different than you think it is. What is actually above you in the sky is very different than you think it is.

The first couple of weeks after all of this sunk in for me I couldn't stop looking up. I kept saying *"Really? Can it really be?"* After the initial shock of it all, a peace began setting in. A peace from the inside out. Not only does God's spirit dwell in me, but God is literally *right up there.* He is so much closer than "the world" would have me believe.

> *The Lord is exalted over all the nations, his glory above the heavens. Who is like the Lord our God, the One who sits enthroned on high, who stoops down to look on the heavens and the earth?*
>
> - Psalm 113:4-6 (NIV)   *(From page 211)*

Yes, at some point in the future the heavens will open and Jesus will descend on clouds.

I guess in the end it all comes down to one question;

Who are you going to believe, "the world" or The Word?

©2017 Chad Taylor

WHAT NOW?

Where do we go from here?

²⁶ Remember, dear brothers and sisters, that few of you were wise in the world's eyes or powerful or wealthy when God called you. ²⁷ Instead, God chose things the world considers foolish in order to shame those who think they are wise. And he chose things that are powerless to shame those who are powerful. ²⁸ God chose things despised by the world, things counted as nothing at all, and used them to bring to nothing what the world considers important. ²⁹ As a result, no one can ever boast in the presence of God.

- 1 Corinthians 1:26-29 (NLT)

Suggestions for sharing this book with people:

Q: I would like to share this book with people.....how do I do it? What should I do?

A: I would have the same desire to share this book with others as you may have right now.   One thing that can slow us down from following through with action is our *fear of rejection*. The fear of rejection can be a deep resistance to what we really want to accomplish. It can stop us in our tracks and leave us saying to ourselves; *"What are they going to think of me?"*

I have really good news for you!

Whether you are good at talking to people or not,

whether you are confident about this subject or not,

whether you are sharing this with someone close or a stranger,

this should be much easier than you think.

Listed below are *five simple steps* for sharing this book. I suggest that you keep things simple and use these steps as a guide. I have learned many valueable lessons in my years of working with people. These steps are a culmination of countless lessons learned, mostly the hard way. Obviously I can't guarantee what your experience is going to be in using these steps as a guide. In my opinion and from my experience this is the best way to share this book....*with anyone.*

The five simple steps:

STEP 1. It's not about you.

STEP 2. Give genuine compliments and ask questions.

STEP 3. Give or loan them this tool.

STEP 4. Follow up with them.

STEP 5. Point them to more information.

Turn the page for more details

The five simple steps in more detail:

I remember being nervous the first few times I shared this subject with people, especially people close to me. I didn't have anything to hand them that would do the work for me. It was all up to me and my words. For the most part I could tell I wasn't really getting through to people. I could easily picture the images you have seen in this book in my mind, but getting others to see what I saw was easier said than done. Other than pointing out some verses, I had nothing physical to hand someone that would help explain things. Until now.

Now, with this book that all changes. No longer is it up to you or me to share this subject. Now there is a tool that will do the work for us.......*this tool.* Using this book as a tool, sharing this subject couldn't be easier.

We are going to go through *the five simple steps* in more detail to see how easy sharing this book can be. Using the steps as a guide should help you in sharing this book with family, friends and strangers. It is only natural to think you can shortcut these steps with family and friends. Keep in mind, just because you know them doesn't make their foundational beliefs any smaller than everyone else's. We must understand that the beliefs this world has given us are as entrenched as any politics or religion can be.

Do you think you could walk up to someone with a different political view or religion than you and say: *"Read this book, it'll prove I'm right and you're wrong. You'll see!"*

How would this go over? What good would come from going this route? You may be perfectly correct in your statement, but how likely is the person to even open the book? Even if by some miracle the person happened to open it, they already have a defensive wall up. They will go into it with a negative attitude and a closed mind. More than likely the person would read until they disagreed with something and that's as far as they go. You will probably never hear from them about the subject again.

The worst way of sharing this book is to blindside someone with details, expecting them to change their foundational beliefs overnight. It does not work. Please do not think your friend or family member is the exception and that they will immediately forget years and years of deeply held beliefs in an instant.

With a little bit of planning, you can help them open this book *without* being defensive. They can read this book *without* being closed minded. This is the purpose of *the five simple steps.* To allow people to read this book in a natural, open minded way.

Another benefit of following these steps is avoiding awkwardness between you and the other person. Are you ready to see how this is done? *Here we go.*

<u>STEP 1.</u> It's not about you

First thing's first. *It's not about you.* It is about *them* and connecting *them* to this book. That's it. *The five simple steps* are easy when pride is not in the way. When you take yourself out of the picture, all you really do is connect A to B. It is not about proving you are right and they are wrong. *"I told you so"* has no place in this process. If this is your attitude, change it.

When it's about *you* and proving *you* are right, *you* put the other person in a position of having to be wrong. If you do this, they are most likely going to react one of two ways. Their most likely reaction is to get defensive and defend their position. They will avoid the topic with you in the future and maybe even avoid you altogether. The other reaction is very un-likely; they admit to being wrong their entire life.

It is vital to have empathy. Try to see things from the other person's point of view. If you act superior and hammer the person to prove your position, *you <u>both</u> lose.* All you accomplish in acting prideful is ensuring they will probably never talk to you about this subject again. If you have already made this mistake the only answer is humility. *You* being humble, meeting the person face to face and apologizing for treating them poorly. In doing this, there is a chance they may come to you in the future wanting to hear more from you. The only reason this would happen is because they know you are not going to treat them that way again.

Be humble. Remember, you were once ignorant too. Treat people with the patience and understanding you would have wanted for yourself. I could hammer people all day long with details to *prove them wrong,* but nothing good would come from it. After all, it's not about *me* and it's not about *you,* it's about *them.*

After we understand **STEP 1**, now it's on to **STEP 2.** Before sharing this book willy-nilly, I suggest doing a Proverbs 3:5-8. Ask God who you should share this book with and go with how you feel led. Some people may not be ready for this book and some people will.

> Trust in the Lord with all your heart and lean not on your own understanding; in all your ways submit to him, and he will make your paths straight. Do not be wise in your own eyes; fear the Lord and shun evil. This will bring health to your body and nourishment to your bones.
>
> - Proverbs 3:5-8 (NIV)

STEP 2.   Give genuine compliments and ask questions

Below are two examples of what you could say to a friend, relative or stranger. You certainly don't have to follow this word-for-word, it is just meant to give you a basic understanding of how simple **STEP 2** can be when you keep it simple.

An example talk with a friend or relative:

"I have always liked to hear your point of view. I recently came across a book that I find very interesting and I would love to get your opinion of it. It is about what the Bible has to say regarding earth and where heaven is. It is an easy read with lots of images. I value your opinion and I'd love to hear your thoughts. If I loaned it to you would you read it and tell me what you think?"

An example talk with a stranger:

Our natural instinct is to talk to friends and family first. However, it may actually be easier to share this book with strangers. If nothing else, it's good practice before talking to friends and family. Most likely you will only have 60-90 seconds with a stranger. It could be the person pumping gas beside you or someone you bump into while shopping. The point is, it is going to be a short conversation. *Which is what you want.*

I suggest complimenting them on their car, shoes, pet, clothes, etc. Be genuine and sincere. Everyone loves a compliment. It's a great ice breaker and a good way of connecting with people. **(Good job complimenting them, they are smiling and saying thanks).** At this point would it be weird to ask them if they've seen the latest popular movie? Of course not, so why would you make this weird?

After a very brief chit-chat, you can say something like; *"This may seem out of the blue but have you read the new book called 'Where are We'?"* If they say yes, you can ask them what they thought of it. Statistically, they will say *"No."* Then all you have to say is something like; *"I read it recently and it blew my mind. It's about what the Bible says regarding earth and where heaven is. I was just curious if you've read it."*

Now stop talking. This may seem weird, but I tend to picture it like fishing. You just cast your line and are waiting for a bite. If they don't bite, no biggy. You wish them a nice day and go on with yours. No awkwardness at all. However if they show interest, *fish on.* They may say something like *"That sounds interesting. Where'd you get it?"* If you happen to have a copy of this book with you at the time, you could show it to them, loan it to them, or give it to them. If not, you could just refer them to **www.wherearewethebook.com** to get their own. If you don't keep a copy of this book in your vehicle, you could show them a screenshot of the book, just a thought.

Whether talking to family, friends or strangers, *there should be no awkwardness to what you say.* It is only awkward if you make it about you and *it's not about you, remember.* You read an interesting book and would like their opinion. That's it. I suggest you avoid telling them your opinions beforehand. This also allows them to open the book *bias-free.* The more you tell them before they read it, the more rope you give them to hang themselves with. What is the point of this book if you are going to try *proving your point* before they even open it?

Remember **STEP 1.** It's not about you. You are just helping connect A to B. Some A's don't want B and some A's do. No matter what happens, don't take it personal. Also, keep in mind some people may eventually come back and want to hear more from you. Some seeds can just take longer to grow than others.

<u>STEP 3.</u> Give or loan them this tool - *Do not vomit on them!*

Imagine this book as a tool. There are many different types of tools. A hammer for instance is made for driving in nails, while a flashlight is made for shining light. You may be able to use a flashlight to drive in a nail, but that is not the best use of a flashlight.

This book is like a flashlight. It works great for shining light on the subject, but it makes a lousy hammer. Do not use this flashlight to beat people over the head in an attempt to drive in your point. Allow this tool to do what it is meant to do; shine light.

After **STEP 1** and **STEP 2**, you are ready for **STEP 3**. At this step, we have already concluded the person is interested in reading this book. Maybe the conversation you had with the person on **STEP 2** was over the phone, or maybe it was in person. Regardless, there is one extremely important factor when giving or loaning someone this tool, *do not vomit on them!*

What does that mean? It means that when you hand somebody a copy of this book, don't spend half an hour continuing to sell them on what they are going to read.

Let me give you an example. I have *thousands* of hours into making this book. I know it better than anyone. There is not a chance I am going to say more than a couple of sentences in an enthusiastic way as I hand them a copy. If I were to share everything I know, eventually they would hear something they didn't agree with and then they would stop being interested in the book.

Would you want someone to spoil the details of a good movie before you had a chance to watch it? Of course not, so don't do that with this book. If they start asking questions, just remind them that is why you want them to read it, so you can hear *their conclusions.* We must allow them to come up with *their own* conclusions. Do not hamstring them by sharing your understandings before they have even gotten to page one. If you have a hard time with this, go back to **STEP 1**. *It's not about you.*

When you give them a copy you can say something like; *"I look forward to hearing your thoughts about it."* If you are going to loan them the copy, it is best that you give them a rough time frame to get it back to you. *"This book is a pretty quick read, would I be able to get it back in a week?"*

Regardless if you are loaning them a copy or giving them a copy, you want to make sure they know you are wanting to hear their thoughts about the book. Otherwise, life could get in the way and they may never open it. You are keeping them accountable to reading it by wanting to hear their opinions of it.

I am not saying to ask for their thoughts just to help them get through the book, I am serious. I can't wait to hear people's thoughts and questions about this book. I can't wait to watch light bulbs go off. I look forward to hearing people's reactions. When I hand someone a book and ask them for their thoughts about it, I mean it.

Allow the tool to do the work. Do not stand there and answer question after question prior to them reading the book. You are actually helping them by sticking to these steps.

Lastly, if you get the feeling the person is not going to read it and/or get it back to you, it may be best to not give them a copy. It could get frustrating trying to retrieve a loaned copy from a flaky person.

<u>STEP 4.</u> Follow up with them

In this step, we get back in touch with the person to get their input. As we have already discussed, there should be no awkwardness and no pressure from you. Regardless of the person's current views of this book, you are very unlikely to change their mind in one conversation. Throughout the steps, we must remain humble and pressure free. It's not about us, it's about them and the information we helped put in front of them.

This may be redundant, but is worth mentioning. In keeping things not about us, even if they hated the book, they can't think negative about you. You didn't beat them over the head with it before you gave it to them. You didn't preach to them about your understandings before you gave it to them. You gave them this tool in a gentle, humble manner. In doing so, they will most likely discuss the book with you in an open way.

I want to hear people's thoughts and where they are without them filtering it. Getting people's genuine thoughts may actually be harder for me because my name is on the cover. However, you will be able to hear unfiltered opinions. You haven't identified your level of belief in what this book contains, because again...*it's not about you,* and you never made it about you.

If you gave them their own copy, contact them after a week or two and get feedback. No matter what they say, do not get upset. Regardless if you loaned them a copy or gave them a copy, you want feedback. You can learn something from everyone, what can you learn from their conclusions?

<u>Some questions you may want to ask them</u>...

- ☐ **What interested you the most?**

- ☐ **Did the Bible say what you thought it did about earth and heaven?**

- ☐ **Were there surprises to what you read? What were they?**

- ☐ **Did the book get you to question things you haven't questioned before? What were they?**

- ☐ **What did you agree or disagree with?**

- ☐ **Do you think there is any validity to what was in the book?**

- ☐ **Would you want to learn more about the subject?**

Don't be surprised or offended by any responses you get. It wasn't that long ago I would have found much of this book hard to swallow. It is hard to say how people will react when their foundational beliefs come into question. It is only natural for some people to be offended or angry at first, while others may be excited and very happy. We must give people their time and space to examine *their own* beliefs.

After you ask them questions like the ones above, allow them to speak. Don't interrupt them. People will be much less likely to give you their thoughts if you immediately start correcting them. After all, you wanted to hear their thoughts didn't you? If they start asking you questions, feel free to answer appropriately.

You may be the only person they feel comfortable discussing this subject with, so be there for them. If you told them you were loaning this book to them, get it back. Make sure you contact the person within a week or two at the most. Do not leave things in a strange silence by purposely not talking to them.

If you contact them and they haven't touched it and seem uninterested, I suggest you get it back from them, (with a good attitude) and move on.

<u>STEP 5.</u> Point them to more information

After getting the person's thoughts, the next step is to give them more information *if they want it.* Some people will want more info, while others may not. Just because someone does not want any more info at the moment, does not mean they are not interested. Some people just take more time to come around than others. Someone you loaned the book to last week may contact you in six months wanting to know more. The great thing is that since it's about them and not you, you are not affected by whether or not people are interested in learning more. Yay!

Refer to page 287 for my suggestions for more information.

<u>Final thoughts:</u>

Sowing and Reaping

One of the many themes in the Bible is the idea of sowing and reaping. Regarding this book, I imagine planting a seed, watering and at some point harvesting. The seed planting would be the process of giving this book to someone and them reading it. Over time the watering occurs, this is when the person grows in understanding and belief. This could take days, months or years. The final step is the harvesting, this is the point when the plant is now bearing fruit and is ready to be harvested. I picture someone at the harvesting stage when they start sharing this subject and/or book with others.

I mention planting a seed, watering and harvesting because almost all of us want this process to happen instantly. I picture standing there vomiting information all over someone as you hand them this book like planting a seed and then taking a fire hose to it. Then after a half hour of forceful flooding, expecting it to be harvest time. This route is fruitless and ignorant, please do not take it.

Personally, when I discuss this subject with people, I am not trying to convince them of anything. My point is only to plant a seed that helps them start to question. Questions are the tool that begin the process of chipping away at the foundation most of us have built our lives on.

This process takes time. We must be patient. We are dealing with deeply rooted foundational beliefs. You are just doing the job of planting a seed and maybe watering it once in a while. It is not up to you if the seed grows, that is between them and God.

What else you can do to help:

If the idea of sharing this book seems a little scary at first, don't worry. There are other important things you can do to help that don't require you to talk to anyone. Regardless of your confidence level or abilities, below are five things *you*, yes *you* can do to help, if you would like to.

1. Consider leaving an honest review online. Every review is helpful and you can leave it anonymously. Thank you in advance for any reviews you leave. If I may ask, please keep the reviews shorter and please don't give away any spoilers. Long reviews that give away spoilers may turn people away before they have had a chance to read the book for themselves and come up with their own conclusions.

2. Visit my website at **wherearewethebook.com**, as well as my YT channel *Chad Taylor*. Consider subscribing to the YT channel and sharing the videos and/or website with people. Subscribing to the channel will help you not miss anything. It will also help promote the channel, which in turn helps share this book with others.

3. If you happen to make content online, (videos or blogging for instance), consider making a short review of this book. This can be a big help as well. You can keep it anonymous, or not. Please give an honest review and again if I may ask, please don't give away any spoilers. Spoilers could turn people off before they have had their chance to go on their own journey through this book and come up with *their own* conclusions.

4. Consider giving others a copy of this book. Whether you give a copy to someone face to face or anonymously, giving away copies of this book is obviously a great way of sharing it. Besides face to face, some suggestions of sharing copies can be to leave one at church, a coffee shop, a waiting room, a community center, a break room at work, a hotel lobby, a restaurant lounge, a truck stop, etc. You can be creative with this. Think about places where people tend to sit for a while. You can also mail copies to people. Please be respectful and obey any laws with sharing this book. Paperback copies are available in bulk at a discount on the website, (see the website for details). Please be responsible and do not spend money you shouldn't in order to share copies of this book with people.

Additional copies of this book are available at: wherearewethebook.com

5. Every effort was made to ensure this book is as accurate as possible. If you happened to notice any errors at all, please let me know. Whether it's something as small as a word spelled wrong or a larger error, please let me know. I greatly appreciate you bringing any errors to my attention so they can be corrected as soon as possible. Please email the information about any errors to: suggestions@wherearewethebook.com

If you would prefer to send regular mail, here is the address:

Attn: Chad Taylor
Rustic Trail Productions LLC,
14241 NE Woodinville Duvall Road
Suite 190
Woodinville, WA 98072

Thank you in advance for your help, I greatly appreciate it.

For More Information:

The people listed below have been a big help to me and are the first places I would suggest for more information.

Suggestions:

1. Visit my website - whearewethebook.com

For additional copies of this book please visit **whearewethebook.com** Copies are available in both 8.5"x 11" paperback, as well as eBook format. You do not have to have a tablet to get the eBook, you can also view the eBook on most computers or smartphones as well, (with the proper app). Paperback copies are also available in bulk at a discount on the website, (see the website for details).

Please check back on the website from time to time as it will be updated with more videos and other info. Lastly, if you want to remain in the loop, you can add your email address on the website underneath **"Join our mailing list."** I will be sending out updates to this email list as I put out new content.

2. Visit my YT channel - I will be uploading video content to my YT channel under my name, Chad Taylor.

I may or may not have these videos listed on the website, so please check both locations. Please consider subscribing to this channel so you can stay up to date with new videos as they come out. Also, please consider liking and sharing the videos if you indeed like them and want to share them.

3. Rob Skiba - Website: testingtheglobe.com

If you are interested in learning more about how the Bible and other ancient texts describe earth and heaven, Rob Skiba is a wealth of knowledge. He is also very well versed about the giants found in the Bible, (another fascinating subject). He has a popular YT channel as well.

4. Mark Sargent - Website: enclosedworld.com

Mark Sargent brings a great balance to this subject. He tends to bring alot of current events and daily observations into the discussion. He interviews a variety of guests that provide even more information. He also has a popular YT channel.

5. Robbie Davidson - Website: celebratetruth.org

Robbie at Celebrate Truth is another great source for more information. Celebrate Truth also has a popular YT channel. This is another great channel for learning how the Bible relates to the world we live in, the world God created.

Definition Reference:
Sources and page numbers

Above: "Above." in or to a higher place   P. 46, 50, 60, 64, 70, 113, 129,
Above: "Above." in or to a higher place than / over   P. 4, 32, 41, 42, 45, 80,
Above: "Above." in the sky / overhead   P. 54, 58, 115, 116, 134, 164,
About: "About." on every side of   P. 151,
Abroad: "Abroad." over a wide area   P. 53, 75,
Abundance: "Abundance." a large amount of something   P. 25,
Across: "Across." from one side to the other   P. 10, 30, 193,
Afraid: "Afraid." filled with fear   P. 151,
After: "After." later in time   P. 147, 169, 191,
Again: "Again." for another time   P. 48, 118,
Ahead: "Ahead." in a forward direction or position   P. 142,
All: "All." the whole, entire, total amount, quantity, or extent of   P. 13, 42, 53, 60, 64, 68, 70, 72, 75, 92, 116, 121, 134, 137, 144, 147, 151, 171, 185, 195,
Alone: "Alone." without anyone or anything else   P. 53, 54, 99,
Always: "Always." Forever   P. 169,
Among: "Among." in the presence of   P. 195,
And: "And." plus   P. 68, 104, 115, 173, 191, 197,
Another: "Another." one that is different   P. 188,
Any: "Any." any person or persons / anyone   P. 156,
Anyone: "Anyone." any person   P. 156,
Appear: "Appear." to come into sight   P. 6,
Are: "Be." to have a specified qualification or characterization   P. 197,
Around: "Around." in a circle   P. 48,
Around: "Around." on all or various sides / in every or any direction   P. 151,
As: "As." in the way that   P. 104, 173,
Ascend(ed)(ing): "Ascend." to move upward   P. 57, 113, 153, 154, 164, 170, 182, 187,
Ascending: "Ascending." rising or increasing to higher levels, values, or degrees   P. 80,
Assembly: "Assembly." a company of persons collected together in one place usually for some common purpose   P. 113,
Astray: "Astray." away from what is right, good, or desirable   P. 185,
At: "At." used to indicate the place where someone or something is   P. 60, 95,
Attention: "Attention." the way a soldier stands with the body stiff and straight, heels together, and arms at the sides   P. 54,
Authorities: "Authority." persons in command; *specifically* : government   P. 62,
Back: "Back." to, toward, or in the place where someone or something was previously   P. 48, 118,
Backward: "Backward." in a reverse or contrary direction or way   P. 118,
Bare: "Bare." open to view / exposed   P. 97,
Bases: "Base." the bottom or lowest part of something   P. 30,
Be: "Be." to occupy a place, situation, or position   P. 45,
Below: "Below." in or to a lower place   P. 50, 58, 115,
Before: "Before." forward of / in front of   P. 138, 142,
Beneath: "Beneath." in or to a lower position   P. 58, 100,
Between: "Between." in the space that separates (two things or people)   P. 4, 132,
Borders: "Border." an outer part or edge   P. 34,
Boundaries: "Boundary." something that indicates or fixes a limit or extent   P. 34, 46,
Bounds: "Bound." something that limits or restrains   P. 26, 34,
Bow: "Bow." something bent into a simple curve   P. 72,
Bowed: "Bow." to stop resisting / yield   P. 97,
Breadth: "Breadth." something of full width   P. 193,
Bright: "Bright." filled with light   P. 188,
Bring: "Bring." to cause (something or someone) to come   P. 126,
Broad: "Broad." having ample extent from side to side or between limits   P. 193,
Burst: "Burst." to open suddenly   P. 124,
Came: "Come." to move toward something   P. 84, 88, 90, 97, 154,
Cannot: "Cannot." can not   P. 22, 37, 58,
Canopy: "Canopy." something that hangs or spreads out over an area   P. 50,
Cast: "Cast." throw   P. 176,
Cast Out: "Cast out." to drive out / expel   P. 185,
Caught up: Past tense of: "Catch up." to pick up often abruptly   P. 166, 169,
Center: "Center." the middle point or part of something   P. 137,
Channel: "Channel." the bed where a natural stream of water runs   P. 97,
Circle: "Circle." a closed plane curve every point of which is equidistant from a fixed point within the curve   P. 26, 46, 50,
Circle(s): "Circle." a path that goes around a central point   P. 48,
Circuit: "Circuit." a boundary line around an area / an enclosed space   P. 25,
Circuit: "Circuit." the route traveled   P. 32, 48,
Come(s)/Coming: "Come." to move toward   P. 124, 156, 169, 187, 188, 191,
Coming: "Coming." an act or instance of arriving   P. 195,
Company: "Company." a body of soldiers   P. 151,
Compass: "Compass." an instrument for drawing circles or marking measurements consisting of two pointed legs joined at the top by a pivot   P. 46,
Compassed: compass. (n.d.). *Dictionary.com Unabridged.* Retrieved July 9, 2016 from Dictionary.com website http://www.dictionary.com/browse/compass Definition #14: to make curved or circular.   P. 26,
Compassed: compass. (n.d.). *Dictionary.com Unabridged.* Retrieved November 26, 2016 from Dictionary.com website http://www.dictionary.com/browse/compass Definition #11: to extend or stretch around; hem in; surround; encircle.   P. 193,
Comprehend: "Comprehend." to understand fully   P. 104,
Congregation: "Congregation." an assembly of persons / gathering; *especially* : an assembly of persons met for worship and religious instruction   P. 113,
Corners: "Corner." a private, secret, or remote place   P. 100, 108, 193,
Cornerstone: "Cornerstone." a stone that forms part of a corner in the outside wall of a building and that often shows the date when the building was built   P. 30,
Cosmic: "Cosmic." of or relating to the cosmos, the extraterrestrial vastness, or the universe in contrast to the earth alone   P. 62,
Cottage: cottage. (n.d.). *Dictionary.com Unabridged.* Retrieved January 27, 2017 from Dictionary.com website http://www.dictionary.com/browse/cottage Definition 1: a small house, usually of only one story.   P. 115,

Course: "Course." the path or direction that something or someone moves along **P. 32, 48,**

Cover: "Cover." to put something over, on top of, or in front of (something else) especially in order to protect, hide, or close it **P. 134,**

Cover(s)(ed): "Cover." to be spread over or on top of (something) **P. 25, 41,**

Crystal: "Crystal." made of or being like a clear colorless glass of very good quality **P. 128,**

Curtain: "Curtain." a piece of cloth or other material that is hung to protect or hide something/ a hanging screen usually capable of being drawn back or up **P. 41, 50,**

Dark: "Dark." having very little or no light **P. 111, 138,**

Darkened: "Darken." to make dark **P. 111, 138, 147,**

Deceive/Deceiving: "Deceive." to make (someone) believe something that is not true **P. 185, 191, 193,**

Deep: "Deep." extending far downward **P. 2, 104,**

Delayed: "Delay." a situation in which something happens later than it should **P. 95,**

Departed: "Depart." to go away **P. 173,**

Depth(s): "Depth." the perpendicular measurement downward from a surface **P. 104, 113,**

Descend(s/ed/ing): "Descend." to go or move from a higher to a lower place or level **P. 80, 86, 116, 153, 154, 162, 164, 169,**

Discovered: "Discover." to see, find, or become aware of (something) for the first time **P. 97,**

Dissolved: "Dissolve." break up, disperse **P. 36, 115,**

Divide: "Divide." to separate (something) into two or more parts or pieces **P. 4,**

Divided: "Divided." separated into parts or pieces **P. 4,**

Dome: "Dome." a large rounded roof or ceiling that is shaped like half of a ball / a large hemispherical roof or ceiling **P. 4, 8, 10, 25, 128,**

Down: "Down." from a higher to a lower place or position **P. 38, 64, 75, 78, 86, 88, 90, 95, 97, 113, 116, 124, 137, 154, 156, 162, 164, 169, 176, 185, 188, 191, 193, 195,**

Down: "Down." below the horizon **P. 48,**

Draw: "Draw." to make (a picture, image, etc.) by making lines on a surface especially with a pencil, pen, marker, chalk, etc., but not usually with paint **P. 46,**

Drop: "Drop." to fall **P. 173,**

Dwell(ing): "Dwell." to live in a particular place **P. 195,**

Each: "Each." every one of two or more people or things considered separately **P. 121,**

Edges: "Edge." the line or part where an object or area begins or ends **P. 102,**

Empty: "Empty." containing nothing **P. 26,**

End(s): "End." the part at the edge or limit of an area **P. 32, 57, 100, 102, 108, 137, 147, 159,**

Entire: "Entire." having no element or part left out **P. 70,**

Established: "Establish." to begin or create (something that is meant to last for a long time) / to bring into existence / to make firm or stable **P. 22, 37,**

Established: "Establish." to put (someone or something) in a position, role, etc., that will last for a long time **P. 46,**

Eternal: "Eternal." lasting forever **P. 154, 156,**

Everlasting: "Everlasting." lasting forever **P. 122,**

Every: "Every." including each of a group or series without leaving out any **P. 13, 64, 171, 173, 195,**

Everyone: "Everyone." every person **P. 154, 173,**

Everything: "Everything." all that relates to the subject **P. 13,**

Expanse: "Expanse." Firmament / great extent of something spread out **P. 4, 8, 10, 129,**

Expired: "Expire." to come to an end **P. 193,**

Face: "Face." any of the plane surfaces that bound a geometric solid / an inscribed, printed, or marked side **P. 2, 13, 26, 46, 59, 70, 75,**

Face: "Face." the front part of the head **P. 173,**

Fall(eth/ing)/Fell: "Fall." to descend freely by the force of gravity **P. 116, 147, 173, 178,**

Fallen: "Fall." to come or go down quickly from a high place or position **P. 113,**

False: "False." not real or genuine **P. 231,**

Far: "Far." to a great extent **P. 60, 113,**

Firm: "Firm." securely or solidly fixed in place **P. 46,**

Firmament: "Firmament." the vault or arch of the sky **P. 4, 8, 10, 32, 128,**

Firm(ly): "Firm." securely or solidly fixed in place **P. 22, 36, 37,**

First: "First." before any other **P. 169, 195,**

Fixed: "Fixed." securely placed or fastened / stationary **P. 34,**

Flood: "Flood." a large amount of water covering an area of land that is usually dry **P. 25,**

Floodgates: "Floodgate." a gate for controlling the flow of water from a lake, river, reservoir, etc. **P. 68, 115,**

Footing(s): "Footing." the base or foundation on which something is established **P. 30,**

Footstool: "Footstool." a low stool used to support the feet **P. 55,**

Forces: "Force." a body of persons available for a particular end **P. 62,**

Forever: "Forever." for a limitless time **P. 156, 169,**

Forth: "Forth." onward or forward in time or place **P. 53, 128,**

Foundation(s): foundation. (n.d.). *Dictionary.com Unabridged.* Retrieved August 7, 2016 from Dictionary.com website http://www.dictionary.com/browse/foundation - the natural or prepared ground or base on which some structure rests **P. 20, 30, 38, 41, 46, 54, 58, 59, 97, 115,**

Founds: "Found." to set or ground on something solid **P. 59,**

Fountains: "Fountain." the source from which something proceeds or is supplied **P. 46, 68,**

From: "From." used to indicate the place that something comes out of **P. 156, 187, 188,**

From: "From." used to indicate the starting point of a physical movement or action **P. 38, 64, 78, 95, 97, 113, 124, 126, 137, 147, 153, 154, 164, 169, 178, 182, 191, 193, 195,**

Garment: "Garment." a piece of clothing **P. 41,**

Gate: "Gate." a means of entrance or exit **P. 80,**

Give: "Give." to make a present of / to yield as a product, consequence, or effect **P. 111, 122, 134, 147,**

Given: "Given." presented as a gift **P. 178,**

Glory: "Glory." brilliance, splendor **P. 132, 151, 160, 188, 197,**

Habitation: "Habitation." a place to live **P. 140,**

Hang(eth/s): "Hang." to attach or place something so that it is held up without support from below **P. 26,**

Hard: "Hard." very firm or solid **P. 28,**

He: "He." that male one **P. 178,**

Head: "Head." to be the leader of (something) **P. 138,**

Heavenly: "Heavenly." appearing or occurring in the sky **P. 62,**

Height(s): "Height." distance upward **P. 25, 38, 104, 113, 137,**

Heights: "Height." a high point or position **P. 45,**

Her: "Her." of or relating to her or herself especially as possessor, agent, or object of an action **P. 111, 134, 147,**

High(er): "High." rising or extending upward a great distance **P. 25, 38, 104, 144,**

High: "High." located far above the ground or another surface **P. 42, 62, 97, 113, 115, 121, 129,**

Highest: high. (n.d.). *Dictionary.com Unabridged.* Retrieved July 7, 2016 from Dictionary.com website http://www.dictionary.com/browse/high Definition #38; a high or the highest point, place, or level; peak **P. 45, 98, 113, 151,**

Him: "Him." *objective case of* he **P. 178,**

His: "His." that which belongs to him **P. 13, 111,**

Home: "Home." one's place of residence **P. 195,**

Host(s): "Host." Army / a great number / multitude **P. 16, 45, 92, 111, 115, 116, 121, 129, 138, 151,**

Hurled: "Hurl." to throw (something) with force **P. 176,**

Hut: "Hut." a small and simple house or building **P. 115,**

Illuminate(d/s): "Illuminate." brightened with light **P. 188, 197,**

Immediately: "Immediately." without any delay **P. 147,**

In: "In." used to indicate location or position within something   P. 4, 8, 10, 50, 62, 64, 88, 90, 95, 115, 134, 182,
In: "In." within a particular place   P. 32, 60, 116, 140, 147, 169, 185,
Into: "Into." used as a function word to indicate entry, introduction, insertion, superposition, or inclusion   P. 113, 164, 170,
Into: "Into." to the inside of   P. 159, 160, 166, 191,
Into: "Into." to a position of contact with   P. 176, 185,
Into: "Into." in the direction of (something)   P. 151,
Is: "Be." to have a specified qualification or characterization   P. 197,
Is: "Be." to equal in meaning   P. 191, 197,
Its: "Its." relating to or belonging to it or itself   P. 111, 134, 147,
Laid: "Lay." to put or set down   P. 54,
Laid: "Lay." to bring to a specified condition   P. 97,
Let Down: "Let down." to allow to descend gradually   P. 162,
Lifted: "Lift." to raise from a lower to a higher position   P. 132, 159, 180,
Lightened: "Lighten." to make light or clear / illuminate   P. 188,
Like: "Like." similar to   P. 104, 173,
Limit: "Limit." something that bounds, restrains, or confines   P. 46,
Lofty: "Lofty." rising to a great height   P. 25,
Lowered: "Lower." to let descend   P. 162,
Mark(ed): "Mark." to make or leave a visible mark on (something)   P. 46,
Meet: "Meet." to come into the presence of   P. 169,
Messiah: "Messiah." a professed or accepted leader of some hope or cause / a person who is expected to save people from a very bad situation   P. 231,
Middle: "Middle." the part, point, or position that is equally distant from the ends or opposite sides   P. 95, 137,
Midst: "Midst." the middle or central part   P. 4, 95, 137,
Most: "Most." greatest in amount or degree   P. 97, 113,
Mount: "Mount." a high hill / mountain   P. 113,
Moved: "Move." to go from one place or position to another   P. 22, 37, 41, 173,
Multitude: "Multitude." a great number / host   P. 16, 151,
Myself: "Myself." Alone   P. 53,
Never: "Never." not ever   P. 22, 37, 41,
New: "New." having recently come into existence / being other than the former or old   P. 195,
No one: "No One." no person   P. 104,
Nothing: "Nothing." not any thing   P. 26,
On: "On." to a position that is supported by   P. 41, 70, 113, 147,
On: "On." used to indicate the location of something   P. 26, 78, 153, 176,
On: "On." touching and being supported by the top surface of (something)   P. 20, 25, 50, 59, 129, 173,
One: "One." being a single unit or thing   P. 6,
Only: "Only." excluding all others / nobody or nothing except   P. 197,
Open: "Open." open air   P. 10,
Opened: "Open." to cause (something) to no longer be covered, sealed, or blocked   P. 68, 124, 153, 160, 162,
Open(ed): "Open." to move (as a door) from a closed position   P. 115,
Or: "Or." either   P. 191,
Our: "Our." relating to or belonging to us / made or done by us   P. 13,
Out: "Out." away from a particular place   P. 53, 78, 191, 193,
Out: "Out." in or to a place outside of something   P. 187, 195,
Over: "Over." Above   P. 26, 42, 95, 128, 134, 142,
Parted: "Parted." divided into parts   P. 97,
Passed: "Pass." to move or go into or through a particular place   P. 170,
Passed Away: "Pass Away." to go out of existence   P. 195,
Pillars: "Pillar." a firm upright support for a superstructure   P. 20, 26, 36, 99,
Place: "Place." a building, part of a building, or area occupied as a home   P. 142,
Place: "Place." (Out of Place): not in the proper or usual location   P. 111,
Place: "Place." a certain area or region of the world   P. 6,
Place: "Place." a particular portion of a surface   P. 46,
Plain: "Plain." a broad unbroken expanse   P. 193,
Powers: "Power." a person or organization that has a lot of control and influence over other people or organizations   P. 62, 115, 147,
Prevailed: "Prevail." to gain ascendancy through strength or superiority   P. 70,
Principalities: "Principality." the state, office, or authority of a prince   P. 62,
Prophet: "Prophet." a person who predicts the future / an effective or leading spokesman for a cause, doctrine, or group   P. 231,
Punish: "Punish." to impose a penalty on for a fault, offense, or violation   P. 115,
Quake: "Quake." to shake violently   P. 36, 57, 138,
Quarters: "Quarter." any of various units of length or area equal to one fourth of some larger unit   P. 108, 126, 193,
Radiance: "Radiance." warm or vivid brightness   P. 151,
Rained: "Rain." to cause (something) to fall in large amounts   P. 78,
Rainbow: "Rainbow." a curved line of different colors that sometimes appears in the sky when the sun shines through rain   P. 72,
Raise: "Raise." to lift up   P. 60, 92, 113, 180,
Reach: "Reach." to extend to   P. 75,
Realms: "Realm." kingdom   P. 62,
Reappearance: reappearance. (n.d.) *K Dictionaries*. (2013). Retrieved August 14 2016 from http://www.thefreedictionary.com/reappearance Definition: to appear again.   P. 187,
Receded: "Recede." to move back or away   P. 173,
Reel(s): "Reel." to behave in a violent disorderly manner   P. 115,
Religion: "Religion." a cause, principle, or system of beliefs held to with ardor and faith   P. 236,
Removed: "Removed." away from something   P. 173,
Rend: "Rend." to become torn or split   P. 124,
Rest: "Rest." to cease from action or motion   P. 142,
Return(s/eth/ing): "Return." to come or go to a place again   P. 48,
Returned: "Return." happening or done for the second time   P. 118,
Returned: "Return." the act of coming or going back to the place you started from or to a place where you were before   P. 151,
Rise: "Rise." to assume an upright position especially from lying, kneeling, or sitting   P. 169,
Rises/Ariseth: "Rise." to appear above the horizon   P. 48,
Rise/Rising/Rose: "Rise." to move upward   P. 57, 70, 84, 187,
Roll: "Roll." to wrap round on itself   P. 116, 173,
Round: "Round." encircle, encompass   P. 48,
Rulers: "Ruler." a person (such as a king or queen) who rules a country, area, group, etc.   P. 62,
Runs(s): "Run." to go without restraint   P. 32,
Same: "Same." in a way that is alike or very similar   P. 159,
Sang: "Sing." to produce musical tones by means of the voice   P. 30,
Scroll: "Scroll." a long piece of paper that rolls around one or two cylinders and that usually has something written or drawn on it   P. 116, 173,

Seal: "Seal." a medallion or ring face bearing such a device incised so that it can be impressed on wax or moist clay **P. 102,**

Secure: "Secure." to put (something) in a place or position so that it will not move **P. 37,**

See: "See." to perceive by the eye **P. 147, 153, 171,**

Separate: "Separate." to stop being together, joined, or connected : to become separate **P. 4,**

Set: "Set." to place with care or deliberate purpose and with relative stability **P. 20, 34, 41, 113,**

Set: "Set." to put or fix in a place or condition **P. 8, 46, 59,**

Sets: "Set." to pass below the horizon / go down **P. 48,**

Shake(n/s): "Shake." to move sometimes violently back and forth or up and down with short, quick movements **P. 111, 115, 138,**

Shed: "Shed." to give off or out **P. 111,**

Shone: Past tense of: "Shine." to give off light **P. 151,**

Sight: "Sight." something that is seen **P. 137,**

Sign: "Sign." something (such as an action or event) which shows that something else exists, is true, or will happen **P. 147,**

Sign: "Sign." something material or external that stands for or signifies something spiritual **P. 72,**

Skirts: "Skirt." the rim, periphery, or environs of an area **P. 102,**

So: "So." to a degree that is suggested or stated **P. 104,**

Spanned: "Span." to form an arch over **P. 54,**

Splendor: "Splendor." great brightness or luster **P. 188,**

Spread: "Spread." to open or expand over a larger area **P. 50, 53 (X2),**

Spread(s)(ing) out: "Spread out." to open, arrange, or place (something) over a large area **P. 26, 28, 53 (X2), 54, 99, 128,**

Springs: "Spring." a source of supply **P. 68,**

Stable: "Stable." firmly established / fixed **P. 22,**

Stand: "Stand." to be in an upright position **P. 54,**

Standing/Stood: "Stand." to be in an upright position with all of your weight on your feet **P. 80, 160,**

Standup: "Stand up." to rise to a standing position **P. 54,**

Stayed: "Stay." the state of being stopped **P. 95,**

Still: "Still." not moving **P. 95, 129, 140,**

Stood/stand: "Stand." to maintain one's position / to remain stationary or inactive **P. 129, 140,**

Stood/stand: "Stand." an act of stopping or staying in one place **P. 142,**

Stopped: "Stop." to cease moving especially temporarily or for a purpose **P. 95, 142,**

Stretched/ Stretches: "Stretch." to extend in length **P. 26, 30, 53, 128,**

Stretch(ed)(es)(ing) out: "Stretch–out." the act of stretching out / the state of being stretched out **P. 41, 50, 53, 57, 99,**

Strong: "Strong." not easy to break or damage **P. 28,**

Surrounded: "Surround." to be on every side of (someone or something) **P. 151,**

Sway: "Sway." to swing slowly back and forth or from side to side **P. 115,**

Tabernacle: "Tabernacle." a dwelling place **P. 32, 195,**

Tear: "Tear." to separate parts of or pull apart by force **P. 124,**

Tent: "Tent." something that resembles a tent or that serves as a shelter **P. 32, 41, 50, 115,**

Terrified: "Terrify." to cause (someone) to be extremely afraid **P. 151,**

Their: "Their." of or relating to them or themselves especially as owners or as agents or objects of an action **P. 173,**

Then: "Then." next in order of time **P. 147, 169, 173,**

Third: "Third." occupying the number three position in a series **P. 166,**

Throne: "Throne." the position of king or queen / the special chair for a king, queen, or other powerful person **P. 55, 129, 173, 185, 195,**

Through: "Through." into one side and out the other side of (something) **P. 170,**

Throw: "Throw." to propel through the air by a forward motion of the hand and arm **P. 176,**

To: "To." used to indicate the direction of something **P. 173, 178, 185,**

To: "To." in the direction of **P. 84, 92, 113, 120, 154, 160, 162, 180, 182,**

To: "To." used as a function word to indicate contact or proximity **P. 137, 166,**

Together: "Together." with each other **P. 169,**

Token: "Token." something that is a symbol of a feeling, event, etc. **P. 72,**

Top(s): "Top." the highest point, level, or part of something **P. 75, 80, 86, 113, 137,**

Totters: "Totter." Sway **P. 36,**

Touched: "Touch." to be in contact with (something) **P. 137,**

Toward: "Toward." in the direction of **P. 159, 180,**

Tremble: "Tremble." the act or a period of shaking **P. 57, 111, 115, 138,**

Two: "Two." being one more than one in number **P. 8,**

Under: "Under." in or into a position below or beneath something **P. 4, 6, 57, 70, 92, 100, 102, 106, 129,**

Unsearchable: "Unsearchable." not capable of being searched or explored **P. 104,**

Until: "Until." up to (a particular time) **P. 191,**

Unto: "Unto." To **P. 75, 84, 92, 137, 173, 178, 185,**

Up: "Up." from a lower to a higher place or position **P. 76, 82, 84, 86, 132, 144, 154, 164, 185, 187,**

Up: "Up." toward the sky or ceiling **P. 92, 121, 159, 160, 182,**

Upon: "Upon." on **P. 30, 78, 95, 129, 153, 162, 176,**

Upward: "Upward." toward the ceiling, sky, etc. **P. 70, 120,**

Us: objective case *of* WE; We: "We." I and at least one other **P. 13, 75,**

Uttermost: "Uttermost." outermost **P. 159,**

Utmost: "Utmost." the highest point or degree that can be reached **P. 113,**

Vanished: "Vanish." to pass quickly from sight **P. 173,**

Vast: "Vast." very great in size, amount, or extent **P. 151,**

Vault: "Vault." an arched structure of masonry usually forming a ceiling or roof **P. 4, 8, 10, 25, 59, 129,**

Vaulted: "Vaulted." built in the form of an arch **P. 25,**

Visible: "Visible." able to be seen **P. 137,**

Void: "Void." not containing anything **P. 26,**

Went: Past tense of: "Go." to move on a course **P. 76, 82, 84, 142, 159, 182,**

Whoever: "Whoever." whatever person / no matter who **P. 154, 156,**

Whole: "Whole." not lacking or leaving out any part **P. 13, 70, 75, 92, 100, 137, 185,**

Whosoever: "Whosoever." Whoever **P. 154,**

Windows: "Window." an opening especially in the wall of a building for admission of light and air that is usually closed by casements or sashes containing transparent material (as glass) and capable of being opened and shut **P. 68,**

Windows: window. (n.d.). *Dictionary.com Unabridged*. Retrieved July 24, 2016 from Dictionary.com website http://www.dictionary.com/browse/window Definition 5: anything likened to a window in appearance or function, as a transparent section in an envelope, displaying the address. **P. 115,**

With: "With." in the company of **P. 195,**

Wrath: "Wrath." violent anger / rage **P. 173,**

Part Five Sources:

1. **From page 236:** https://en.wikipedia.org/wiki/Kola_Superdeep_Borehole

2. **From page 252:** NOAA National Centers for Environmental Information. "Wandering of the Geomagnetic poles" https://www.ngdc.noaa.gov/geomag/GeomagneticPoles.shtml

3. **From pages 254, 255 & 256:** New York Times: 16 AREAS RESTRICTED UNDER ANTARCTIC TREATY http://www.nytimes.com/1985/10/20/us/16-areas-restricted-under-antarctic-treaty.html

4. **From pages 254 & 256:** U.S. Department of State: Antarctic Treaty https://www.state.gov/t/avc/trty/193967.htm

5. **From page 254 & 256:** High-altitude nuclear explosions by Wm. Robert Johnston http://www.johnstonsarchive.net/nuclear/hane.html

6. **From pages 254 & 256:** Wikipedia: Operation Deep Freeze https://en.wikipedia.org/wiki/Operation_Deep_Freeze

7. **From page 254:** U.S. Department of State: Inspections https://www.state.gov/e/oes/ocns/opa/inspection/index.htm

8. **From page 256:** United States Coast Guard: CHRONOLOGY OF U.S. COAST GUARD POLAR AND ICE OPERATIONS https://www.uscg.mil/history/uscghist/USCGPolarIceOpsChron.pdf

Acknowledgments

An entire book could be written about the people I would like to thank who have helped me over the years. Unfortunately, I have to narrow down the list to fit in this book. I have listed those that have played a key role in my life and without each of them, this book would not exist. I don't know if I will get another opportunity to share my love and appreciation for each of them publicly, so I want to do it here.

First and foremost, I must thank and acknowledge our Heavenly Father and his Son, Jesus Christ. All of the honor and glory for this book and the fruit it will bring goes to them and their spirit which helped guide me in assembling this book. I am eternally humbled and grateful for all they have blessed me with in this life and the one to come.

To my Wife; You are a true gift from God. You are the partner and helpmate I have always prayed for. You are an amazing wife and patient mother. Thank you for the love and support you have shown while I spent the time assembling this book. I know it was not easy spending countless hours apart while I worked on this. You never complained about it and were always proud of what we were accomplishing. Thank you for being you. A Jesus loving Wife and Mother, with such a beautiful spirit. I love you so much.

To my Son and future kids; You inspire me to be better every day and I am so blessed to be your dad. I pray I am as good of an example for you as my Dad was for me. I can't wait to see you grow and watch you turn into the awesome adult I know you will be. I don't know what the future holds but I pray it includes many years of us hunting, fishing and horsing around together. I thought of you and your Mom alot while I spent the countless hours on this book. One big reason I pushed so hard to put this book together is to inspire you in your future endeavors. I wanted to show you an example. An example that the right path and the popular path are usually not the same. The right path can be challenging and hard. The right path may come with alot of rejection and criticism, even from those close to you. How do we know which path is the right path? It's the one God wants you to go down. One of the biggest turning points in my life was learning not to rely on my understanding, but on God and His understanding. When you trust Him and rely on Him, He will direct you. He will be right there beside you as you walk down your own path. What is too hard for God? Absolutely nothing. In your life, if/when you find yourself going down the wrong path, He will always be there for you. He loves you more than we can comprehend. Be humble, be respectful and question everything. Questions will lead you to The Truth. Jesus is Truth. Your Mom and I love you so much.

To my Dad; Thank you for being the best Dad any kid could ask for. You have always been my hero and have always been there for me. You taught me so much, mostly by how you treated others and the way you lived your life. You were always there for anyone needing help. You always got us out of the woods, even when things looked bleak. I watched over the years as you helped countless people who couldn't help themselves. You were a true neighbor to everyone you met. You inspire me to this day. I am so impressed by you.... a quiet, humble country boy at heart. When you had to make a decision you knew would bring difficulty, you sucked it up and did the right thing. I watched you push yourself out of your comfort zone and grow, many times. You were a man of less talk and more action. I can't think of a single time I didn't see you live by the golden rule. The gentle and meaningful way you lived your life goes on. With Mom, your sons, your grandchildren, and also with the countless people you made a positive impact with over the years. I see you in my son when I look at him. Your legacy lives on. It's not goodbye, it's see you later. We love you Dad.

To my Mom; You have always been there for us. Even though we are 'all grown up', you are just as available and loving as ever. We are so blessed to have you as our mom. I know raising us boys was not easy. We would not be who we are today without your loving example. I can only imagine the patience it took to raise us rambunctious kids. Most women would have caved to the pressure I've seen you faithfully go through over the years. You are a great example of what it means to be a loving wife, a loving mother, a loving grandmother and a person who loves Jesus. We always look forward to seeing you and we think of you daily. We look forward to the days when we can see you more often. We love you Mom!

To my Brothers; Our time growing up together has helped form who I am today. I care and love you both very much. I sure miss you both and love any opportunity we have to get together. It is hard to not picture us as little kids riding around the neighborhood on our bmx bikes. I look forward to spending more time with you in the future, especially playing in the woods or on the lake. I love you both.

To my third Brother; God has worked through you to play an integral part in my life. Your humility, empathy and work habit have inspired me so much. There is no way I would be where I am today without you. I know you say I have helped you alot over the years, but believe me, it is mutual. This book would not exist had you not been there for me over the years. Thank you for saving my life at least twice that I am aware of. I love you.

To Dale; I look at you like a second father. Maybe it's more like an uncle because my Dad thought of you like a brother. I would not be where I am today without the influence and guidance of you and your wife. I do not want to imagine where or how I would be without you and your example. I'm pretty sure broke and frustrated would be two words that would describe it. You are another great example of what a Jesus follower looks like and I am so grateful God put you in my life. I love you Dale.

To Victor; You and your wife have played such an instrumental role for my family and I. You are a true brother in Christ and such an amazing example of what a Jesus follower looks like. Thank you for all of our talks and the time you continue to spend with us. We are so blessed to know you and call you our friend. I love you.

To Rob Skiba; This book would not exist if you didn't have the guts to share things you knew would bring objections and ridicule. You are a great example of love and humility. I have spent countless hours putting this book together and to show you my appreciation, you will receive the first copy printed after publishing. I greatly appreciate the work you have done and continue to do.

To Mark Sargent; Thank you for your diligence and willingness to tackle a subject that most people wouldn't even consider. I have learned much from you and I greatly appreciate your dedication to sharing your mind with others. I love your sense of humor and your dedication to finding answers.

To those of you who are saying.... What about me? Yes, I thank you. God has blessed me by putting so many wonderful people in my life over the years. Countless people have helped me along the way, in small and big ways. Maybe it was an encouraging word when I needed it or a friendly discussion. Just know that each of you in your own way have helped get me to a point that made this book possible.

Lastly, to you, the reader that has taken the time to read this book. Thank you for having the willingness to continue reading on, even after the moments that had you scratching your head. I don't know your name, but you have also been an inspiration to ensure this book was finished. One big thing that kept me going through this process was knowing that God was going to use this book to give you something. What that specifically is for you is between you and Him. I am just doing what I believe He wanted me to do. He loves you more than words can express and more than any of us can possibly understand.